THE CHOICE TO
LEAVE
ABUSE

THE CHOICE TO
LEAVE
ABUSE

RYAN ANDERSON, PhD, LMFT, MEDFT

CFI

An imprint of Cedar Fort, Inc.
Springville, Utah

ISBN 13: 978-1-4621-4179-1

Published by CFI, an imprint of Cedar Fort, Inc.
2373 W. 700 S., Springville, UT 84663
Distributed by Cedar Fort, Inc., www.cedarfort.com

Library of Congress Control Number: 2022930450

Cover design by Shawnda T. Craig
Cover design © 2022 Cedar Fort, Inc.

Printed in the United States of America

10 9 8 7 6 5 4 3 2 1

Printed on acid-free paper

*For Rebecca, and for everyone who has
ever needed to hear these words.*

Contents

CHAPTER 1

CORE TRUTHS ABOUT ABUSE AND DELIVERANCE

THE MOST IMPORTANT THINGS TO KNOW

I want to start this book by saying the most important things for you to hear:

- Abuse is a serious, damaging sin that requires a firm response from individuals, the Church, and society.
- The damage of abuse can be passed down from generation to generation if it is not stopped.
- God does not want you or anyone to be abused. ***God strongly condemns any form of abuse***.
- Those who abuse are frequently experts at hiding the abuse.
- There are many kinds of abuse, including physical, emotional, mental, sexual, and spiritual. Many types of abuse are hard to detect from the outside.
- Part of almost every pattern of abuse is a psychological effort to make the victim doubt that what is happening is abuse and to feel that he or she is responsible for the abuse he or she is receiving.
- Anyone who engages in abuse is in grave violation of their covenants and is accountable to God, the Church, and the society they live in.
- Abuse is not the victim's fault. Ever.
- Abuse is not about the victim; it is about the abuser.

- God's first priority and the first priority of the Church when there is abuse or suspected abuse is to **protect and help those who have been abused** and to do everything possible to keep them from being abused again.
- The abuser's needs are secondary to the needs of the victims.
- *It is okay for you to leave an abusive situation.* God values and prioritizes your need for physical, emotional, social, and spiritual safety, and He knows that in abusive relationships all of these are at constant risk.
- Just because an abuser repents does not mean you have to return to them.
- Choosing to stay in continued abuse does not make you somehow more celestial or bring you extra blessings.
- The principle of forgiveness does not include you returning to a situation that is abusive or emotionally toxic.
- *In many circumstances, leaving an abusive relationship permanently is what is needed for safety and healing*, and God will endorse and bless this course of action.
- Fully repentant abusers accept the damage they have done to you, understand and empathize with why you needed to leave or have boundaries, and honor your boundaries, even if it means their contact with you or your children is limited or ended.
- There are promises of healing for those who have suffered abuse.
- There is a future for those who leave abuse that is brighter than their past.
- If you have been abused, *the role of the Church is to believe you when you report it, help you find safety, and provide you with support, resources, and connections to help you build a life where you are no longer being abused.*

You may choose to close this book and not read another word, and you hopefully will have already heard what you need to hear. The rest of this book will build on these important truths, help through the emotional and mental snags and snares that can keep people in abuse, and provide ideas and practical resources for those experiencing abuse or worried that someone they love is being abused. Guidance for local Church leaders for how to respond to reports of abuse will also be expounded upon.

MISTAKES OF THE PAST

I am fully aware that many of the people who read the points listed above may have had a difficult emotional reaction to some or all of them. Many of these concepts I listed likely touch tender points of pain, heartache, disappointments, and deep despair that readers have experienced. In reading through these concepts, I know there are many people who will find themselves saying inwardly, "But that's not what I have experienced at all!"

What they have experienced instead is heartbreakingly all too familiar, although they almost certainly feel entirely alone in their tribulation. People who speak up about abuse hope to be believed and to receive help. Unfortunately, far too often that is not the case. Frequently, what they experience is significant pushback, minimization, dismissiveness, and lack of support and help. Sometimes they are even accused or punished. Often, they are told that it is their religious duty to bear the abuse—if it is even acknowledged as such—for as long as it may last. They often experience being interrogated about the accuracy or truthfulness of the reports of the abuse they are suffering. They frequently find themselves being told that they are the ones who need to change. Sometimes, they are admonished by the supposedly consoling precept that when their mortal life is done, all will be made right through the Atonement and their currently abusive marriage or parent/child relationship will become celestial.

For people of faith who are dedicated to keeping their covenants, these experiences are paralyzing. The empowering and ennobling gospel of Jesus Christ that teaches of faith, hope, charity, and redemption through the Atonement of Christ transforms itself into an austere and psychologically damaging form of pseudo-spirituality based on perpetual and non-redemptive suffering and humiliation. A living hell on earth becomes the apparent price for the hope of someday obtaining heaven, with an eternal companion, parent, or other family member who will supposedly love and honor them in that more exalted sphere, whereas their actions now are filled with contempt and harm. And for far too many people, finding that their efforts to receive help from local religious leaders are met by responses that enable or even endorse the abuse is such a spiritually jarring experience as to shatter even the strongest of testimonies.

These experiences lead many victims of abuse to believe that the concepts of marriage and family are held sacred within the Church— even worshiped, as it were—at the price of sacrificing the individual well-being of people within those marriages and families. They are erroneously taught to believe that the institutions of marriage and family are greater in the eyes of God than the worth of souls who are suffering under the mistreatment of another. These perversions of true doctrines are particularly insidious, since they are designed as snares of the adversary to turn someone's faith and willingness to be obedient into shackles of hopeless suffering.

Mental health professionals and law enforcement officers responding to reports of abuse by Latter-day Saints have commonly heard many variations on the following experiences:

- "I was counseled by a bishop/stake president to stay with my spouse after I told them about the abuse."
- "I was told by a priesthood leader that this sort of thing is very common, that it's not as big of a deal as I am making it out to be, and that I need to be more supportive of my spouse."
- "I was told by my local leader that my spouse is under a lot of pressure, and I just need to do a better job of not adding to their stress."
- "My bishop told me that I had made a covenant to submit to the will of my spouse, and in refusing to do so I was sinning."
- "I was told by a Church leader that if I lost weight, took better care of myself, made more of an effort to be attractive, and was more attentive to my husband's needs that the abuse would stop."
- "A priesthood leader I spoke to about the abuse told me that I had made a covenant when I was sealed to my spouse, and if I left I would be breaking that covenant."
- "When I told my bishop/stake president about the abuse, they

told me what a great guy my spouse is and how they have a testimony of how much God loves him."

- "My priesthood leader acted as if he thought I was exaggerating or even making the whole thing up."
- "When I went to my priesthood leader for help, I was told that the solution was to counsel with my spouse."
- "The advice I received from my bishop was to increase my scripture study, prayer, fasting, and temple attendance, and that the Lord would provide the solution."
- "My priesthood leader accused me of being a liar, home-wrecker, and covenant breaker."
- "When I separated from my spouse because of the abuse, my local priesthood leader treated me like I was sinning. I wasn't allowed to have a calling, speak in church, pray in church, or have home or visiting teachers."
- "When I told my bishop/stake president about what was happening, they told me I should be very cautious about talking about such things, because I could potentially damage my spouse's career and/or ability to hold callings within the Church."
- "When I told my priesthood leader that I felt I needed to get out to get safe, I was told that if I left, I was breaking my covenant and my children would be sealed to my spouse, but I would lose them in the eternities."

How can we possibly reconcile these oft repeated, soul-rending stories with the idea that God does not want anyone to be abused, that He considers abuse to be a terrible sin and a deep offense against His laws and plan? How can we resolve the dissonance between what these people are reporting and an understanding that the role of the Lord's servants is to stand in His place and act as He would to be a judge in Israel? This includes protecting the victims of abuse and holding those who abuse accountable for their actions.

The answer that reconciles these two disparate sets of precepts is found in something Elder Uchtdorf (2013) taught regarding struggles people have when learning about the history of the Church. "[To] be perfectly frank, there have been times when members or leaders in the

Church have simply made mistakes. There may have been things said or done that were not in harmony with our values, principles, or doctrine."

To state it as plainly as possible, any time any member of the Church has responded to a report of abuse by counseling the victim to stay in the abuse, implying spiritual punishment for leaving the abuse, implying that the abuse was the fault of the victim and he or she was the one that needed to change, or not giving emotional and practical support to help secure their safety, *that person has made a mistake*, and their counsel and actions were not in harmony with the doctrines of Jesus Christ. That is true whether the person in question is a member or a leader within the Church.

There are a wide variety of reasons that mistakes in this area have been made, ranging from repetition and tradition, to culture, to overemphasizing some doctrines (the sacredness of the marriage covenant, the necessity of faithfulness to temple ordinances) while under-emphasizing other doctrines (the worth of an individual soul, the value of a daughter of God, the gravity of the sin of abuse), and more. While there can be some utility in understanding why mistakes in the past were made, there is much greater urgency and importance in understanding the corrections we have been given in the present and the choices these guide us towards making, both as those who have been the victims of abuse and those who receive reports of abuse.

CONTINUING REVELATION AND THE LORD'S CORRECTION

The Church of Jesus Christ of Latter-day Saints is based upon the principle of continuing revelation. President Spencer W. Kimball (1977) taught, "Of all things, that . . . we should be most grateful [for] is that the heavens are indeed open and that the restored church of Jesus Christ is founded upon the rock of revelation. Continuous revelation is indeed the very lifeblood of the gospel of the living Lord and Savior, Jesus Christ." The concept that God will continue to provide revelation is core to our very understanding of the relationship between Him and His children during their mortal sojourn. We understand that revelation is given "line upon line, precept upon precept" (2 Nephi 28:30), and as such our collective understanding of doctrines and their application grows and evolves over time. This happens at all levels.

One of the reasons for continuing revelation is that God knew that members of the Church, including leaders, would make mistakes. He was fully aware that continued guidance, correction, and direction would need to be given to correct those mistakes. Consider the words of the Lord in His own preface to the Doctrine and Covenants:

> Behold, I am God and have spoken it; these commandments are of me, and were given unto my servants in their weakness, after the manner of their language, that they might come to understanding.
>
> ***And inasmuch as they erred it might be made known;*** And inasmuch as they sought wisdom they might be instructed. And inasmuch as they sinned they might be chastened, that they might repent; And inasmuch as they were humble they might be made strong, and blessed from on high, and receive knowledge from time to time. (D&C 1:24–28; emphasis added)

In the area of responding to abuse, many errors have been made for generations, not just within the Church but within our societies as a whole. The Lord has made the errors we have been making known to us and has provided wisdom that we collectively might be instructed, made strong, and blessed from on high. We are all meant to move on from the past, leaving behind the mistakes and misconceptions, and move forward in new and better ways.

In 2018, the general handbook of The Church of Jesus Christ of Latter-day Saints was updated, with clarification and clear direction given in the policy that discusses abuse and how to respond to it. The policy states, ***"Members should never be encouraged to remain in a home or situation that is abusive or unsafe*** [emphasis added]. Church leaders should never disregard a report of abuse or counsel a member not to report criminal activity to law enforcement personnel."

Furthermore, the policy lays out important guidelines and principles, including:

- "Most . . . allegations of abuse are true, and should be taken seriously and handled with great care."

- "The doctrine of the church commits all leaders and members to protect each individual."
- "Abuse in any form is sinful, tragic, and in total opposition to the teachings of the Saviour."
- "Those who commit abuse in any way are accountable to God."
- "When abuse occurs, *the first and immediate responsibility of Church leaders is to help those who have been abused and protect vulnerable persons from further abuse* [emphasis added]."
- "Church leaders should *never disregard a report of abuse or counsel a member not to report criminal activity to law enforcement personnel* [emphasis added]."
- "Church leaders and members should fulfill all legal obligations to report abuse to civil authorities."
- "Priesthood leaders should help those who have committed abuse to repent and cease their abusive behavior."

There is something else worth exploring about this policy. President Russel M. Nelson has become renowned for leading out on helping the Church move forward with a wide variety of inspired changes, including many that clearly prepared the Church and its members for the 2020 COVID-19 pandemic. From the time he assumed the mantle of President of the Church to March 2021, he led out in more than forty significant updates to Church structure, policy, and guidelines.

However, it is worth noting that of all those revelations and all those changes, the one the Lord chose to give to him to act on first was the update on the Church's policies and guidelines for preventing and responding to abuse that has been discussed here. While I am not in a position to speak for President Nelson, it seems to me that the fact that the Lord made this the first of many changes can teach us something about how much of a priority it is to God to protect His children from abuse and help them find safety and recovery when they have fallen victim to it.

THE MOMENTUM OF OLD WAYS

History, scripture, and experience teach us that when new light and knowledge are given, individuals and societies go through what is often a difficult period of adjustment, even if the new clarification is received with joy and gratitude. As a result, some people find themselves trying to inhabit some sort of middle ground between what they feel they have been taught their whole lives and the new information that is given. Other people are more deeply entrenched in their old mindset and habits, and feel that the change is somehow an affront on what they consider to be gospel truths. People in this position can often be prone to quote from the scriptures in a way intended to defend their position, or cite quotes from General Authorities that they believe contradict the new guidance and directives.

Sadly, for far too long, quotes from the scriptures or from modern-day General Authorities have been used to support the idea that people who are being abused within the bonds of a temple sealing must stay within that abusive relationship, and that doing otherwise is a breach of their most sacred covenants. It is not within the scope of this book to document commonly used scriptures and quotes that have been employed in such a fashion. However, it does bring up the bitter parallel that the name of Christianity has been used to justify a wide variety of atrocities throughout history. It's a very clever and subtle tactic of the adversary to try to soil the name of something sacred by getting people to use it to support courses of action that are violent, profane, or dehumanizing.

While there is a much larger discussion to be had about what actually constitutes doctrine and about the temptation to try to dismiss or reshape new revelation based on what has been taught in the past officially or otherwise, for the purpose of this discussion we will highlight one crucial point. The whole purpose of continuing revelation is to move beyond our limitations with what we knew previously. True continuing revelation will perpetually refine, change, and even significantly shift old points of view. That's the purpose of it. In our efforts to understand the fulness of what the Lord has revealed, we are to look to the most recent revelation given through those in positions of appropriate stewardship. To do otherwise is to fall into the trap of wresting the scriptures (see Alma 13:20).

With all of this in mind, it is worth reiterating these important, core truths that are at the core of the most recent light and knowledge the Lord has revealed on the subject of abuse:

- No matter what has been done in the past, no matter how people have supported the practices by scriptures or quotes, no matter what the traditions have been in our lifetimes and before, *God does not look upon the sin of abuse with any degree of allowance.*

- To commit any form of abuse is to break one's most sacred covenants.

- The Lord requires those who participate in abusive attitudes and actions to repent and to cease all forms of abuse. This includes attempting to control, punish, or coerce the victims of the abuse as they determine how they are going to move forward with their own healing process.

- In responding to abuse, *the focus should never be on protecting the abuser from the potential consequences of his or her actions.* Accepting, working through, and living with the consequences of having abused someone else is a part of the repentance process.

- God does not hold the victims of abuse responsible for it.

- Our Father in Heaven forbids His servants from counseling people to stay in abusive relationships or to forbear from reporting criminal forms of abuse to the civil authorities.

- *God's children are free to leave abusive relationships if they choose to do so.*

- Making the choice to leave an abusive situation is not a sin or a violation of covenants.

- In any abusive situation, *the Church's first priority is to protect the victims of abuse and help them create the circumstances they need to heal and move forward with their lives.*

CHAPTER 2

HOW GOD FEELS ABOUT ABUSE

THE SOUL WOUND OF ABUSE

Abuse of all kinds tends to create perhaps the most damaging, gangrenous wound of the soul: doubt. Those who have suffered abuse find that it creates doubts about all of the most crucial things in their mortal lives and in eternity. These doubts tend to target their understanding of themselves (like their own sanity, judgment, worth, likeableness, and so on), their understanding of the world (this is just the way things are, there is nothing better out there, all people will ultimately behave this way, and so on), and their understanding of relationships. Perhaps most damaging of all is the doubt that tends to get lodged within their understanding of God and how God feels about them.

This doubt becomes the crafty servant of the abuse, allowing it to fester and expand in a way that is so stealthy that the person who is the victim of the abuse comes to doubt their own senses and question their own ability to understand what is happening to them. And, even in the moments when they are able to experience clarity in understanding that what they are experiencing is abusive, the doubt binds them to thoughts that they somehow deserve it.

Anything that causes us to doubt God's love for us and His desire for our well-being is not of God but is a tool of the adversary intended to bind us down to whatever misery he has schemed to enslave us with. A proper understanding of true doctrines about God's attitude about abuse is a powerful tool in beginning to find liberation from the doubt that keeps us captive.

GOD'S POSITION: THE ULTIMATE OPPONENT OF ABUSE

The Lord speaks out strongly against abuse in the scriptures. For example:

- "But whoso shall offend one of these little ones which believe in me, it were better for him that a millstone were hanged about his neck, and that he were drowned in the depth of the sea." (Matthew 18: 6; see also Mark 9:42 and Luke 17:2)
- "Let no corrupt communication proceed out of your mouth, but that which is good to the use of edifying, that it may minister grace unto the hearers. And grieve not the holy Spirit of God, whereby ye are sealed unto the day of redemption. Let all bitterness, and wrath, and anger, and clamour, and evil speaking, be put away from you, with all malice." (Ephesians 4:23–31)
- "But now ye also put off all these; anger, wrath, malice, blasphemy, filthy communication out of your mouth." (Collosians 3:8)
- "For men shall be lovers of their own selves, covetous, boasters, proud, blasphemers, disobedient to parents, unthankful, unholy, Without natural affection, trucebreakers, false accusers, incontinent, fierce, despisers of those that are good, Traitors, heady, highminded, lovers of pleasures more than lovers of God; Having a form of godliness, but denying the power thereof: from such turn away." (2 Timothy 3:2–5)
- "Wherefore, my beloved brethren, let every man be swift to hear, slow to speak, slow to wrath: For the wrath of man worketh not the righteousness of God." (James 1:19–20)
- "If any man among you seem to be religious, and bridleth not his tongue, but deceiveth his own heart, this man's religion is vain." (James 1:26)
- "Therewith bless we God, even the Father; and therewith curse we men, which are made after the similitude of God. Out of the same mouth proceedeth blessing and cursing. My brethren, these things ought not so to be." (James 3:9–10)
- "Behold, there are many called, but few are chosen. And why are they not chosen? Because their hearts are set so much upon the things of this world, and aspire to the honors of

men, that they do not learn this one lesson—That the rights of the priesthood are inseparably connected with the powers of heaven, and that the powers of heaven cannot be controlled nor handled only upon the principles of righteousness. That they may be conferred upon us, it is true; but when we undertake to cover our sins, or to gratify our pride, our vain ambition, or to exercise control or dominion or compulsion upon the souls of the children of men, in any degree of unrighteousness, behold, the heavens withdraw themselves; the Spirit of the Lord is grieved; and when it is withdrawn, Amen to the priesthood or the authority of that man. Behold, ere he is aware, he is left unto himself, to kick against the pricks, to persecute the saints, and to fight against God. We have learned by sad experience that it is the nature and disposition of almost all men, as soon as they get a little authority, as they suppose, they will immediately begin to exercise unrighteous dominion. Hence many are called, but few are chosen." (D&C 121:34–40)

- "No power or influence can or ought to be maintained by virtue of the priesthood, only by persuasion, by long-suffering, by gentleness and meekness, and by love unfeigned; By kindness, and pure knowledge, which shall greatly enlarge the soul without hypocrisy, and without guile." (D&C 121:41–42)

Consider the following quotations from General Authorities and General Officers of the Church and what they teach about God's feelings about abuse.

- "A priesthood holder who would curse his wife, abuse her with words or actions, or do the same to one of his own children is guilty of grievous sin." (Ezra Taft Benson in Conference Report, Oct. 1983, 61–62; or *Ensign,* Nov. 1983, 42).
- "Any form of physical or mental abuse to any woman is not worthy of any priesthood holder. . . . This, of course, means verbal as well as physical abuse." (James E. Faust in Conference Report, Apr. 1988, 44; or *Ensign,* May 1988, 37)
- "A husband who would never dream of striking his wife physically can break, if not her bones, then certainly her heart by the brutality of thoughtless or unkind speech. Physical abuse is uniformly

and unequivocally condemned in The Church of Jesus Christ of Latter-day Saints. If it is possible to be more condemning than that, we speak even more vigorously against all forms of sexual abuse. Today, I speak against verbal and emotional abuse of anyone against anyone, but especially of husbands against wives. Brethren, these things ought not to be." (Jeffrey R. Holland, "The Tongue of Angels," *Ensign*, May, 2007)

- "Those who verbally or physically abuse their wives or husbands or those who degrade or demean or exercise unrighteous dominion in a marriage are not keeping the covenant." (F. Burton Howard, "Eternal Marriage," *Ensign*, May, 2003)

- "No man who abuses his wife or children is worthy to hold the priesthood of God. No man who abuses his wife or children is worthy to be a member in good standing in this Church. The abuse of one's spouse and children is a most serious offense before God, and any who indulge in it may expect to be disciplined by the Church." (Gordon B. Hinckley in Conference Report, Oct. 1998, 92–93; or *Ensign*, Nov. 1998, 72)

- "I have in my office a file of letters received from women who cry out over the treatment they receive from their husbands in their homes. They tell of the activity of some of these men in Church responsibilities. They even speak of men holding temple recommends. And they speak of abuse, both subtle and open. They tell of husbands who lose their tempers and shout at their wives and children. They tell of men who demand offensive intimate relations. They tell of men who demean them and put them down and of fathers who seem to know little of the meaning of patience and forbearance with reference to their children." (Gordon B. Hinckley in Conference Report, Apr. 1990, 68; or *Ensign*, May 1990, 52)

- "To our Heavenly Father, children have *never* been secondary—they have *always* been primary. He trusts us to value, respect, and protect them as children of God. That means we never harm them physically, verbally, or emotionally in any way, even when tensions and pressures run high. Instead, we *value* children, and we do all we can to combat the evils of abuse.

Their care is primary to us—and to Him." (Joy D. Jones, "Essential Conversations," *Liahona*, May, 2021)

- "Certainly we have more material blessings than any other generation in history, but in 21st century culture generally and too often in the Church, we still see lives that are in trouble, with compromises resulting in too many broken covenants and too many broken hearts. . . . Or perhaps we see other forms of abuse and indignity. How doubly careful we have to be as disciples of the Lord Jesus Christ not to participate in any such behavior. In no case are we to be guilty of any form of abuse or unrighteous dominion or immoral concern—not physical or emotional or ecclesiatical or any other kind. I remember feeling the fervor of President Gordon B. Hinckley a few years ago when he spoke to the men of the Church regarding those he called 'tyrants in their own homes.'" (Jeffery R. Holland, "Not as the World Giveth," *Liahona*, May 2021)

- "We warn that individuals who violate covenants of chastity, who abuse spouse or offspring, or who fail to fulfill family responsibilities will one day stand accountable before God." ("The Family: A Proclamation to the World," *Ensign*, Nov. 1995, 102)

- "We know that many of you are innocent victims — members whose former spouses persistently betrayed sacred covenants or abandoned or refused to perform marriage responsibilities for an extended period. Members who have experienced such abuse have first-hand knowledge of circumstances worse than divorce. . . . When a marriage is dead and beyond hope of resuscitation, it is needful to have a means to end it." (Dallin H. Oaks, "Striving Together Towards Perfection," *Ensign*, May 2007)

In addition to these direct quotations from General Authorities, consider the following information—endorsed by the First Presidency and Quorum of the Twelve Apostles—on the Church's web page about abuse at https://www.churchofjesuschrist.org/get-help/abuse

- "Your safety is the most important consideration in a situation of abuse. No one is expected to endure abusive behavior… **There are situations where it is advisable to leave** [emphasis added]."

- "Abuse is the neglect or mistreatment of others (such as a child or spouse, the elderly, the disabled, or anyone else) in such a way that causes physical, emotional, or sexual harm. *The first responsibility of the Church in abuse cases is to help those who have been abused and to protect those who may be vulnerable to future abuse* [emphasis added]. Church leaders and members should be caring, compassionate, and sensitive when working with victims and their families."

- "When working with offenders, priesthood leaders should help them repent, *accept the full consequences of their actions* [emphasis added], and cease their abusive behavior."

- "If another one of your family members is the offender, you may need to consider removing him or her from the home. While this may feel like the family is being torn apart, the separation is an important step that can lead to the eventual healing of everyone involved. In some situations, family reunification may eventually be possible through help from civil authorities and professional counselors. In other situations, family reunification may not be advised."

Additionally, the Church released the following statements on abuse through its online Newsroom at https://newsroom.churchofjesuschrist.org/article/how-mormons-approach-abuse

- "Abuse is a matter the Church takes very seriously. When we learn of abuse, our first priority is to help the victim and stop the abuse."

- "The Church has a *zero-tolerance policy when it comes to abuse*. This means that if we learn of abuse, *we cooperate with civil authorities to report and investigate the abuse*. Offenders are also subject to the laws of God. *Whether or not someone is convicted of abuse, offenders are subject to Church discipline and could lose their membership in the Church* [emphasis added]."

- "A victim of abuse is a child of a loving Heavenly Father. We must do everything we can to protect and love them. *We urge our local leaders and members to reach out to victims, comfort and strengthen them, and help them understand that what happened was wrong and that the experience was not their fault* [emphasis added]. We encourage leaders and members to make efforts to prevent it from happening again."

There is much more that could be included, but for the purposes of this chapter, these references will suffice. In reading them, there are several important themes that emerge that demonstrate to us God's feelings about abuse.

GOD OPPOSES ABUSE IN ALL FORMS

There is no type of abuse—physical, sexual, mental, emotional, verbal, social, or spiritual—that God does not strongly condemn. People or societies may attempt to explain away abuse under certain circumstances. For example, people may claim that it is impossible for a married man to sexually abuse his wife, even in circumstances in which she clearly indicates that she is not giving consent. Alternatively, people may excuse some types of hitting as not qualifying as abusive. Or, people may try to explain away verbal abuse as being a form of humor. However, the Lord accepts no such justifications. He sees them as what they are: rationalizations for grievous, sinful behavior.

God does not tolerate abuse, even in small doses. It is not something He is willing to excuse or sweep under the rug. He opposes it. He condemns it. He requires real and complete repentance and a cessation of the abuse. Those who refuse to do so will ultimately be held accountable before Him for their actions.

GOD KNOWS THAT THE ABUSERS ARE THE ONES RESPONSIBLE FOR THE ABUSE

Almost inevitably, those who engage in abusive behavior blame other people and other circumstances for the abuse, if it is admitted to at all. In particular, the victims of the abuse are most often blamed by abusers as the cause of the abuse. How common are the refrains, "They provoked me. They are such a difficult/crazy/unreasonable person. Anyone in my circumstances would have done the same. They have no sense of humor. They just can't take a joke! They bring this on themselves. If they just did x, I wouldn't have to act that way."

Abuse is a sin against many sacred things, including the body, mind, and spirit of God's children. It is also a sin against the sacred principles of agency and accountability, which are central to God's plan of salvation for His children. It is interesting to note that accusations seem to be a central feature of abuse and that one of the descriptions given of the adversary in the scriptures is "the accuser" who "accused them before our God day and night" (Revelation 12:10). In fact, the word *Satan* directly translates into English as "accuser." Is there any wonder that the adversary would seek to influence us to do the same?

In an *Ensign* article on spouse abuse, licensed social worker and BYU associate professor Anne Horton stated, "Abusers need to know their behavior is a choice. Every time they hit someone, every time they slam a door in someone's face, they've made a choice to do that and they need to take responsibility for their actions" ("A Conversation on Spouse Abuse," *Ensign*, October, 1999).

God's position is clear: those who abuse are the ones responsible for it. No one made them do it. No one else is to blame. Their choice to engage in abusive behaviors is theirs to own, and they must be accountable for it.

GOD KNOWS THAT MANY FORMS OF ABUSE ARE NOT PHYSICAL

Did you notice how often in the scriptures and quotations included in this chapter that abuse is spoken of as being more than just physical violence? Words, contemptuous attitudes, constant anger, intimidation, efforts to control and compel, isolation, disregard for feelings and needs, disrespect, objectification, and neglect are all included, as well.

Many times, people try to deny the existence of abuse by holding up the supposed evidence of a lack of bruises, abrasions, and broken bones to "prove" that no abuse has occurred. This is the equivalent of saying food only has flavor if it is sweet, ignoring the wide variety of other varieties of taste.

It is fair to say that most types of abuse do not leave physical marks. This is true in part because even when physical abuse has occurred and has left forensic evidence, it is almost always accompanied by the other, more subtle, but even more powerful forms of abuse that wound the mind and the soul.

Abuse is about far more than physical impacts. It is about the impact of patterns of attitude and behavior that erode one's very sense of self. God knows this and will not turn a blind eye to forms of abuse that carefully avoid traceable bodily harm so as to avoid detection and accountability. God does not consider the other forms of abuse to be lesser than physical abuse.

GOD KNOWS THAT ABUSE CAN HIDE BEHIND AN IMAGE OF RESPECTABILITY AND HONOR

Far too often, members of the Church who are suffering abuse seek out help, only to be met with shock and disbelief. The reasons given are usually variations of the idea that the person that is being abusive has fulfilled certain roles or held certain offices or seems to present themselves well publicly, and therefore the reports of abuse must be exaggerated or entirely false. Statements might include:

- "But they are a returned missionary, and their mission president has said they were an amazing missionary."
- "But they seem so good with the kids in their Primary/Young Men/Young Women calling."
- "But they've been a [fill in the blank with a leadership calling]. Twice. There's just no way."
- "They just seem so personable and friendly. This just doesn't sound like them."

The sad truth is, most people who abuse others do not seem like "the sort of person who would be an abuser," or at least the shared social construct that we seem to have of what an abuser looks like. A majority of abusers are charismatic and good at making a positive impression.

The fact that someone has held a prominent calling is not a reason to think they are incapable of being abusive. In fact, as the scriptures quoted from Doctrine and Covenants 121 indicate, the Lord knows that the temptation to unrighteous dominion is a common strategy of the adversary for those who are placed in any positions of authority.

Abuse is about many things, but it is always about efforts to exercise power and control over another child of God.

Abuse can happen anywhere. The fact that it is being reported that someone in a prominent position is engaging in abuse is not a reason to believe it isn't happening. It is simply a manifestation of the fact that people can have a "form of godliness, but deny the power thereof" (2 Timothy 3:2–5). God has warned that we would face "spiritual wickedness in high places" (Ephesians 6:12). While this may have reference to secular high places, it is also a warning that wickedness may exist in high places for members of the Church, as well.

In fact, people who abuse who also hold certain prominent callings or fulfill certain religious practices often use that fact as a way to explain away the abuse. "But I am a temple worker!" "But I read my scriptures!" "But I'm in the elders quorum presidency!" The fact is, position or status within the Church is irrelevant, both when it comes to how much God loves us and also in whether or not someone in that position may be engaging in abuse.

GOD KNOWS THAT ABUSERS ARE BREAKING THEIR COVENANTS

Simply stated, it is impossible to abuse someone without breaking your covenants. There is not a single covenant we enter into—be it the baptismal covenant, the oath and covenant of the priesthood, the covenants made in the temple endowment, the sealing covenant, or any other covenant available to disciples of Christ—that is compatible in any way whatsoever with abuse.

Historically, members of the Church suffering abuse at the hands of their spouse have frequently been told that to leave the abusive relationship would be to break their covenants. This is completely false. In fact, the situation is quite the opposite. Those who are the victims of abuse are facing circumstances in which the abuser has broken their own covenants. The choice the victim has is not whether or not to break their own covenants; it is what to do with the knowledge that their spouse has broken theirs.

GOD KNOWS THAT ABUSE IS COMPLETELY INCOMPATIBLE WITH HOLDING THE PRIESTHOOD

Any person engaging in abusive behavior is not worthy to hold or exercise the priesthood. Abuse is the antithesis of the priesthood. Force, coercion, and manipulation are all ways the adversary tempts God's children to try to exercise power, control, and dominion over others. These efforts to control and force others hearken back to the arguments in the great War in Heaven, in which Satan sought means to exercise power and control over others to the point of removing their agency entirely. These efforts, combined with his rebellion against God's correction and his determination to stir others up in rebellion, led to Lucifer's fall.

God does not exercise control and coercion over His children. He does not "pull rank" when He sees us making poor decisions. He does not override our agency or force our thoughts or feelings. The priesthood literally cannot be used to do so, because doing so is a violation of the virtues that make God divine. Instead, He operates by "persuasion, by long-suffering, by gentleness and meekness, and by love unfeigned; By kindness, and pure knowledge, which shall greatly enlarge the soul without hypocrisy, and without guile" (D&C 121:41–42).

Sadly, there are those who have attempted to wrest the meaning of the next verses, which read, "Reproving betimes with sharpness, when moved upon by the Holy Ghost; and then showing forth afterwards an increase of love toward him whom thou hast reproved, lest he esteem thee to be his enemy; That he may know that thy faithfulness is stronger than the cords of death" (D&C 121:43–44). There are those who have claimed that the "sharpness" spoken of is the Lord endorsing harshness of language and action, and have used this as an excuse for verbal and even physical abuse.

Millet and Newell (2001) observed:

Our pride may prompt us to lash out and reprove harshly. Our own insecurity and fear may precipitate unkind responses. Possibly, we may truly misunderstand or have a stilted notion of reproof. Perhaps we have let it fester until the situation has become much larger than it warrants. Reproving with sharpness does not merit callous disregard for the sensitivities of the other person or heartless actions that demean.

It is possible that far too often we are "moved upon," not by the Spirit, but by our own emotions—or even by the adversary, the author of contention. The Master taught His Nephite disciples that "he that hath the spirit of contention is not of me, but is of the devil, who is the father of contention, and he stirreth up the hearts of men to contend with anger, one with another" (3 Nephi 11:29). The Holy Ghost must dictate the need for reproof to us, or else we reprove improperly and for the wrong reason. That requires the personal righteousness of the reprover, a loving and patient disposition, and a sincere desire to help rather than to harm and to bless rather than to damage.

To help correct perversions of the doctrine taught in this section of the Doctrine and Covenants, the Church published an article entitled "Doctrine and Covenants 121:41–43" in the June 2011 *Ensign*. In the article, the words are defined and expounded upon as follows: "*Reproving*—scolding or correcting gently; expressing disapproval. *Betimes*—speedily; early; before it is too late. *Sharpness*—clarity."

To provide more insight, Jackson and Hunt (2011) explored the meanings attributed to the word *sharpness* in Joseph Smith's lifetime. They found that it included connotations of "acuteness of intellect; the power of . . . discernment; quickness of understanding" and "quickness of sense or perception."

They concluded, "Joseph Smith was explicit when he added that we reprove 'when moved upon by the Holy Ghost,' which is not present when harshness and anger are used. And the subsequent '*increase* of love' suggests that love must already be present when the reproving takes place. The Holy Ghost inspires a person to higher degrees of intellectual power and discernment, quickness of understanding, and quickness of perception. These are among the qualities embodied in the word *sharpness.*"

Harshness, anger, and contempt have no place in efforts to correct, guide, or seek to resolve problems or differences. To resort to these things is to surrender one's right to wield the priesthood.

GOD WILL PERSONALLY HOLD ABUSERS ACCOUNTABLE

Those who commit abuse will answer to God for it. Even if they manage to talk their way out of accountability with every religious and civil authority throughout the entirety of their mortal lives, this is not something God will let pass without firm accountability to Him. There is no diplomatic immunity for this, no matter what other good deeds may have been done by that person in their lives. God does not fall for rationalization, justification, or excuses. Known to Him are all the pains of those who have suffered abuse. There is no way to put a spin on it in His presence.

Those who abuse will either be accountable for their abuse through a thorough and complete repentance process—including making amends and doing everything in their power to allow the victims of the abuse to heal—or they will be held accountable at the tribunal of our Father in Heaven.

GOD WANTS THOSE WHO ABUSE TO BE ACCOUNTABLE TO THE SOCIETIES IN WHICH THEY LIVE

The updated policies in the Church's handbook and the information on the Church's website about abuse are very clear that those who commit abuse are not only accountable to ecclesiastical authority but to civil authority as well. Under no circumstances should a Church leader ever counsel a victim of abuse to not report the abuse to legal authorities, regardless of what the consequences of an investigation or conviction may be for the person committing abuse. It may prevent an abuser from holding certain callings. It may cost an abuser a career. It may result in an abuser being placed on a sexual offender list that they will never be removed from. It may result in jail time for the abuser. This is because abuse is not just a sin; most types of abuse are also a crime. If these are the results of someone who commits abuse being held accountable for their actions, we are not to seek to intervene to buffer or remove this form of accountability from them.

The wording from the Church's statement on their online newsroom bears repetition: "This means that if we learn of abuse, we cooperate with civil authorities to report and investigate the abuse." Note that the statement does not say that we debate, ponder, or weigh out whether we should alert civil authorities.

Doctrine and Covenants 134:8 deals with the relationship between religion and government: "We believe that the commission of crime should be punished according to the nature of the offense; that murder, treason, robbery, theft, and the breach of the general peace, in all respects, should be punished according to their criminality and their tendency to evil among men, by the laws of that government in which the offense is committed; and for the public peace and tranquility all men should step forward and use their ability in bringing offenders against good laws to punishment."

GOD EXPECTS ABUSERS TO ACCEPT THE FULL CONSEQUENCES OF THEIR ACTIONS AS A PART OF REPENTANCE

The Church's website on abuse offers clear counsel on what is required from someone who has committed abuse: "When working with offenders, priesthood leaders should help them repent, accept the full consequences of their actions, and cease their abusive behavior."

True and full repentance for someone who has committed abuse has several crucial elements. First, they must recognize that their actions have done real harm to the victims of their abuse. They must be able to acknowledge this without minimization, rationalization, or justification. They must learn to accept the fact that they have done deep damage that in many cases can permanently redefine what is possible in that relationship in the future. This is a difficult truth to accept, but to do less is to misunderstand the true nature of their actions.

Second, they must come to accept that healing for others is required and is a higher priority than their own personal feelings. Part of abuse is a disregard for the feelings, dignity, and needs of another person. Part of truly repenting is learning to put the needs of that other person ahead of their own desires or needs. Once a person has wounded another's soul, the victim's needs for healing take precedence over the needs and desires of the person who committed abuse. The abuser may desperately want the relationship to be renewed, but the victim may need the relationship to end to heal. The victim's needs are the deciding factor. True repentance from abuse requires accepting this fact.

Anne Horton, a professor at Brigham Young University and a licensed social worker, stated in the *Ensign*, "But while the Lord commands us to forgive, He doesn't tell us to forget any lessons we have learned or demand that we trust an abuser. We can forgive someone without putting ourselves in the position to be victimized again. Love can be achieved and so can forgiveness, but we still must protect ourselves" ("A Conversation on Spouse Abuse," *Ensign*, October 1999).

A truly repentant abuser will understand that their repentance may not restore trust from the victims. He or she will accept that the victims are fully within their God-given rights to not place themselves in a position to be vulnerable with the abuser ever again, even if the abuser has had an entire change of heart and the abuse has fully stopped.

Third, someone who has committed abuse needs to understand and accept that their actions may have, in fact, disqualified them from being able to be a part of that healing in ways other than giving the abuse victims distance, respecting their boundaries, and letting them be in control of what they need to feel safe and to feel like they can move forward with their lives. If this is all that they can contribute to the healing, then they must accept it. It is the victim who should decide what they can and cannot receive from the abuser. With time, what is possible may change in some cases. But a repentant abuser will not coerce, argue, or try to force that change. They will accept what the victim needs.

One significant challenge is that people who have fallen into a pattern of committing abuse often struggle with issues of power and control. When faced with the consequences of their abusive actions, many will still face a significant temptation to try to control, define, dictate, or limit what those consequences are, especially when it comes to the boundaries and emotional needs of the victims of abuse. It is not uncommon for an abuser to say, "But that happened a long time ago. They shouldn't still have hard feelings about it," or, "I've repented. They need to forgive me and give me another chance. We are commanded to forgive. If they refuse to forgive, then they are sinning." These attitudes are actually a continuation of the mindset that led to abuse in the first place. They are based on emotional entitlement, a lack of respect for the emotional reality of the other person, and a desire to place their own comfort ahead of the needs of those they have hurt.

In response to these common arguments, Elder Jeffery R. Holland (2018) has given some apostolic clarification: "'Forgive, and ye shall be forgiven,' Christ taught in New Testament times. And in our day: 'I, the Lord, will forgive whom I will forgive, but of you it is required to forgive all men.' It is, however, important for some of you living in real anguish to note what He did not say. He did not say, 'You are not allowed to feel true pain or real sorrow from the shattering experiences you have had at the hand of another.' Nor did He say, 'In order to forgive fully, you have to reenter a toxic relationship or return to an abusive, destructive circumstance.'"

When someone who has committed abuse demands that the victims forget, restore trust, and allow them back in, they are insisting on something that the Lord neither requires nor states they are entitled to. There may be circumstances under which the victims of the abuse heal in a way that leads to them choosing to grant these things to the person who abused them, but it is the victim's choice if and when they feel ready for it.

GOD WANTS HIS CHILDREN TO ESCAPE ABUSE

God does not want any of His children to subject themselves to abuse. Our covenants are meant to draw us to God, not to bind us down to some perversely obligated suffering at the unrighteous exercise of agency of another person. To suggest that the sealing covenant not only excuses abuse but obligates children of God to stay within an abusive relationship is a profound perversion of what should be an exalting doctrine.

Consider the following loving counsel given by Elder Jeffery R. Holland (2003): "I would not have you spend five minutes with someone who belittles you, who is constantly critical of you, who is cruel at your expense and may even call it humor. Life is tough enough without having the person who is supposed to love you leading the assault on your self-esteem, your sense of dignity, your confidence, and your joy. In this person's care you deserve to feel physically safe and emotionally secure."

While Elder Holland was speaking of dating relationships, how much more true is this counsel of what is needed within a marriage? A temple sealing does not suddenly negate the requirements for a healthy relationship; if anything, it amplifies them. Being sealed to someone does not reverse the wisdom of the counsel to choose not to associate with someone who will treat you with cruelty. While marriage is more complex than dating, we should expect and deliver more reciprocal love, compassion, selflessness, and care in a marriage, not less. In fact, when we are sealed, we covenant to do so. Using a temple sealing as an excuse to lower one's standard of behavior to the point of unkindness and abuse is sullying the sacredness of that ordinance and is entirely out of harmony with all that is entailed in that covenant. Covenants are commitments, not entitlements.

The standard works of the scriptures include an overarching theme of deliverance from oppression and abuse that includes God commanding his people to physically remove themselves from the oppressive situation, with Him providing for their needs as they flee. There are more examples of this than can be shared here in the interest of space, but consider the following:

- Abraham left a corrupt society to seek out a better life (see Abraham 1).
- The Israelites were delivered out of bondage in Egypt (see Exodus).
- The Israelites returned to Jerusalem from the long Babylonian captivity (see Ezra).
- The Savior warned His followers to flee to safety from the violence and oppression of the Romans at the fall of Jerusalem (see Matthew 25; Joseph Smith—Matthew).
- Lehi and his family fled from Jerusalem, where they were being oppressed for Lehi's prophecies (see 1 Nephi 2).
- Nephi and his followers left the land of Lehi-Nephi to escape the hatred, oppression, and violence of Laman, Lemuel, and their followers (see 2 Nephi 5).

- Alma fled the oppression of King Noah (see Mosiah 18).
- King Limhi and his people escaped the oppression of the Lamanites in the land of Lehi-Nephi (see Mosiah 22).
- Alma and his people fled the abuse and slavery of Amulon and the Priests of Noah (see Mosiah 24).
- Amulek and the other survivors fled from the violence of the people of the city of Ammonihah. Alma takes Amulek into his own home (see Alma 14–15).
- God commanded Ammon to lead the Anti-Nephi-Lehies out of the reach of the Lamanites and to safety. The Nephites provide lands for them and protect them from the Lamanites (see Alma 27).
- The maid servant of Morianton ran away from his physical abuse and went to Captain Moroni for safety (see Alma 50).
- On many occasions, early Latter-day Saints left behind cities, towns, and colonies to escape the oppression and violence of local mobs (see, for example, D&C 124).
- Following the martyrdom of Joseph Smith, the Latter-day Saints travelled deep into the wilderness to settle in the
- West, where they would be far from oppression.

Notice that these examples span each of the standard works of Latter-day Saint canon. Fleeing out of oppression, persecution, and abuse is not foreign or contrary to the teachings of the gospel. In fact, it isn't even a rare occurrence. Rather, as these examples demonstrate, it is a constant and recurring theme of God's work to bless His children in mortality and to provide healing and redemption for them.

GOD KNOWS THAT HEALING FROM ABUSE MAY REQUIRE A PERMANENT END TO A RELATIONSHIP

In speaking of abusive relationships, President Gordon B. Hinckley lamented:

I regret to acknowledge that some husbands are abusive, some are unkind, some are thoughtless, some are evil. They indulge in pornography and bring about situations which destroy them, destroy their families, and destroy the most sacred of all relationships.

I pity the man who at one time looked into the eyes of a beautiful young woman and held her hand across the altar in the house of the Lord as they made sacred and everlasting promises one to another, but who, lacking in self-discipline, fails to cultivate his better nature, sinks to coarseness and evil, and destroys the relationship which the Lord has provided for him." (Gordon B. Hinckley, "Walking in the Light of the Lord," *Ensign*, Nov. 1998, 99)

In these statements, President Hinckley used very clear language: abuse destroys relationships. The things that lead to abuse—like poor emotional regulation, selfishness, aggression, narcissism, unkindness, thoughtlessness, and addiction to things such as pornography or drugs—destroy relationships. When the abusive actions of another have destroyed your relationship, God does not simply expect you to wallow in the ashes of the radioactive wasteland of that relationship while it poisons you. Your life, your dignity, your ability to seek happiness and meaningful relationships are important to God. If a relationship—even one sealed in the temple—has become something in opposition to all of those priorities, God does not expect nor ask you to stay. Any marriage that has become abusive cannot rightfully be called a celestial marriage because the covenant made at marriage has been broken by an abusing spouse. The marriage may have started as a celestial one, but it is not so now in both substance and in spirit.

Elder Robert D. Hales illuminated this important truth when he said, "As taught in this scripture [D&C 132:19], an eternal bond doesn't just happen as a result of sealing covenants we make in the temple. How we conduct ourselves in this life will determine what we will be in all the eternities to come. To receive the blessings of the sealing that our Heavenly Father has given to us, we have to keep the commandments and conduct ourselves in such a way that our families will want to live with us in the eternities" (Conference Report, Oct. 1996, 87; or *Ensign,* Nov. 1996, 65).

It bears great emphasis that trying to reconcile with someone who is continuing abusive patterns in attitude and actions is both emotionally and physically dangerous and should be strongly cautioned against. Abuse is a cycle very much like an addiction. If someone who has committed abuse has not been able to make substantial and sustained changes in both behavior, mindset, emotional regulation, and willingness to take personal accountability, then it is unrealistic to expect that the patterns of abuse will not return and escalate. Family law attorney and judge Brent Bartholemew stated in the *Ensign*, "An abused spouse shouldn't feel she has to return to a relationship with someone who is unwilling to repent of destructive behavior" ("A Conversation on Spouse Abuse," *Ensign*, October, 1999).

It should be acknowledged that in some cases of abuse, there may be genuine repentance, lasting change, and enough emotional safety established that the victim of the abuse can reconcile with the perpetrator of the abuse, heal the relationship, and move forward. The relationship may return to a close association. Or, the victim of the abuse may find that they cannot have the same relationship they once had, but a more distant relationship with more boundaries is possible, if they so desire. That being said, victims of abuse have no obligation whatsoever at any point in time to return to or re-establish regular contact with those who have abused them.

However, in many cases of abuse, the nature of the abuse has had such an effect as to make reconciliation and a continuation of the relationship impossible or unwise. This can still be the truth even when the perpetrator of the abuse has repented. When this is the case, discontinuing the relationship is not a failure to forgive; it is an establishment of the boundaries and distance needed to establish and secure physical and emotional safety, allow for healing, and allow for a better future for the victims of abuse.

Particular care should be taken when children have been victims. Imagine the impact upon a child who has suffered physical abuse, sexual abuse, threats of harm, intimidation, or verbal abuse when they are told that the non-abusive parent is trying to reconcile with the abuser, with the intention of eventually bringing them back home to live together. This situation often feels to the child like a betrayal from the non-abusing parent and destroys their sense of trust and safety. If a spouse has abused a child, the child's need for safety should be given precedence over any marital considerations.

Needing to end a relationship that has become abusive is not a failure for the victim. It is a recognition of a truth about what they, as a child of God, have a right to seek: peace, safety, hope, and healing.

CHAPTER 3

RECOGNIZING ABUSE

HOW COMMON IS ABUSE?

What a blessing it would be to report that abuse is rare! Sadly, that is far from the truth. Having a full account of how frequently abuse occurs is difficult because a large amount of abuse goes unreported. Furthermore, most abuse that is reported is limited to physical violence. So, even the best data we have on abuse rates are a significant underrepresentation of the actual amount of harm being done. With that caveat, consider the following statistics:

- In the United States, an average of 20 adults are abused per minute, totalling 10 million adults abused per year.
- 33 percent of women and 25 percent of men have experienced severe physical violence from an intimate partner or spouse.
- 14 percent of women and 4 percent of men have been significantly injured by violence from an intimate partner or spouse.
- Only 34 percent of people injured in a domestic violence incident end up receiving medical treatment for their injuries.
- Intimate partner violence is responsible for 15 percent of all violent crime.
- 19 percent of reported domestic violence episodes involve the use of a weapon.
- The presence of a gun in a home during a domestic violence incident increases the chances of it escalating to homicide by 500 percent .

- In 94 percent of domestic violence murder/suicides, the victim is female.
- 6 percent of children are exposed to incidents of domestic violence, with 90 percent of these children being direct eyewitnesses of the violence.
- Victims of domestic violence and abuse are at an elevated risk of depression and suicide (National Center for Injury Prevention & Centers for Disease Control and Prevention, 2010).

WOMEN AT ELEVATED RISK

In an examination of how commonly abuse occurs, there is a very important fact to emphasize. While both men and women can be the victims of abuse, women are much more likely than men to be the target of abusive patterns. Additionally, injury and fatality rates for women who suffer abuse are six times higher than for men who suffer abuse.

Unfortunately, there are many societal factors that influence people to doubt women and to protect men when reports of abuse are made. Sadly, we are not immune to these same societal attitudes within the Church. Many women who report abuse to their religious leaders state that instead of being helped, they are told that "they are the problem" (Moore, 1999). They are accused of being "home-wreckers," told that the abuse is their fault for being "sexually cold" and unavailable, or counseled to dress more attractively, fix their own behaviors, attend the temple more, lose weight, or alter their appearance to be more physically appealing to their husbands. They have also been frequently told to not do anything that would endanger their husband's career or reputation (Stack, 2018).

This is not good counsel. It ignores the real problem and places the blame on women for being insufficiently spiritual and/or stereotypically sexy. These are not the causes of abuse. These attitudes are diabolical in nature. They demonstrate priorities that are vastly out of order. They are at odds with prophetic counsel to believe the sisters when they report abuse. They enable abusers to continue to wound their own souls along with the souls of those they target. To state it plainly, these attitudes compound suffering and cost lives, and end up becoming an additional source of trauma themselves. That is why the counsel given by the leaders of the Church is to believe reports of abuse and take action to protect the person seeking help.

FALSE REPORTS OF ABUSE ARE EXCEEDINGLY RARE

In research on abuse, the data are quite clear about an important truth: virtually all reports of abuse are valid. For example, Jones & McGraw (1987) found that only 1 percent of cases of children alleging abuse were the result of the child fabricating a story. Similarly, Oates, Jones, Denson, Sirotnak, Gary, and Krugman (2000) found that only 2.5 percent of children's allegations of abuse were based on mistaken concerns, and only 1.5 percent were made falsely or in collusion with a parent. There is a vast body of research that replicates and reinforces these findings (see Dallam & Silberg, 2006 for a review).

Let that fact sink in for a moment: between 97.5 percent and 99 percent of cases of alleged abuse are truthful. Conversely, that means that when people who are accused of abuse protest their innocence, they are lying 97.5 percent to 99 percent of the time. This number is astonishing, especially considering that we live in an age where people put the victim of abuse on trial in the court of public opinion instead of the alleged perpetrator and a time when we hear many people opine about the need to protect "promising young men" from false allegations of abuse that will rob them of what is otherwise sure to be a sterling future, all while disregarding the very real suffering they have caused. This attitude ought to be reversed. It must be reversed. We must develop a culture of believing those who report abuse. It is the only attitude aligned with the reality that the statistics clearly demonstrate. It is the only rational position on this matter.

ABUSE IS AS COMMON INSIDE THE CHURCH AS IT IS OUTSIDE THE CHURCH

Given the Church's teachings on family, peace, and the nature of contention, one would fervently hope that this would mean that rates of domestic violence and abuse are lower in the Church than in the general population. Unfortunately, this is not the case. In general, there is very little difference between rates of abuse for members of the Church compared to non-members.

For example, in 2010, the domestic violence rates in Utah—with 66.7 percent of its population identifying as Latter-day Saints— showed that 32.4 percent of Utah women had experienced some form of domestic violence at some time in their lives. This was actually somewhat higher than the national average of 28.8 percent (National Center for Injury Prevention and Control, 2010). This is an area in which the members of the Church are not "a peculiar people," as we have been commanded to be. We are not acting as the city on a hill or the lighted candle on a candlestick. Rather, we are right on par with the world. While this is a difficult truth to accept, we must accept it in order to begin to make progress in changing it.

And we can change it. Sage Williams, an advocate for victims of sexual abuse and collaboror in Harvard's "Faith and Flourishing" symposium, noted that research indicates that in communities where abuse is reported and responded to consistently, occurrences of abuse decrease (Jones, 2021). Providing hope for victims of abuse that they will be believed and assisted and letting people who might commit abuse know by example that they will be held accountable is effective in reducing abuse. Applying the gospel principle of choice and accountability—without fear and without respect of persons—is a part of the solution. We can do better with this. We must. And it will make a difference.

IT'S HARD TO SEE THAT IT'S HAPPENING: THE ROLE OF SHOCK AND GRIEF

If a person is being abused, it seems like they would be aware of the fact. As a result, many people are surprised to learn that victims of abuse often struggle to recognize that what is happening to them is, in fact, abuse. This is not because they are not intelligent or honest with themselves. This veiling of the truth is one of the common effects of abuse. There are several aspects of the nature of abuse in intimate relationships that make it difficult to recognize and accept.

In dating, friendship, or familial relationships, there is an expectation of emotional safety. These relationships are based on the idea that the people in them care about each other and are invested in each other's well-being. These types of relationships involve a certain degree of emotional vulnerability and trust. As such, when abuse happens in a close relationship, it is a big shock to the whole system. It is an experience that is diametrically opposed to what the relationship should be. Not only is the victim's sense of security rocked, but their confidence in their perception of reality is shaken.

As a result, many victims of abuse find themselves entering what has been identified by social scientist Elizabeth Küble-Ross (1969, 2005) as the first stage of grief: denial. To say that is not to pathologize or blame the victim of abuse in any way. The denial is a natural defense mechanism, like the emotional equivalent of an airbag in an automobile. It serves the purpose of providing some kind of cushioning between the full impact of the horrifying truth that someone who should be a loved one has just done something deeply injurious.

It is a natural reaction, then, for the victim of abuse to wonder if they remember the incident of abuse correctly. In fact, it is not uncommon for memories of abusive incidents to be partially or even fully repressed into the subconscious parts of the mind. The memories of abusive incidents can seem fuzzy, shadowy, dreamlike, surreal, or as if they had happened to someone else. Important details seem scrambled, and it is often very hard to relate the experience to someone else in a way that feels coherent, chronologically accurate, and realistic.

If the event is fully remembered, the mind of the victim of abuse often searches desperately for some other explanation. Maybe it really was an accident. Maybe what they heard is not what the other person meant to say. Maybe the victim said or did something wrong that made the incident happen. Maybe the things they did to communicate that they did not consent were not clear enough. Maybe it was wrong of them to express their needs and ask for something from the other person. In its attempt to protect itself from the agonizing realization that the abuse was real, that it was intentional, and that it has implications for the survivability of the relationship, the mind of the victim tries to find some way to take the experience and make it fit some other sort of explanation. As a result, victims of abuse often struggle greatly to feel any degree of confidence in their memories and in their judgment about the abuse, even if they are 100 percent spot on with the details.

GASLIGHTING: THE MIST OF DARKNESS

To further complicate the situation, most perpetrators of abuse engage in a psychological process known as gaslighting. Gaslighting is a form of manipulation in which one party works to make the other party doubt his or her own perceptions by inserting "alternative facts," attacking the credibility of the other person, twisting facts to fit a different narrative, making the other person seem unstable or crazy, or denying the reality of what happened altogether (Abramson, 2014). It should be noted that gaslighting in and of itself is a very damaging form of emotional abuse. There are many phrases that are frequently used as a part of gaslighting efforts. These are just a few:

- "You're crazy."
- "Don't be so sensitive."
- "Don't be paranoid."
- "You probably have bipolar, or maybe borderline personality disorder. You need to get on some pills or something."
- "I was just joking! Don't take it so personally!"
- "You're always imagining things."
- "That never happened."
- "You're remembering it wrong."
- "Why do you keep bringing that up? That was nothing!"
- "I don't remember doing that."
- "That's not the sort of thing I would ever have done."
- "There's no legitimate reason for you to feel the way you do."
- "I never said that."
- "When did I ever do that?"
- "You always make up these lies about me!"
- "I'm not the sort of person who would ever abuse anybody."
- "You're the one who is being manipulative."
- "Nobody would ever believe you if you told them that. They know I'm not like that."

- "I think I'm behaving very reasonably for the way you are acting."
- "It was your fault."
- "Anybody in my situation would do the same thing. You are just impossible to live with."
- "No wonder nobody likes you."
- "You have a terrible grasp of reality."
- "You are such a liar!"
- "My mom/dad/sibling/friend/priesthood leader all think you are crazy. I'm beginning to think they are right."
- "If it was that bad, then why didn't you do something about it?"
- "That's not the way it happened. This is what happened . . ."
- "I'm sorry you feel that way, but I didn't do anything wrong."
- "Now you are just attacking me."
- "You can't complain about getting what you deserve."
- "Don't pretend for one minute that someone else wouldn't do exactly what I have done if they had to live with you. In fact, I think I'm doing a better job at it than anyone else ever would."
- "I was talking to x person the other day, and they agree with me about this."
- "If anyone's being abusive here, it's you!"
- "Of course your mom would agree with what you are saying! The two of you are so codependent! She's as much of a liar as you are!"
- "You're the one who put those ideas in the kids' heads. You are trying to alienate them from me."
- "You have no idea how lucky you are to have me. No one else would put up with all of your garbage."

In addition to the direct gaslighting efforts from the abuser to the victim, the perpetrator of the abuse and gaslighting often uses other relationships and societal structures to reinforce the gaslighting. Abusers can use cultural and social stereotypes (women are stereotyped as irrational, hysterical, overreacting, and overly emotional), differences in social structure (men are overtly ordained to the priesthood and hold priesthood offices and women are not), social manipulation (isolating the victim from friends, family, and other supporters while the abuser builds a network of supporters for himself/herself), and power imbalances (the husband has a closer relationship to the bishop because of their associations through quorum activities) to enroll other people in reinforcing the efforts to undermine the victim's memories of what really happened and overwrite them with the perpetrator's explanations (Sweet, 2019).

This frequently ends up looking like an abused spouse feeling deeply confused about what has been happening and then finally reaching out to a mutual friend or a priesthood leader. Frequently, the abuser has been in contact with that friend or priesthood leader and has been laying a foundation of doubt about the credibility of the victim of abuse, all while being warm, engaging, and charismatic. So, when the victim of abuse finally speaks up, he or she is met with incredulity. Often, the response is something like, "I have a hard time imagining your spouse would do that to you. That just doesn't really seem like them at all." Those words and attitudes accelerate the confusion and fear of the victim.

A BROKEN HEART, A PARALYZED MIND, AND A CRUSHED SPIRIT

The victim's reaction to the abuse, gaslighting, and social alliance that keeps the truth from being seen is both deeply emotional and physical. They may feel like the world is spinning or like they've been hit in the head with a shovel and can't think straight. Their senses will often feel fully overwhelmed, as if their brain is incapable of handling the stimulus present in their world anymore. Their body can get locked in an endless cycle of the fight, flight, or freeze response (Webster, Brough, & Daly, 2016). This is an all-encompassing, paralyzing experience.

As this continues, the victim sinks deeper into a state in which they struggle to trust their own thoughts, perception, and judgment. They fear that others would never believe them, feel compassion for them, or do anything to help them. They begin to internalize the blame that is being constantly piled on them. They feel ashamed, dirty, worthless, unworthy, and hopeless. All of this makes them even more vulnerable to a continuation of the abuse and the gaslighting.

By the time they try to talk to someone about it, they can come across as scattered, flighty, flaky, or unstable. They may have a hard time articulating what they are trying to say. They may struggle to put together a coherent narrative, and their sense of chronology may seem chaotic. They may find themselves beginning to discuss something but then freezing up due to an overwhelming sense of anxiety or panic. These are all natural responses to trauma and a fully activated fight, flight, or freeze response. Unfortunately, this is far too commonly used as a way to plant doubt about what they are saying, since they are having trouble expressing themselves in a way that feels consistent. Perpetrators of abuse are often adept at using this as a way to paint the victims as dishonest or mentally unstable.

Alternatively, victims of abuse may come across as very calm, clinical, articulate, and almost detached when they try to speak about the abuse they have suffered. These signs are usually an indication that the victim is experiencing a degree of dissociation, which is a way that the mind responds to try to protect itself from trauma. In dissociation, people experience a sort of break or distance between what they are experiencing and their consciousness (Vonderline et al., 2018). They can feel as if their thoughts, feelings, and experiences are happening at a distance, through a filter, or in a fog. Dissociation often disrupts a person's sense of time and also their perceptions of their own identity. Sometimes, this can elevate itself to the point where the victim feels almost as if the things they went through happened to someone else, or as if they observed it from the outside.

Dissociation can even be elevated to the point where a person pushes their memories of the abuse into their subconscious and experiences a form of amnesia. The mind may consciously forget what has happened, but the information is not erased. What the conscious mind may struggle to store or comprehend, the body remembers through a mechanism known as somatic memory, and it plays itself out in a person's sense of security and safety (Rothschild, 2000). This is true even if abuse happened at a young enough age that the average person might be tempted to think there is no way the victim could possibly have memories of the abuse.

In any of its forms, people unfamiliar with dissociation are often confused by it. As a result, Church members and leaders may feel like the emotion that an abuse victim is demonstrating is inconsistent with what someone who has been abused would actually display, and therefore conclude that the victim's report is false. Or, they may conclude that the fact that the victim says that they feel unsafe with someone but cannot articulate specific memories of abusive situations means that the victim is being irrational, overdramatic, or dishonest. Understood correctly, these are frequently signs of dissociation as a psychological defense against the trauma of the memories of these experiences.

INADVERTENT CONTRIBUTORS

For many victims of abuse, this cycle of abuse, gaslighting, doubt, fear, and rescripting of facts and reality feels a lot like being caught in an emotional riptide, with waves of aggression, anger, blame, and violence pounding against them from one direction while an undercurrent of doubt, fear, and isolation pulls at them from another. It is disorienting, frightening, and feels a lot like drowning.

In this cycle, it has not been uncommon for victims of abuse to receive counsel from Church members and local leadership that the way to solve their problem—and notice that here it is framed as their problem and not the problem of the abuser—is to increase their personal spiritual practices of fasting, praying, scripture study, temple attendance, service, participation in missionary work and family history, and so forth. It is not uncommon for this to be accompanied by admonitions to be Christlike by forgiving the abusive actions.

Inadvertently, these dynamics send an implied message that the solution to the abuse is for the victim to be the one to change. It also carries an implied blame that the abuse may be occurring because of the victim's lack of spirituality. While this is not usually directly stated (although some victims may bear sad testimony to the fact that sometimes it is), this message of spiritual inadequacy tends to be felt, absorbed, and internalized by victims of abuse, and it often becomes a powerful contributor to why they surrender themselves to the fate of a never-ending cycle of mistreatment.

While there is tremendous value in the aforementioned religious practices, they are not the solution for abusive actions, attitudes, and uses of personal agency by someone else. While it is true that victims of abuse would do well to hold close to their personal religious practices, these should never be considered sufficient in and of themselves to deal with the problem of abuse.

DIFFERENT FORMS OF ABUSE

It is important to recognize that different forms of abuse do not exist in a total vacuum; there is almost always some crossover between one type of abuse and others. Some are easier to detect, and others are much stealthier. However, all forms of abuse include an emotional and physical impact, even if there is no physical contact whatsoever between the abuser and the victim.

To understand this point, it can be helpful to have some familiarity with what is known in modern psychology as the biopsychosocial model (George & Engle, 1980). A brief summary of this model is that the different aspects of our humanity—our bodies, minds (thoughts and feelings), and social interactions—interact with each other in a mutually influential way.

For example, social isolation can lead to changes in neurochemistry, which then affects our thoughts and emotions in a negative way. Or, having brain damage, an abnormality in brain structure, or atypical brain functioning (such as in Autism Spectrum Disorder) can affect perception and emotional regulation, which then has an impact on our social interactions. From another angle, having negative perceptions about ourselves can lead to complicated relationships with others, which then has an impact on important body functions such as sleep and immune system response. And yes, our social interactions—including uplifting relationships or abusive relationships—affects our emotional and even our physical functioning. These interactions tend to form circular, mutually causing, mutually reinforcing patterns. Researchers have expanded on this idea into a biopsychosocial-spiritual model (Sulmasy, 2002), noting that our spirituality also falls into this mutually influencing and influenced pattern. In this way, abuse can actually come in the guise of spirituality, and it also has substantial spiritual implications that will be discussed later.

Just as we cannot drop a stone into a pond without producing ripples throughout the water, abuse in any of its forms sends waves cascading throughout the whole soul of the victim of the abuse. Oftentimes, incidents of abuse are ignored or downplayed because they did not leave a visible, external, recognizable mark. One problem with this thinking is that it does not recognize how all abuse has a physical impact in the way it restructures neural pathways and functioning (Coates, 2010). These deeper, hidden, but very real and physical wounds of all forms of abuse are much more challenging to heal than broken bones, torn ligaments, crushed cartilage, and bruised limbs.

Any examination of different types of abuse should be punctuated by a clear doctrinal point: "The Lord condemns abuse in any form" (*Protecting Children and Youth*, 2019). God does not look upon one form of abuse with any greater degree of allowance than another. All of them are repugnant to Him and in total opposition to His gospel. We must be careful, then, as people in a position to help prevent abuse and help other people to heal from it, that we do not find ourselves in the position of minimizing or excusing any type of abuse.

Consider the clarity of the directive, "Anyone who knows or has cause to believe that a child has been or is a victim of physical, emotional, or sexual abuse has a solemn responsibility to do something that can ensure protection for the child. . . . Do not tolerate abuse in any form" (*Protecting Children and Youth*, 2019). It does not state, "If it is physical or sexual then do something, but if the abuse is emotional, give it time and be cautious to not make trouble for the person that is potentially engaging in emotional abuse." All forms of abuse are harmful. All victims of abuse need help and protection.

PHYSICAL ABUSE

The specific legal definitions of physical abuse vary from state to state, but they share common factors. Consider the following selection of legal statements defining physical abuse:

- "Any intentional act causing ***injury or trauma*** [emphasis added] to another person or animal through way of bodily contact." (https://barprephero.com/legal-terms/family-law/physical-abuse/)

- "The willful action of inflicting ***bodily injury or physical mistreatment*** [emphasis added]. Physical abuse includes, but is not limited to, striking with or without an object, slapping, pinching, choking, kicking, shoving, prodding, or the use of chemical restraints or physical restraints unless the restraints are consistent with licensing requirements, and includes restraints that are otherwise being used inappropriately." (https://www.lawinsider.com/dictionary/physical-abuse)
- "Physical abuse is the use of ***physical force, body posture or gesture or body movement*** [emphasis added] that inflicts or threatens to inflict pain." (https://definitions.uslegal.com/p/physical-abuse/)
- "'Abuse' means intentionally or knowingly causing or attempting to cause a cohabitant physical harm or ***intentionally or knowingly placing a cohabitant in reasonable fear of imminent physical harm*** [emphasis added]." (Utah Code § 78B-7-102)
- The occurrence of one or more of the following acts between family or household members, sexual or intimate partners or persons who share biological parenthood:

  "(1) Attempting to cause or intentionally, knowingly or recklessly causing bodily injury, serious bodily injury, rape, involuntary deviate sexual intercourse, sexual assault, statutory sexual assault, aggravated indecent assault, indecent assault or incest with or without a deadly weapon. (2) Placing another in reasonable fear of imminent serious bodily injury. (3) The infliction of false imprisonment . . . (4) Physically or sexually abusing minor children . . . (5) Knowingly engaging in a course of conduct or repeatedly committing acts toward another person, including following the person, without proper authority, under circumstances which place the person in reasonable fear of bodily injury." (Penn. Cons. Stat. tit. 23, § 6102)

  - "(a) For purposes of this act, "abuse" means any of the following: (1) To intentionally or recklessly cause or attempt to cause bodily injury. (2) Sexual assault. (3) To place a person in reasonable apprehension of imminent serious bodily injury to that person or to another. (4) To engage in any behavior that has been or could be enjoined pursuant to Section 6320. (b) *Abuse is not limited to the actual infliction of physical injury or assault.* [emphasis added]" (Cal. Fam. Code §6203, Cal. Fam. Code § 6209-6211)

- "An act by a member of a family or household against another member of the family or household that is intended to result in physical harm, bodily injury, assault, or sexual assault or that is a threat that reasonably places the member in fear of imminent physical harm, bodily injury, assault, or sexual assault, but *does not include defensive measures to protect oneself.* [emphasis added]" (Tex. Fam. Code § 71.004)

- "Inflicting, or attempting to inflict, physical injury on an adult or minor by other than accidental means, *placing an adult or minor in fear of physical harm, physical restraint, malicious damage to the personal property of the abused party* [emphasis added], including inflicting, or attempting to inflict, physical injury on any animal owned, possessed, leased, kept, or held by an adult or minor, or placing an adult or minor in fear of physical harm to any animal owned, possessed, leased, kept, or held by the adult or minor." (Tenn. Code § 36-3-601)

- For a full list of legal definitions by state in the United States, see: https://www.ncsl.org/research/human-services/domestic-violence-domestic-abuse-definitions-and-relationships.aspx

A discussion on this specific topic could fill volumes all by itself, but for the purpose of our focus, there are several important points to emphasize. First, notice the broad definition of what constitutes physical abuse. The action does not have to cause a physical injury that can be seen and identified as such in order to qualify as abuse. It is not just hitting with an open or closed palm, punching, kicking, or hitting with objects. It can include such things as using body posture in a threatening way, doing things which make the other person afraid of being physically harmed (such as throwing objects in a rage or punching walls or furniture close to the body of the other person or making threats about hurting or killing them), making threats against another family member (such as a child) as a way to try to control the actions of the targeted family member, destroying property of the targeted person, using pain or the fear of pain as a supposed disciplinary method, and so forth.

At the core of physical abuse is the willingness to employ physical force, physical presence, pain, and the fear of pain as tools to be used in controlling or punishing another person. It not only consists of what an abuser actually does to the other person but what the abuser leads them to believe may happen next. Creating fear in the victim that the abuser will escalate into the use of physical force against them or another loved one (including animals) or their personal property is an integral part of the power and control dynamics of abuse. What is silently implied or explicitly threatened is just as much a part of the abuse as what is actually done.

Some people try to draw a justifying line, making the argument that as long as they don't use physical pain or the threat of physical pain in a specific way, their actions do not constitute abuse. This line of thinking is legally incorrect and psychologically erroneous. More than that, it is an indication that the person's heart is in the wrong place and that they are spiritually misaligned in their desires and intentions. The Christlike question is not, "In what ways can I use physical force, pain, fear, and the threat of pain to make this other person do what I want them to without crossing a line?" If those are the desires of a person's heart, that person is already deep in spiritual error.

The Christlike questions are, "How do I refrain from causing any harm to this other person? More than that, how do I help guide, nurture, correct, and support this person in a loving way? How do I work through concerns and conflicts with my spouse as an equal? How do I teach and correct my children using Christlike methods? How do I shun the temptation to exercise unrighteous dominion? How do I develop the Spirit as my guide in challenging matters? How do I shed the natural man?"

Furthermore, many perpetrators of abuse try to create an emotional trap for the victims of their abuse, stating, "You hit me back!

You were being abusive, too. If you report me for abuse, I'll just tell them what you did to me. You are no better than me." Please note that in the legal definitions of abuse, there is almost always a clause that states that physical actions taken to defend oneself or another person from the aggressions of someone else do not constitute abuse. Reacting in self-defense against the physical aggression of another person is not abuse. This accusation by an abuser is just another form of trying to use fear, shame, and threats to control the targets of their abusive behavior.

VERBAL ABUSE

Words have a power that reaches beyond the physical realm; they have psychological and even spiritual aspects. Speaking is used as an activating power in all of the saving ordinances. The creation of the world was initiated by God speaking. It is worth noting that one of the spiritual titles for the Savior Jesus Christ is "the Word" (see John 1:1). Words have the ability to create, as well as the ability to destroy. Words play a large role in the very way we think. They form the internalized dialogue that we use to understand ourselves, others, and the world around us. Words can be a tool or an instrument of torture. We should never minimize the impact of words, for good or for ill.

It should be no surprise, then, that words can be misused for abuse and that doing so can have deep, long-lasting effects on those who are the targets of verbal abuse.

In an *Ensign* article focused on domestic abuse, Dr. John Nelson described verbal abuse as follows: "Abuse may also include the use of threats, name calling, yelling, and intimidation" (A Conversation on Spouse Abuse, *Ensign*, October, 1999).

Elder Jeffery R. Holland (2007) instructed us about the immense power present in words:

> The Prophet Joseph Smith deepened our understanding of the power of speech when he taught, "*It is by words . . . [that] every being works when he works by faith.* God said, 'Let there be light: and there was light.' Joshua spake, and the great lights which God had created stood still. Elijah commanded,

and the heavens were stayed for the space of three years and six months, so that it did not rain. . . . All this was done by faith. . . . *Faith, then, works by words; and with [words] its mightiest works have been, and will be, performed.*" Like all gifts "which cometh from above," words are "sacred, and must be spoken with care, and by constraint of the Spirit." . . .

There is a line from the Apocrypha which puts the seriousness of this issue better than I can. It reads, "The stroke of the whip maketh marks in the flesh: but the stroke of the tongue breaketh the bones."

Elder Holland further expanded on verbal abuse by stating,

Husbands, you have been entrusted with the most sacred gift God can give you—a wife, a daughter of God, the mother of your children who has voluntarily given herself to you for love and joyful companionship. Think of the kind things you said when you were courting, think of the blessings you have given with hands placed lovingly upon her head, think of yourself and of her as the god and goddess you both inherently are, and then reflect on other moments characterized by cold, caustic, unbridled words.

Given the damage that can be done with our tongues, little wonder the Savior said, 'Not that which goeth into the mouth defileth a man; but that which cometh out of the mouth, this defileth a man.' A husband who would never dream of striking his wife physically can break, if not her bones, then certainly her heart by the brutality of thoughtless or unkind speech. . . . Today, I speak against verbal and emotional abuse of anyone against anyone, but especially of husbands against wives. Brethren, these things ought not to be.

Relationships are built with words. They can also be destroyed by words. Words work their way into our very hearts. The words chosen to describe us and interact with us by those whom we should be able to safely love and trust work their way into our internal dialogue and become a part of the way we perceive everything. They are not to be taken lightly. Harsh, caustic, dismissive, mean-spirited words are not harmless.

It should be noted that in all marital relationships, there will be disagreements and even arguments. But there is a very big difference between discussions that happen in disagreements in a healthy relationship and verbally abusive tactics. Consider the following "red flag" dynamics:

- Threats. The threats don't have to be physical in nature (for example, "I'm going to punch you in the face if you don't shut up!"). They can target anything that is important to the other person.
- Insults. Simply put, there is no room for insults in a healthy relationship. Perpetrators of verbal abuse may use insults and try to pass it off as "just joking" or accuse their target as simply "having no sense of humor."
- Circular arguments.
- Personal criticisms.
- Yelling and screaming.
- Throwing things, punching walls, or other acts of force.
- Displays of contempt.
- Humiliation and attacking the person's worth.
- Twisting the other person's words.
- Setting emotional traps.
- Blaming the other person for one's own actions.
- Seeing the discussion as a competition.
- Demanding credit for not having done something worse ("Hey, I didn't hit you. You need to give me credit for that," or "It's not like I'm watching child porn") (Healthline, 2021).

On the other hand, in healthy relationships conflicts are approached with compassion, care about the other person's feelings, a willingness to open up space for the other person's thoughts and feelings, the ability to accept influence from one another, and a desire to work through the differences in a way that respects the dignity of all involved.

EMOTIONAL/PSYCHOLOGICAL ABUSE

In an *Ensign* article, Talley Nanon of LDS Social Services wrote, "Emotional abuse is one person's attempt to remove another's agency and gain control over them with words or behaviors that manipulate emotions or choices. Emotional abuse can happen in any kind of relationship: between spouses, between parents and children, in friendships, in dating relationships, or among co-workers" (October 2020).

As previously mentioned, although abuse can take many forms, a common factor of all types of abuse is the desire to control another person in a variety of ways. It is a violation of the fundamental gift of agency and a reenactment in microcosm of the adversary's attempts to strip the children of God of their ability to choose for themselves. The more intimate our relationship with someone else is, the more aware we become of the thoughts and feelings that drive their motivations and actions. This can be misused when an abusive person uses their knowledge of another person's fears, insecurities, pains, traumas, interests, dreams, hopes, and desires to try to create beliefs or emotional states within that person to make them easier to manipulate and control.

Emotional abuse can happen in large incidents, like a parent publicly humiliating their child, filming the humiliation, and posting it to social media as a way to shame their child in an effort to change the child's behaviors. Emotional abuse can also accumulate in countless small incidents, including:

- Dismissing a family member's feelings.
- Demeaning a family member in small but constant ways.
- Frequent lies and deception.
- Overpressuring.
- Rejecting.
- Neglecting others' need for time and attention.
- Blaming the victim.
- Twisting the other person's words.
- Making the victim responsible for fixing the abuser's attitudes and behavior ("If you would just change this thing about you, I wouldn't have to treat you this way").
- Isolating.
- Intimidating.
- Coercing or threatening the other person but telling them they still have a choice.

- Insulting.
- Bullying
- Frequent criticism.
- Displays of contempt.
- Withholding love or support.
- Treating the other person like they are worthless or unloved.
- Treating the other person like they only exist to fulfill the abuser's wishes and priorities.
- Trying to convince someone that nobody likes them and they are lucky the abuser puts up with them.
- Emotional blackmailing or hostage taking.
- Threatening to do something unkind or damaging to another friend, family member, pet, or possession as a way to elicit a specific behavior from the other person.
- Terrorizing in any other way (Brassard, Hart, & Hardy, 2000; Children's Bureau, 2019; Haraman & Bernet, 2000; Trickett, Mennen, Kim, & Sang, 2009).

Emotional abuse can take place in private, where there are no witnesses. It can also take place in plain sight but be disguised and passed off as any number of things, including humor, natural competitiveness, "boys being boys," and so forth. In either case, it is often difficult for people suffering from emotional abuse to find anyone willing to believe that the problem they are experiencing is actually happening or is really all that serious. In fact, the abusive partner can be well liked and considered charming by other people. Says one woman, "People from our ward often tell me how lucky I am to be married to such a nice guy. I am confused by this. It is very painful for me to be with him" (Judy Olsen, "The Invisible Heart-breaker," *Ensign*, June 1996).

The fact is, emotional abuse has serious consequences. It can have substantial and long-lasting effects on a person's sense of security, their self-esteem, their emotional well-being, their ability to trust other people, their sense of self-efficacy, their ability to form healthy relationships, their risk of addiction and other self-destructive behaviors, and their overall psychological and social development and adjustment (Sturge-Apple, Skibo, & Davies, 2012).

SOCIAL ABUSE

One of our fundamental human needs is to be connected with other people and to be emotionally and physically safe in those connections. Many mental health issues are caused, contributed to, and exacerbated by having those connections and that safety disrupted, corrupted, or severed (Leigh-Hunt, Bagguley, Bash, Turner, Turnbull, Valtorta, & Caan, 2017). Conversely, part of good mental health treatment is facilitating the establishment of these kinds of connections (Imber-Black, 1992; McDaniel, Hepworth, & Doherty, 1992; McGoldrick & Hardy, 2019). Isolation even impacts physical health, including things such as coronary heart disease, stroke, infections, cognitive functioning, diabetes, hypertension, cancer, kidney disease, arthritis, emphysema, asthma, and general risk of death (Purrsell, Gould, & Chudleigh, 2000; Evans, Martyr, Collins, Brayne, & Clair, 2019; Tomaka, Thompson, & Palacios, 2006; Valtora, Kanaan, Gilbody, Ronzi, & Hanratty, 2016).

This provides some context to understand the seriousness of the social isolation that is frequently a part of abuse cycles. An *Ensign* article on spouse abuse noted, "Abuse victims may be isolated a lot; they may not be allowed to take part in community activities, and the people they see and how their time is spent may be closely monitored by the spouse. Those are some indicators we worry about" ("A Conversation on Spouse Abuse," *Ensign*, October, 1999).

People engaging in abuse rely on isolation for several purposes. First, it distances the victims of abuse from anyone who could witness the abuse and would speak up against it. Second, it creates an insulating social layer that the abuser can control. Abusers are often expert at determining whom they have managed to win over to the story they tell about their situation. By surrounding themselves and the victims of their abuse by people they have convinced to see them in a positive light, they create what is essentially a chamber of voices that will speak up in a variety of ways to cast doubt on the victims' experience of being abused. Third, in the absence of contrasting perspectives from friends and family of the victims who would be willing and able to see the abusive patterns for what they are, victims of abuse become increasingly vulnerable to questioning their own perceptions, thoughts, and feelings and having their own experience molded, changed, superimposed, and corrupted by the assertions of the person perpetrating the abuse.

Another result of this isolation is that it can be used to create the false impression that the abuser is a healthy, well-adjusted individual. After all, the perpetrator of abuse has social connections and is accepted and often well liked by the social circle which they allow the family to have. At the same time, the pattern of purposeful isolation paints the pernicious picture that the victims of abuse are poorly adjusted or even crazy. They are not well known by anyone in the social circle allowed by the abuser. The abuser is often the one who has controlled the narrative about their victims to the other people within the social circles they permit. The victims have often become anxious and unsure of themselves as a result of the abuse. So, if and when they do speak up or ask for help, the abuser has already laid a foundation that leads others to doubt the truthfulness or the sanity of the victims of abuse.

Besides isolation, another form of social abuse is spreading false, misleading, humiliating, or damaging information about a person with the goal of destroying the targeted person's reputation. This is usually done with the purpose of providing some kind of excuse for the abuser's actions. ("Well, yes, I screamed at her, but she is so neurotic and stubborn, I think I actually responded in a much more responsible way than anyone else would have if they had to put up with her!") It also serves the purpose of encouraging others to view the victim of abuse in a negative light, which is a preemptive strategy to discredit and please for help from the victim.

It also serves the psychological function of allowing the abuser to feel justified in mistreating the victim by getting other people to agree that the targeted person is somehow deserving of mistreatment or contempt. In addition, these forms of character assassination are frequently used by abusers to twist actions that the victim of abuse is taking to defend themselves into seeming like a form of abuse, thus portraying the abuser as the victim.

For example, in once case, a husband had a habit of calling various family members and discussing his sex life with his wife in great detail. As a part of this, he made accusations that his wife was too "Molly Mormon" in all ways, including in their sexual relationship, since she was unwilling to play out his pornography-inspired fantasies with him. His complaints to his family members garnered their support, which reinforced his anger and sense of victimhood about the boundaries his wife had.

These conversations with his family members escalated in intensity and negative tone. As the husband found that his parents and siblings were willing to align with his negative portrayal of his wife, he began to find ways to accuse her and blame her for other things, as well, even when he knew that he was exaggerating or even completely fabricating. For example, he tried to portray her as being an out-of-control spender, when in reality she was scrimping and saving to make the financial ends meet for their family while he was spending money without telling her to fund his pornography habit, refusing to work with her on the budget, and screaming at her about the financial situation. Rather than working on his relationship with his wife, recognizing his contributions to the problems he was complaining about, and making changes in his behavior and attitude that would improve the situation, he used phone calls with his family to assassinate his wife's character, scapegoat her as the cause of the problems, build up a false narrative of his victimhood and innocence, and garner support from his siblings and parents for his criticisms of his wife.

When the wife learned that he was doing this, she was deeply hurt by his accusations and embarrassed by his violation of personal boundaries in talking about their sexual relationship. She asked him to not discuss their sex life with his family. She pointed out the falsehoods he was spreading regarding the reasons for their financial struggles and inability to take time off of work for extended family activities, and she asked him to work on correcting the lies and misinformation that he was telling his family about the nature of their struggles and about her. However, he continued to engage in these phone calls with his family and carry on the same conversations.

Finally, the wife stated that she was very uncomfortable with what he was doing and hurt by his continued betrayal of trust and violation of marital boundaries. She asked that when he spoke with his family on the phone that he would place the phone on speaker so that the conversation was audible to her in order to hold him accountable for what he was saying. She saw no other option to try to counteract his continued campaign of blame and defamation.

Rather than being willing to see how he was betraying and hurting his wife and how his efforts at coping were actually destructive, the husband decided to use her efforts to protect herself as more ammunition for his rationalization, justification, and denial of his own behaviors. The husband claimed that his wife putting this boundary in place was actually isolating him from his family and that he was in fact the victim of her being abusive to him.

While there are many ways social abuse can play out, at its core is the desire to distance or cut off a targeted person from social support and anyone whose perceptions, beliefs, and emotions that abuser is unable to sufficiently manipulate and control. It also involves cultivating a negative and blaming perception of the victim of the social abuse to undermine their credibility and the degree to which other people see them as a sympathetic figure. Other common forms of social abuse include:

- Forcing a spouse to drop out of school/technical training against their will. This is often done as a way to keep the spouse from being in a position where they could potentially be financially independent and where they are making multiple social contacts with people that the abusive spouse cannot control.
- Forcing a spouse to quit a job against their will. Again, this keeps a spouse financially dependent and removes him/her from a social network.
- Forcing a spouse to ask for release from a church calling against their will.
- Telling a spouse who they can and cannot have as friends.
- Criticizing a spouse to other people.
- Spreading untrue or exaggerated stories about a spouse.
- Interrogating a spouse's friends, colleagues, or coworkers.
- Withholding funds (when they are within the budget) from a spouse to prevent them from engaging in reasonable social activities or personal development opportunities.

- Creating a hostile environment for a spouse's friends, family members, or colleagues to try to get them to distance themselves from the targeted spouse.

Besides its utility in protecting abusers from being caught and held accountable while simultaneously sapping the emotional strength of the victim, social abuse occurs in part as an attempt by the abuser to help himself or herself feel justified in their mistreatment of the other person. A human being mistreating someone while seeing them for who they are, as a real person with thoughts, feelings, dreams, and needs, creates a tremendous amount of cognitive and moral dissonance. We see the truth that we are hurting one of God's beloved children. This is a devastating truth. Indeed, we know that God weeps when He sees His children mistreating or abusing one another (see Moses 7:32–41).

The dissonance created in our hearts when we harm another person is exquisitely painful. It is in violation of our divine heritage and a mockery of the Savior's Atonement for that person's pains and sorrows. It is a wound to the soul of the abuser as well as to the victim. The natural and healthy way to resolve it is to repent, change, make amends, do what is necessary to help the other person heal, and treat the other person as we should in the future.

However, people often fall into the trap of attempting to resolve this dissonance by finding ways to blame the other person, to see the victim of their mistreatment as less than a real person, to objectify them, to create a false caricature of the victim and villainize this misrepresentation of them. In this process, abusers magnify the faults of their victims and invent new flaws and accusations against them. The abuser develops a narrative that portrays the other person as deserving the mistreatment they are suffering at the abuser's hands, thus making the victim responsible for the abuse. The harmful thoughts, feelings, and actions of the accuser are transformed in his or her own eyes into something that is excusable or even the right thing to do.

This psychological sleight-of-hand to keep a person's conscience at bay so they don't have to repent can be very fragile. Even a moment of being honest with themselves about the way they are falsely portraying and mistreating another person can lead to a breakdown of the false sense of self-assurance and a return of pangs of conscience, with a knowledge that they need to repent. The more a person has abused and mistreated other people, the more painful these truths are to them in the moments they break through their psychological armor. For those who have carried on long patterns of abuse, the temptation to flee from these feelings that the truth brings is magnified.

As a result, when someone is engaged in this pattern of rationalizing their own misdeeds and accusing others to keep themselves from admitting that they are being abusive, they often seek out allies. They value those whom they can win over to their self-justifying narrative and their blaming misrepresentation of the victim. In finding others that they can get to agree with their story, abusers find a dark sort of comfort and consolation and a sense of vindication that they are right, or at least justified, in their accusations against their victims. Their conscience is lulled back into an inert state, and they find a sense of strength in their self-justification. This often leads to an intensification of their mistreatment and abuse (Ferrell & Boyce, 2015).

Social abuse is both directly damaging—with impacts on mental and physical health—and also a tool through which the abusing person degrades the victim's sense of hope that other people could see the abuse, believe it, care about it, and be willing to do something to help. This is made even more complicated and harmful when members of the social circle that has been manipulated by the abuser include teachers, ecclesiastical leaders, mutual friends, family members, and even therapists or law enforcement personnel. No group of people is immune to the possibility of being caught up in the narrative of an abuser engaged in social isolation and character assassination against their victims, and that is true even of people who are in priesthood positions of authority and stewardship over abusers and their victims.

It is vital that we remember an important research finding: ***the vast majority of all allegations of abuse turn out to be true***, with only between 1 percent and 4 percent of all cases of reported abuse demonstrated to be fabrications (O'Donohue, Cummings, & Willis, 2019; Trocmé & Bala, 2005). Therefore, when someone reports abuse, the logical and correct choice is to believe them and to take action to assist them. A reason frequently cited for the failure of family, friends, and Church leaders to do so is fear that the accusations may be false and that the allegations could be harmful to the person being accused of abuse. However, this mindset is not aligned with the priority set forth by the Church in the General Handbook of instructions: "The first responsibility of the Church in abuse cases is to help those who have been abused and to protect those who may be vulnerable to future abuse."

Given that false accusations of abuse are extremely rare, and given the difficulty in substantiating abuse to the point that it would be litigated, the risk of doing some sort of harm to an innocent person accused of abuse is very low and is outweighed by the great and pressing needs of victims of abuse. If there is any question about whether or not abuse is occurring, it should be reported and acted upon, not debated as to whether anything should be done. As stated in the preamble to the "Church's Protecting Children and Youth" (2019) training, "The Lord expects us to do all we can to prevent abuse and help those who have been victims of abuse." Those are the priorities and guidelines set forth by the apostles and prophets of the Lord.

SPIRITUAL ABUSE

President James E. Faust (1987) felt impressed to teach of Satan as "the Great Imitator." In his discussion of the adversary's deceptive tactics, he noted that Satan can take things that are good and twist them to serve his diabolical agenda. Indeed, one can only imagine that the fallen son of the morning takes great pleasure when he manages to set in motion great evil in the guise of good. Consider the millions who were killed in the Christian Crusades, the torture and death wrought at the hands of the Spanish Inquisition, the numerous cultures forced into conversion to adulterated Christianity on the threat of annihilation, the innocent women burned or drowned as witches at the zealous demands of the Puritains, and a long list of other atrocities, all purportedly done in the name of the Savior. What a gross perversion of His name! One can only imagine his contemptuous laughter as the Father of Lies commits crimes for which he frames the Son of God!

President Faust went on to cite a statement by the First Presidency: "He is working under such perfect disguise that many do not recognize either him or his methods. There is no crime he would not commit, no debauchery he would not set up, no plague he would not send, no heart he would not break, no life he would not take, no soul he would not destroy. He comes as a thief in the night; he is a wolf in sheep's clothing."

That wolf in sheep's clothing can present itself in the form of spiritual or ecclesiastical abuse, as well. This can take many forms, including but not limited to:

- A husband telling a wife that she must obey him because "he is the priesthood holder."
- A parent telling children that he or she is the one who will receive all revelation for them and that it will trump or supersede any or all personal revelation they might receive.
- Children being told that they must "honor their father and mother" and obey them without question.
- The misapplication of spiritual principles or teachings to try to control the thoughts, feelings, or behaviors of another person.
- Using covenants as an instrument of control or coercion.
- A person claiming that the fact that they hold a particular calling means they are right and the other person is wrong.
- Excusing abusive or immoral behaviors because of supposed spiritual achievements or status.
- Any form of "pulling spiritual rank."
- Implying that there will be spiritual consequences if another person does not act in the way the abuser is demanding.
- Demanding that other people behave in a certain way so as not to harm an abuser's appearance of righteousness.
- Shaming people for their spiritual feelings, desires, and practices.
- Using coercive methods to get other people to engage in spiritual practices.
- Forbidding other people to engage in spiritual practices without the presence and control of the abuser.

- Implying that a person's physical or emotional struggles are due to them being unrighteous.
- A person excusing their own sins while being merciless about what they perceive as the sins of others.
- Feeding another person's sense of spiritual inadequacy.

Faithful disciples of Christ who are earnest in their desire to follow Him and are dedicated to obedience can often be vulnerable to being manipulated, hurt, and controlled by those willing to misuse, misinterpret, misrepresent, and misapply gospel principles or practices in the service of hurting, punishing, or controlling other people. This is a doubly damaging form of abuse. On the one hand, it has a tendency to drive a wedge between the victims of abuse and the Church, since the way the gospel and the structure of the Church is being perverted in the abuse can make it feel like the Church endorses the abuse. On the other hand, it can corrupt a person's understanding of spiritual things and make it hard for them to discern the Spirit, tying them down instead to a pseudo-religion of anxiety and fractured agency in which the desires of an abusive person have taken the role of an idol that eclipses the true nature of the Savior and His mission.

SEXUAL ABUSE

In common Latter-day Saint culture, we have traditionally approached teaching about sexuality by emphasizing modesty and abstinence before marriage and fidelity after marriage. These are good principles, but they are not the only principles that govern a healthy and happy sexual relationship between spouses and that protect against sexual exploitation and abuse. What we have not been accustomed to speaking very openly about is the concept of consent, either in lesser matters like kissing a dating partner or in more impactful matters like engaging in a sexual relationship with a spouse. In the absence of overt teachings about consent, certain common patterns and traditions have developed. These range from not even acknowledging consent as a concept to overtly teaching that it is a spouse's duty to provide sex whenever their husband or wife says they want it.

Additionally, for many years discussions about sexuality within the culture of the Church have been dominated by the use of archaic terms that youth no longer use nor understand (such as necking and petting). These discussions have generally focused a great deal on what not to do but have not provided much guidance on how to grow an emotional and physical relationship in a healthy way. Unfortunately, teachings about modesty have sometimes been twisted into a message that boys are not able to control their sexual urges and that girls are responsible for behaving in a way that keeps the boys in check.

Efforts to be modest in our discussions about sexuality have often ended up leaving it mysterious and misunderstood. The missing pieces have had a tendency to be filled in by ignorance, tradition, or secular ideas. Sadly, far too often the pieces are filled in by ideas and concepts that have been generated by pornography use and addiction. With that being the case, there are several important points to acknowledge in order to build an understanding of sexual abuse.

First, being married to someone is not the equivalent of a blanket statement of sexual consent. Spouses have a right to say, "No, not now," or "I'm not comfortable with that," or "I don't want to be touched that way," or even, "Our relationship is not in a spot where I feel open to being sexually active with you at all right now. We've got some things to work on before that could feel good for me." A spouse who says no to engaging in some form of sexuality is not breaking his or her marital covenant. On the other hand, a spouse who insists on sexually gratifying themselves over the objections of their spouse is breaking that covenant.

The proper response to a spouse saying no to sexual activity in part or as a whole is not to seek to coerce their compliance, to assert that sex is a marital duty, or to state that the spouse "owes it" for any reason. In matters of consent, the word "no" is a complete sentence! It does not require justification or explanation. It is not up for debate. The proper, moral response to a spouse saying no to engaging in any form of sexuality is to respect the boundary, learn what is making the other person uncomfortable, and work on building a relationship that is comfortable and safe for both.

This should not be done manipulatively. The question isn't, "What do I need to do so my spouse will be sexually active with me again?" This shows that the person's heart is in the wrong place and that they are viewing their spouse as an object of their own sexual gratification and not as a person, a sacred and special son or daughter of God. It's not about making the spouse available for sex! It's about caring enough about one's spouse to find out what is disrupting his or her sense of safety and being dedicated to doing all in one's power to helping them to heal and feel safe. Anything less than that is not living up to the covenant made at marriage.

Coercing a spouse to have any form of sexual activity when they say no is a form of sexual abuse. This is true whether or not the cooercing partner uses physical force. Use of shame, threats, intimidation, bribery, or other forms of verbal or emotional coercion are equally in violation of how God has ordained the physical relationship between spouses to be.

Second, at the core of almost all definitions of spousal sexual abuse or rape is that one person is coercing the other to engage in a sexual act that they do not wish to engage in. Coercing a spouse into sexual activity is not only wrong, it is a criminal act (Cal Pen Code § 262). Any degree of sexual coercion by a spouse is deeply concerning and should not be tolerated. It is important to acknowledge that sexuality is an entire range of actions and interactions that is much more comprehensive than the act of coitus. It does not matter whether or not the coerced sexual action results in intercourse. Any coerced sexual activity is a form of sexual abuse.

Third, the continued struggle of many members of the Church with pornography use is a problematic contributor to the scourge of sexual abuse. Much of what is portrayed in pornographic material minimizes, normalizes, and promotes sexual coercion as not only acceptable but desirable. Predatory and forceful sexual actions are portrayed as attractive, and the victims of these actions are depicted as actually desiring to be dominated, with their boundaries only being a part of the sexual game being played, designed to be bypassed as a means to pleasure for both parties. These oft repeated concepts become a part of the sexual paradigm for many users of pornography and tend to work their way into their own thoughts and actions in their relationships with their spouses.

Fourth, it should go without saying that any degree of sexual interaction with a child is wrong and should not ever occur. Sadly, the fact that 20 percent of girls and 5 percent of boys admit to being sexually assaulted (and those are just the ones that admit it; the actual numbers are most likely much larger) shows that this is a fact that should be stated much more frequently and far more emphatically than it is right now (US Department of Health and Human Services, 2010). While previous educational approaches regarding the sexual abuse of children have focused on the concept of "stranger danger," research indicates that most child victims of sexual abuse are abused by someone they know, such as a family member, family friend, or trusted adult in their community (Mcalinidin, 2006). It bears great emphasis that using pornography or masturbating in the presence of children, whether or not they are awake at the time, is not only a violation of God's laws but also a violation of the laws of the land.

For example, Utah Code 76-10-1201 specifically deals with laws that protect children from exposure to pornographic and harmful materials and performances. As a part of these laws, children are given legal protection against exposure to sexual conduct, defined as "acts of masturbation, sexual intercourse, or any touching of a person's clothed or unclothed genitals, pubic area, buttocks, or, if the person is a female, breast, whether alone or between members of the same or opposite sex or between humans and animals in an act of apparent or actual sexual stimulation or gratification." Using pornography in the presence of a child or masturbating in the presence of a child is a violation of this and other portions of the law.

Many other sexualized attitudes and interactions can happen with children that—while not falling within the legal statues of a crime—are concerning in nature and create an overly sexualized environment for the children that is developmentally inappropriate and that makes it easier for sexual abuse to develop without a child being aware that boundaries are being crossed. This can range from an adult bragging about their own sexual anatomy or perceived prowess in the presence of a child, an adult making derogatory statements about someone's sexual anatomy of performance in the presence of a child, adults engaging in sexualized conversations around children, and more.

Jeffery R. Holland (2021) warned us about such behavior when he stated, "Consider the coarse language that parallels sexual transgression, both of which are so omnipresent in movies or on television, or note the sexual harassment and other forms of impropriety in the workplace about which we read so much these days. In matters of covenantal purity, the sacred is too often being made common and the holy is too often being made profane. To any who are tempted to walk or talk or behave in these ways—'as the world giveth,' so to speak—don't expect it to lead to peaceful experience; I promise you in the name of the Lord that it won't. 'Wickedness never was happiness,' an ancient prophet once said. When the dance is over, the piper must always be paid, and most often it is in a currency of tears and regret."

One reason to be justifiably worried about people—including adults seen as trusted family members or close family friends who are respected in the church in community—engaging in sexualized conversations around children is that this often is a part of the process of grooming a child to prepare them to be a victim of actual sexual assault (Thornton & Matravers, 2013). By engaging in sexualized conversations around children, a potential abuser can lead the child step by step to be desensitized to sexualized content in the context of their relationship with that adult specifically and with adults in general. That way, the child who has been groomed and desensitized has difficulty discerning sexual actions from adults as sufficiently outside of the norm of their experience to be able to identify it and reach out for support if it happens to them.

It is important to recognize that in many cases of child sexual abuse, it is not only the child who has been groomed, desensitized, and mislead about the intentions and potential actions of an abuser. Many abusers are experts at weaving an image of themselves that creates doubt for other family members, bishops, and even law enforcement officers about the feasibility of them engaging in some kind of abusive behavior (Mcalinidin, 2006). They can present themselves as charming, hard-working, diligent in church callings, model return missionaries, well accomplished, and well liked individuals. That way, when the victim of sexual abuse or an ally of that victim speaks up, they often find themselves confronted with a chorus of voices who tell them that they must be wrong because the abuser is clearly not someone who would ever engage in that type of behavior.

While on this topic, it should also be noted that under-educating children about sexuality also creates vulnerabilities for children being groomed and sexually abused. To illustrate this issue, consider the experiences of one family in which all of the children were being sexually abused by a parent. Within that family there had been no discussion of sexuality with the children. The children had no concept of what sexual behavior was, and as such had no baseline understanding of what it would look like if someone was acting out on them sexually. As a result, the abusive parent carried out a pattern of sexually molesting his children for years while telling them that he was engaging in a part of their personal hygiene that was his duty as their father to help them take care of. It was only when one of the children took a health class in high school that they were able to begin to realize that what their father was doing was sexual abuse.

Fifth, sexual abuse and sexual harassment are not limited to interactions between spouses and between parents and children. Unwanted and unwelcome sexualized comments and interactions are a form of sexual harassment that can happen in any relationship.

For example, I am aware of a situation in which the father of a family of adult children who was considered a respected family patriarch and held a prominent calling in his ward would regularly travel through his house nude in the presence of the spouses of his married children and in the presence of his grandchildren, much to the discomfort of his daughters-in-law. I know of another situation in which a mother-in-law who was in a Relief Society presidency had a pattern of commenting suggestively about the sexual anatomy of her daughters-in-law and making lewd comments about what she perceived as their sexual prowess. I am aware of another family in which the diminutive size of a certain nephew's genitals was an ongoing point of discussion and purportedly "good-natured" derision amongst his extended family members, including some who were temple workers. I also know of other situations in which brothers (one of whom was in an elders quorum presidency and another who had a calling in the Young Men's organization) would share the details of their sexual relationships with each other against the protest of their wives.

Each one of these examples demonstrates a crossing of sexual boundaries, a lack of respect for consent, and an oversexualization of self or other family members. While most of these do not yet reach the legal stature of sexual abuse (although the actions of the grandfather regularly walking nude in front of children may possibly qualify), they can certainly be identified as sexual disrespect and sexual harassment, and could easily be a part of the grooming process. They indicate family systems in which sexual lines and boundaries are blurred, and the risk of grooming and sexual abuse is elevated. These types of attitudes and actions are not in harmony with the Savior's teachings about the dignity and sanctity of each individual and the sacred nature of sexuality.

A COMMON ABUSE CYCLE

Survivors of abuse are often asked, "Why didn't/don't you leave?" This question is often very painful, because by the time someone is being asked this question they have usually been deeply emotionally programmed by the abuser to blame themselves for the abuse, to feel hopeless that things could be any better for them, or to even feel that they deserve anything better. The answer to the question is complex, involving the combination of the effects of the various types of abuse previously discussed. Another contributor to the answer of that question is that abuse often occurs in a predictable cycle that contains powerful psychological mechanisms that can make a victim of abuse feel confused and paralyzed.

The cycle of abuse tends to be divided into four stages (Racovec-Felser, 2014):

Build up stage. In this stage, the early warning signs that the abuser is ramping up emotionally toward acting out abusively appear and begin to grow. They can include things such as increased irritability, increased impulsiveness, increased lies and deceptions, engaging in addictive behaviors, increased blaming of the potential victim, and more. The general sense is that the pot is simmering and working its way up toward a boil.

This is often a time of growing unease and anxiety for potential targets of the abuser's behaviors. They may find themselves engaged in a wide variety of efforts to defuse the abuser's growing tension and anger in an effort to avoid a major incident. Oftentimes, the abuser grows in their accusations toward the victims as the reason for the abuser's emotional disturbance. The fear of physical or emotional violence becomes more and more palpable for the victims.

It should be noted that in this stage, we are already seeing various forms of abuse at play. The fear that the victims feel is already a form of psychological abuse and control. The growing irritability and accusations are already methods of verbal abuse. In general, there are usually abusive behaviors and dynamics in motion well before a major incident of abuse occurs.

Acting out stage. At the acting out stage there is a major incident of abuse. It may be a raging session of screaming and throwing furniture. It may involve acts of physical violence or aggression. It may involve saying deeply hurtful things. It may include some kind of sexual coercion. There is a wide variety of ways that such an incident may play itself out. Furthermore, the acting out stage may not be just a single episode. It may be the beginning of a prolonged series of overt and major abusive actions that stretches on for days, weeks, or even months.

These are the moments of abuse that stand out the most. In fact, they tend to feel so prominent that other forms of abuse that are not as loud or dramatic go unnoticed or unidentified as abuse. Major incidents of abuse are a bit like cockroaches in the sense that if you see one, you can rest assured that there are quite a few more crawling around that you haven't yet found or that aren't being discussed or identified as such.

During the period of acting out, intimidation, the threat of harm, and actual harm (physical, emotional, or otherwise) are very active. Victims may find themselves locked in any number of patterns of fight, flight, or freeze. Abusers often use any actions taken by the victims to defend themselves as further reason for anger and accusations, and may even use this as a way of trying to claim that the victims are the ones who were being abusive.

"Reconciliation" and honeymoon stage. At this stage, the abuser appears to de-escalate and engages in actions designed to keep the abuse

victims from leaving or from reporting the abuse. The abuser may apologize or even beg for forgiveness with grand gestures. They may appear to be genuinely sorrowful about what has happened and make promises that it will never happen again.

At the same time, it is not uncommon even at this stage for the abuser to minimize or even deny what happened while still making efforts to placate the victims of the abuse. If they do admit it, they may still hold fast to their claims that what happened was the victim's fault. There can be confusing, mixed signals.

The general effect of the honeymoon stage is to create within the victims some sense of hope that the abuse is over and will not happen again. This often has the effect of placing the victim in an emotional state in which they are unlikely to reach out for help or report the abuse because they feel like things might finally change and they don't want to do something that could ruin a relationship if it is just about to get better.

Notice the type of thinking the victim often finds themselves utilizing: they are the ones afraid of "ruining" the relationship if they reveal what has happened, rather than recognizing that it is the abuser's actions and attitudes that are harming the relationship. They are the ones who feel responsible for preventing a recurrence of the abuse. All of these are signs that psychological and emotional abuse have been occurring in a way that programs the victims to take responsibility for things that are out of their control and instead are within the realm of the abuser's accountability. This is not a sign of weakness or of consent to the abuse or of some sort of deep psychological desire to be punished by the victims. These are the results of emotional abuse, and part of what needs to be corrected and healed. This psychological downloading of responsibility to the victim is a part of what keeps them from leaving abusive relationships. Furthermore, the hope that the abuser will change is used as a weapon to keep the victims in the line of fire.

Calm stage. After the drama of major abuse incidents or periods and after the intensity of the reconciliation or honeymoon period, the patterns that take place between an abuser and their victims seem calm by comparison. Note that this does not indicate that the relationship has become healthy, mutually supportive, or free of any maladaptive, manipulative, or abusive patterns. It just means that the difference between fully active, highly energized moments of abuse and the "calm" stage are large enough to feel to the victim as if things are peaceful and that the immediate danger is past.

Sometimes in the calm stage, the victims of abuse can have experiences with the abuser that feel loving, deep, and secure, as if the person really has changed and as if the abuse will never happen again. In some ways, these moments of calm in between more dramatic acts of abuse can perversely mirror a dynamic that happens when a woman gives birth: the intense agony of labor is followed by a burst of job and connection that can dampen or even erase the true, full memory of how excruciating the process of labor and delivery has been. Extremes in emotional fluctuation make the moments of joy (or relative joy) seem amplified when following intense suffering. In this way, a natural bonding mechanism designed to connect mother with child is hijacked to connect victim to abuser through the dynamics of the cycle of abuse.

These moments of relative calm feel good, even precious at times, and victims of abuse hold out hope that this is what the relationship could become, even if these moments are few and far between. In this way, the churning cycle of abuse uses hope and these periods of positive emotion as a type of cement, leading victims of abuse to feel that if they leave, they are losing the potential for good in the relationship.

POWER AND CONTROL

Like skinwalkers, shapeshifters, and changelings from mythology and science fiction, abuse has the ability to take on many forms. While the actual structure and expression of the abuse can portray itself differently, all abuse is made up of the same basic element: a desire to exert power and control over another person. Whether it is designed to force a person to think, feel, or behave in a desired way or to erase thoughts, emotions, and choices that the abuser does not want from the other person, abuse is about attempting to override the agency of another.

In that way, our mortal battle with the scourge of abuse is a continuation of the War in Heaven following the great counsel in which Lucifer proposed a selfish pseudo-alternative to the plan of salvation in which he would subvert the agency of all of God's children under His will. He proposed himself to be the supreme ruler, the one mind and the one voice that would be given any sense of expression or autonomy or freedom. He justified this by gilding it in a guise of supposed benevolence, saying, "Behold, here am I, send me, I will be thy son, and I will redeem all mankind, that one soul shall not be lost, and surely I will do it; wherefore give me thine honor" (Moses 4:1).

It is perhaps not surprising at all that the adversary of all that is good would decide to try to tempt so many of God's children to do the very thing for which he was cast out of heaven for trying to do. In so doing, he knows he is capable of causing an inexpressible amount of sorrow and suffering to innocent people who fall victim to abuse while simultaneously bringing abusers under condemnation for repeating his own sin. This diabolical double dipping brings nothing but misery.

Attempting to assert power and control over another person is antithetical to creating a loving, safe, nurturing, and empowering relationship. God loves us for who we are. He seeks to exalt our nature and personality, not to erase it, mold it, or turn it into some sort of clone of Him. Husbands and wives are intended to learn to value each other, to respect each other, and to cherish each other. Neither holds dominion over the other, but both work together for their common good. While teaching, guidance, and direction are necessary parts of parent/child relationships, there is a vast difference between providing these and acting coercively toward children. God does not force anyone to do anything. He who has power to do all things refuses to use that power to control anyone. He is our model to follow.

Consider the contrast between abusive relationships, with their focus on power and control, versus healthy relationships, as conceptualized in the Duluth Model (i.e. Domestic Abuse Intervention Programs, 2021; Bohall, Bautista, & Musson, 2016).

THE CORE OF ABUSE: THE HEART

As this chapter has demonstrated, abuse can take many forms. The possibilities for abuse are so vast that, as mentioned in the scriptures, "I cannot tell you all the things whereby ye may commit sin; for there are divers ways and means, even so many that I cannot number them" (Mosiah 4:29). At the end of the day, whether or not something is abusive is not simply a matter of whether it checks off certain boxes on a list of behaviors or attitudes. At the core of all abuse is the desire and willingness to control others through the use of physical, emotional, social, verbal, or other means. Abuse starts in the heart, and works its way towards outward manifestations.

In the core teachings of the gospel, the Savior Himself spoke about how the state of our hearts matters. He taught that for a person to lust after someone else they are not married to is already committing adultery in their hearts (Matthew 5:27-28). He taught that hating someone is the heart-level equivalent of murder (1 John 3:15; Matthew 5:21-22). He said through His prophets that giving a gift with a grudging heart is the equivalent of withholding the gift (Moroni 7:8). And the Savior also taught in great plainness that whatever we do to someone else, we are doing to Him (Matthew 25:40). In that way, abuse is never just between the abuser and the victim. It is always between the abuser and the Son of God, the Creator of the world, the Redeemer from suffering and death. The pain caused to a son or daughter of God by another is always the Savior's business. His Atonement makes it so. "Behold, I have graven thee upon the palms of my hands; thy walls are continually before me (Isaiah 49:16)."

Who would ask themselves, "How physically, emotionally, socially, or verbally aggressive, controlling, neglectful, or abusive can I be with Christ before I 'cross the line'?" I would hope that no one who claims to be Christian would ever seriously contemplate that question as a guide. And yet, those who abuse others are, in fact, making this calculation with each hostile word, with each controlling gesture, with each moment of cutting the other person down emotionally. How often do those who commit abuse seek to excuse themselves because it does not fit the definition of abuse they are willing to accept? Why do people who abuse feel like they get to be the ones who determine where "the line" is?

Similarly, what person who claims to follow Christ would say in a moment of repentance, "Lord, I've done what I think I need to do in order to repent of this sin. It's been rather uncomfortable for me, if you don't mind me saying so, and I don't really feel like there is more I should be asked to put up with. So, I'm going to consider this squared away between me and Thee. Please don't bring it up to me again, and certainly don't allow those I have hurt through my sins to still have any need for healing, especially if it is inconvenient or uncomfortable for me. Even worse, don't let them feel like they need any kind of boundaries with me. I feel like I have changed, and I deserve to have them see me the way I would like to be seen. Make it so. Amen."

And yet, this is the attitude that is frequently displayed by those who have committed abuse. If they are even willing to admit at all that they have done wrong and need to change, they often fall into a trap of feeling like they should be able to define what that needs to look like and to determine when they are done and when other people can no longer rationally feel any degree of hurt, mistrust, caution, or desire for distance from them. Their thoughts are not on the needs of those they have hurt. Rather, their concerns are about their own feelings, desires, and sense of how they would like things to be. It is this self-centered set of thoughts and emotions that was the seed for abuse in the first place! One cannot repent of abuse by using the same mindset and state of the heart from which the abuse sprung in the first place.

As long as a person still harbors desires to control other people's thoughts, feelings, and behaviors and is willing to use aggression, hostility, and manipulation to achieve these goals, this person is still thinking like an abuser. As long as someone feels they have a right to dictate to other people what they can feel about how they have been treated and what they are allowed to need, that person is still thinking like an abuser. As long as a person continues to seek to justify their own actions and minimize any responsibility for its impact on others, that person is still thinking like an abuser. And, as the Bible teaches, "As a man thinketh in his heart, so is he" (Proverbs 23:7). What is in the heart will work its way outward.

CHAPTER 4

OBSTACLES TO ESCAPING ABUSE

WHY DO VICTIMS OF ABUSE STAY?

Many victims of abuse are met with the same question by other people over and over again: why do they choose to stay? Unfortunately, it is not uncommon for this question to contain some implied accusations: "If what you are saying was true, you would have already left," or "It can't be as bad as you are saying it is," or, "You are just doing this for attention. If it really bothered you this much, you would leave." The answer to the question is that there are many obstacles to leaving an abusive situation. Some of those are practical and logistical. Some of those are based on hopes and dreams for the idea of what the relationship could have been. Some of those are fears and insecurities planted within the victim of abuse through the psychological aspects of the abuse.

Whether internal or external, whether "objectively real" or perceptions caused by the abuse itself, each one of these obstacles plays the role of keeping the victim within the abusive relationship. Unless the target of the abuse is able to see some way to overcome these obstacles, the thought of leaving the abusive situation feels impossible.

THE PERCEPTION OF NO OTHER CHOICE

As much as positive emotions can be used to tie a victim of abuse down in an abusive relationship, negative emotions also play a powerful role. Most victims of abuse stay in the abusive relationship because they simply feel that they have no other choice than to do so. When people feel they have no other choice than to continue to suffer, they can easily fall into a state known as learned helplessness, which is both a damaging weapon by itself and also deepens the harm done by the acts of abuse (Bargai, Ben-Shakhar, & Shalev, 2007). In learned helplessness, the person's experiences lead them to a firm belief that there is no correlation between their actions and what the outcomes of their situation will be. They are powerless, entirely at the mercy of other people and of the vicissitudes of life. No matter how hard they try, those in stations of power, influence, and control will have their way with them. There is no escape. How utterly bleak and depressing! As much as victims of abuse may wish to believe otherwise, their repeated experiences only serve to reinforce this vision of reality for them.

This state of learned helplessness is so profound that even if there is a clear path of escape shown to them, victims of abuse may not be able to perceive it, believe it, or feel like they deserve it. In this case, victims of abuse feel their only options are either to endure the abuse to the end of their mortal lives—another perversion of a true doctrine—or to end their lives. This is one of the reasons that victims of abuse are at an elevated risk of death by suicide (Devris et al., 2011; Kavak, Aktürk, Özdemir, & Gültekin, 2018; Malkesman, Pine, Tragon, Austin, Henter, Chen, & Manji, 2009; Plunkett, O'Toole, Swanston, Oates, Shrimpton, & Parkinson, 2001; Stark, Riordan & O'Connor, 2011).

From a child's point of view. There is an inherent power difference between children and adults. Children rely on adults for their basic survival needs, for access to important services like healthcare and education, for opportunities, and for help learning to grow into mature, well-adjusted individuals. As such, children in our society are recognized as a vulnerable population (Landrigan, 2005).

If one or more adults who have responsibility for the care of a child are either unwilling or unable to fulfill these roles or responsibilities, or if they act in ways which harm the child physically, socially, or emotionally, children are dramatically limited in the choices available to them to try to do something to change their situation or to protect themselves from the immediate harm they face or the risk of future damage being done to them. The younger a child is, the fewer options they have within their own immediate abilities.

If a child is the target of some kind of physical or sexual abuse, the difference in physical strength between them and their abuser is such that even their hardest efforts to escape, run, break free, or fight back are unlikely to have any results beyond angering the abuser, often leading to the abuser being harsher. The abuser punishes the child for resisting, with the implication that in future instances of abuse, they will suffer more if they try to protect themselves. Children's own experience of trying to defend themselves physically teaches them that they do not have the power to stop the abuse.

Children who have lived their entire lives with one or more abusive parents/adults often lack a frame of reference to even understand that what they are experiencing is not normal or healthy. For them, this is the way life has always been. The anger, manipulation, control, and psychological games are all just a part of the world as they have come to know it. Or, the child living in a long-term abusive dynamic may be able to recognize that it is harmful, but may have no understanding of how things could be different. They find their ways of hunkering down trying to survive because as far as they know, this is just the way the whole world is.

Some children living with abuse may try to cope by becoming perfectionistic high achievers, or some variation on that theme (Flett, Druckman, Hewitt, & Werkerle, 2012). These children find that other adults tend to praise them for their accomplishments and interpret their actions as a sign that things are going well in their lives. In fact, it is not uncommon for adults to congratulate and give credit to the abusive parent for doing "such a good job" raising high achieving children. How devastating this praise is for the abused child to hear! Other adults tend to see the veneer of successes, not perceiving the underlying neglect, pain, humiliation, fear, and the deep sense that the abused child carries within them that they must find a way to take care of themselves and put themselves in positions where they cannot be hurt. Their external achievements are driven by an internal motor of despair. These children may dream of someday creating a future for themselves where they can make their own decisions and perhaps be free from abuse and mistreatment. But they know they must continue to suffer so long as they are minors. Their experience has taught them no other option.

Other children living with abuse—both experiencing it themselves and watching it happen to other family members—find that the pain turns to anger and resentment within them. They may start to act out in a variety of ways (Almış, Gümüştaş, & Kütük, 2020; Lloyd, 2018; Dodaj, 2020; Margolin, 1998; Ososfsky, 2018). They may be harsh and unkind to others. They may be disruptive in peer groups. They may engage in risky or self-destructive behaviors. They may develop or exacerbate learning disorders. They may seek to numb themselves with drugs, or hide away from the world in video games or the internet. They may experiment with their sexuality to find ways to feel special and create belonging. They often struggle to succeed in school and may push back against church and things of a spiritual nature.

In their experience, gospel ideas have been used as excuses for abuse and unrighteous dominion, or worse, as weapons. In acting out, these children are often labeled as being problematic, rather than having adults recognize the problem the children are trying to cope with and survive. In fact, abusive parents of children who respond in this way are often approached with empathy and commiseration by other adults for having a "problem child." This often leaves the abused child feeling suspicious and distrustful of adults in general, since they seem to empathize and align with the abusive parents.

When a child who is trying to cope by acting out decides to speak up about their issues with the abusive parent, it is often met with the attitude that they are being unkind, dishonest, and disrespectful of their parent. To be sure, when children speak out in this way, it is often not very articulate, specific, or clear. In fact, it is frequently angry, difficult to follow, and punctuated by profanities. This is all too often met with lectures and consequences about respect for parents and use of appropriate language, rather than with an ear that discerns the message that is being ineloquently delivered in this fashion. These children learn that anything they do to try to change their situation just ends up making them look bad and causes them more trouble.

For the vast majority of abused children, the reality is that they do not have power to change their situation—not without the help of an adult who is willing and able to see what is happening to them, believe what is happening to them, and take action to help ensure that the child's physical and emotional well being is protected and conditions of safety are established. Abused children need adults who are willing to speak up and act courageously so that the needs of the vulnerable are not overshadowed by the agendas of those who have committed abuse but are granted more power due to their status as an adult.

From a spouse's point of view. There are many reasons a spouse may feel that they have no other choice but to stay with an abusive partner (Buel, 1999). It should be noted that these reasons are compounded and amplified when the abused person is a woman. These reasons can include:

- The victim of abuse is often financially dependent on the abuser. As such, the abuser has greater access to resources such as legal representation than the victim does, and the victim is left without recourse for getting daily needs met.
- Abusers often use their position of greater financial stability to threaten that they will take the children away from the victim of abuse if the victim tries to leave.
- Fairly regularly, victims of abuse have not been able to obtain a college degree or technical training certification of their own as a result of being required to drop out of school or leave jobs by the abusive partner. Therefore, job options if the victim were to leave are more limited and financially prohibitive.
- The social isolation/social sabotaging that is often a part of abusive patterns frequently leaves victims of abuse feeling that they have no friends, allies, or anyone who would give them emotional or practical support.
- Victims of abuse often fear that attempting to leave or protect themselves would only lead to greater danger and an escalation of violence. This fear is merited, because one of the most dangerous times is when a victim of abuse tries to speak out against it or leave it (DeKeseredy, & Schwartz, 2009).
- Abusers may also try to convince victims that if they leave, they will be the ones guilty of breaking the family apart.
- Victims may not be able to identify anywhere that they could go if they were to leave.

- Ownership of cars or other means of transportation may be solely in the name of the abuser, putting the victim in a position where they have no means of leaving physically and no means of transportation to assist them in setting up a new living condition.
- Victims of abuse are frequently unaware of resources available to them that would empower them to leave if they choose to do so.
- People who have been abused may still feel that it is their responsibility to try to help the abuser to change.
- As a result of emotional abuse, the victim may believe that they are unlovable and that leaving would be to choose a life of being profoundly alone, lonely, and perpetually rejected.
- Family members and friends may put pressure on the victim of abuse to stay in the relationship, urging them "not to throw the baby out with the bath water."
- The victim may stay out of a conditioned desire to protect the abuser. It is not uncommon that in an abusive relationship, the victim has had to defend the user against the consequences of his or her own actions in a variety of contexts. Learning to let go of the role of being the abuser's safety net can be extremely emotionally challenging.
- The victim of abuse is aware that he or she has not always responded well to the abuse, and may feel that any action he or she takes to leave or protect himself or herself will only result in the abuser using the victim's actions as a weapon against them.

Latter-day Saints, and particularly for Latter-day Saint women, have another foundational layer underneath these other reasons. In her research and clinical experience as a social worker and victim advocate coordinator in a community inhabited predominantly by Latter-day Saints, Betty McMaster noted that Latter-day Saint women have a tendency to see their roles as eternal wives and mothers as superseding all other aspects of their identity (Moore, 1999). Women in the Church have traditionally been taught this precept as a part of their religious experiences, and these self-concepts are deeply tied into their personal testimonies of the gospel.

This is in contrast to men in the Church, who are more accustomed to seeing themselves in other roles in addition to husband and father, such as their careers, friendships, hobbies, pursuits, or church callings. The faithfulness and commitment of many Latter-day Saint women is such that they see themselves as "[Latter-day Saints] first, women second." They are committed to their covenants, and the thought of doing something that could potentially be defined as breaking a covenant is abhorrent to them, even in the face of significant suffering.

Perhaps some of them view the sufferings of their abuse through the lens of stories from the shared Pioneer heritage of the Church. In these histories, brave and committed women are rightfully celebrated for enduring mob violence, carrying their children across frozen rivers, enduring starvation and deprivation, and carving a path through the wilderness with dangers at every turn on an exodus to a desert land they had never seen, all as part of their devotion as disciples of Christ. Certainly this heritage of faith can inspire faithful endurance in the face of trials and opposition. But it can also be twisted from its proper application and misconstrued to reinforce the erroneous idea that leaving an abusive relationship would be breaking a covenant, and that covenants must be kept at all costs. After all, the Pioneer trek West was intended to deliver the faithful out of the hands of those who would abuse them. But this detail can sometimes be lost when contemplating the application of these examples to modern women in abusive relationships.

Perhaps they think of the story of the women and children in the city of Ammonihah. When these women were converted by Alma and Amulek, the men who had not been converted turned on them. While the unbelieving and unrepentant Zoramite men cast the converted men out of the city, they approached the women and children with greater cruelty; they burned them to death, along with the scriptures. I wonder how often we contemplate the horrifying thought that some of the Zoramite men might have been burning their own families in those fires because of their pride and because of their solidarity with the other men who were also riled up to anger against the women.

Perhaps they think of the Anti-Nephi-Lehies, kneeling in prayer as the murderous Lamanite armies attack them, dying in terrible violence without resistance and praising God in the very act of bleeding out. It is easy to focus on this single detail of this story of faithful and repentant converts without remembering that later in their tale, the Lord commanded a prophet of God to remove them from the danger and unite them with a people willing to provide them with a safe place to dwell and willing to defend them against further harm.

Perhaps some victims of abuse have internalized some misleading colloquialisms that have been traditionally used within the culture of the Church, such as referring to homes without an adult male in residence as homes "without the priesthood." These old patterns of speech can make it hard to see the many principles being taught in recent years that faithful men and women have access to the blessings of the priesthood through their temple covenants and their faithfulness.

Perhaps some victims of abuse have come to believe that suffering for another's sins is a way of emulating the Savior. The idea of turning the other cheek, not returning reviling for reviling, and going like a lamb before the slaughter can appeal to their desire to be Christlike. In fact, they may feel that it is somehow their spiritual duty to save the abuser from his or her violent and abusive tendencies. Unfortunately, this set of ideas fails to comprehend an important truth: for something to be antichrist, it is set either in opposition to Christ, or it is set up to try to act as a substitute for Christ. When a victim comes to feel that they must be the savior of an abuser, they have fallen into the trap of a sort of emotional idolatry, letting themselves struggle under the burden of an Atonement that they are not capable of making.

These stories and examples form a powerful narrative that shapes the entire paradigm of Latter-day Saints. And when properly understood and viewed as a whole—rather than subdivided and cherry-picked to support someone's agenda, an act known as wresting the scriptures (Alma 13:20, 2 Peter 3:16)—they provide a liberating understanding of the Lord's desire to deliver His people. Sadly, these very same stories are all too frequently used to compromise the agency of children of God by claiming that their discipleship requires them to stay in abusive relationships.

In her research of abused Latter-day Saint women, McMaster found that when she asked these women about why they stayed in abusive relationships, this turned out to be the wrong question to ask, "because the question implies that she has a choice. Does she think she has a choice? Absolutely not. Over and over I asked women what they can do about it. They feel trapped and unable to move from where they are. Every option has been closed in their minds" (Moore, 1999). When the perceived choice is to stay with abuse or surrender one's chances at exaltation, does that person really have a choice? Not if their faith has any depth to it.

These women reported that they felt trapped financially and logistically, facing what they believed would be a life of poverty and deprivation for themselves and their children. They feared being ostracized by their wards and branches and looked down upon by Church leadership as a sort of spiritual leper for supposedly breaking their covenants by leaving a temple-sealed marriage. Beyond that, these women had come to view divorce as the ultimate failure and a breach of their faithfulness, regardless of the intensity of the abusive behaviors of their spouses. In their minds, leaving their abusive spouse had become the equivalent of betraying God. And that is something they simply would not do, even if they suffered unto death like the early Christian martyrs.

Ultimately, in order to make the choice to leave an abusive relationship, McMaster found these women needed three things. First, they needed to be able to recognize the abuse for what it is. This required working through all the things other people told them and the things they told themselves and reaching the point of being able to say, "This is abuse. It is not my fault. He is choosing to abuse me and/or the children."

Second, they needed to come to a point where they recognized and believed that the Lord and the Church denounce abuse. This can often be difficult, because they have been exposed to a large number of Latter-day Saint teachings that caution against divorce and encourage forgiveness. When they do find teachings about abuse and the Lord's desire to deliver them out of it, they often have a hard time seeing themselves in those teachings.

Third, they needed support from a priesthood leader. "These women are looking for permission from priesthood leaders, and if they don't get permission from them they can't leave. They need to hear it from a Church leader that they are supported in their decision to leave" (Moore, 1999). Note that this is not the same as a bishop or stake president telling them they should leave. That is not a priesthood leader's decision to make. But they need to hear that it is a choice that they can make that is acceptable to the Lord. Furthermore, they need to hear that their priesthood leader will support them if they make the choice to leave. This willingness of priesthood leaders to support a woman's choice to leave an abusive relationship was the most influential factor in helping end cycles of abuse.

GOSPEL PARALLELS

Embedded deeply into the message of the gospel is that each person is in need of help beyond their own to overcome the trials, challenges, and tragedies of mortality. The very nature of our experiences and of our mortal limitations makes it so any attempt to deliver ourselves on our own is bound to failure. Why do we not just deliver ourselves? Because we cannot. The task is beyond us.

Why do people being abused generally not leave on their own? For the same reason. They cannot. They need help to see what is possible. They need assistance to believe that life can be better. And they need real, practical, human help with all of the things they must face in order to make the courageous decision to leave abuse. Even with that, it is a task that challenges their mind, body, and spirit to their extremes. But when they know that deliverance is possible, and when they have confidence that others will be willing to help, what can happen is nothing short of miraculous.

CHAPTER 5

THE EFFECTS OF ABUSE

SHATTERED SOULS

How does the experience of being abused affect a person? While there are many factors that go into determining the exact effects of abuse on a specific individual, it is fair to say that abuse affects every aspect of the victim. It has a powerful molding effect upon their thoughts, often changing the way they see virtually everything. It remodels their emotional world through a process of tearing down their sense of safety and self-worth and rebuilding new emotional realities of fear, anxiety, and despair. It deeply impacts their social lives, both by direct influence of the abuse and by its side effects. It digs deep into their sense of spirituality. And it even changes their bodies in highly influential ways, all the way down to their genes.

Abuse of any kind is a whole-person experience. It is the demolition of a soul. Those who have experienced it know the truth of this statement. That is not to say that there is no means for healing and rebuilding those souls shattered by abuse. But this truth should help build understanding of just how deeply the wounds of abuse dig into its victims and the types of help and support they need in order to heal.

There is far too much research on the effects of abuse to give a comprehensive review of it in this book. However, several important themes about its impact will be covered here.

ABUSE AS PSYCHOLOGICAL CONDITIONING

Studies in psychology in the early twentieth century by scientists such as B. F. Skinner (1963) discovered that certain reinforcement techniques can be used to exert a large amount of control over human thoughts, feelings, and behaviors. While several different techniques have been identified, one of the most influential forms of behavioral control through reinforcement is known as operant conditioning (Skinner, 1971).

The general principle of operant conditioning is that responses that follow a targeted behavior can either greatly increase or decrease the probability of that targeted behavior being repeated—and even becoming a well-entrenched pattern—based on the way the responses activate certain basic learning functions of the brain. In particular, the hard-wired survival instincts that prime humans to seek things that feel good (like eating or being in a safe temperature) and avoid things that provoke pain (like excessive temperature conditions or over-exertion) is tapped into in a way that it creates the same kind of emotional and physical imperatives to a new set of behaviors as it does to basic survival needs. These strategic responses can fall into a few discrete categories:

- **Positive reinforcement:** Following the targeted behavior, a stimulus that feels good is added to the situation, thus increasing the likelihood of the targeted behavior being repeated. For example, a parent may provide a child with a favorite meal after the child has worked hard to study for a test to encourage them in their efforts. The child is then more likely to study in the future.

- **Negative reinforcement:** Following the target behavior, a stimulus that feels unpleasant is removed from the situation, thus increasing the likelihood of the targeted behavior being repeated. For example, a person who is reluctant to wake up in the morning may press the snooze button on their alarm clock, removing an unpleasant stimulus (the sound of the alarm) from their situation. As a result, the person is more likely to use the snooze button in the future, rather than pushing through their reluctance and getting out of bed.

- **Positive punishment:** Following the target behavior, a stimulus is added that feels unpleasant, thus reducing the likelihood of the targeted behavior being repeated. For example, a parent may yell at a child for interrupting them while the parent is using their phone. This reduces the child's likelihood of trying to get their parent's attention while the parent is using their phone.
- **Negative punishment:** Following the targeted behavior, a stimulus that feels good is removed from the situation, thus reducing the likelihood of the targeting behavior being repeated. For example, a parent may ground a child from playing video games because they did not get their homework done.

The naming conventions of operant conditioning can be confusing to some people. For clarity, it can help to think about the word positive meaning addition (adding something to the situation) and negative meaning subtraction (taking something about from the situation). Reinforcement simply refers to something feeling good on a basic, sensory level, and punishment refers to something feeling bad on that same level.

It should also be noted that simply applying one of these strategic responses one time is not the same as fully conditioning a person. For that to happen, the strategic responses must be repeated over time. They do not have to be an exact repetition in order to work; they just need to be close enough in the physical and emotional circumstances that they create. How that repetition is managed has a large impact on the degree of psychological conditioning and behavioral modification that occurs.

Patterns of repetition in operant conditioning are known as reinforcement schedules. The simplest schedule is a basic one-to-one ratio: *every time you do A, B happens*. This is the easiest and quickest schedule to learn. However, when the connection between A and B is broken, it is also the quickest conditioned behavior to stop.

Imagine, for a moment, that we have a monkey in a cage. Monkeys display the same kind of basic learning patterns that humans do. This monkey explores the cage and discovers that when he pushes the red button on the wall, a banana pops out of a chute like a potassium-rich gift from heaven. Upon pressing the button again, the monkey sees another banana appear as if by magic. One press of the button always produces one banana.

The monkey will rapidly learn to press that button whenever he wants a banana. However, let's suppose we decide to deactivate the button. The monkey will press it and no doubt be puzzled and frustrated to find it doesn't work. He will try it several times, but after a relatively small number of experiences with the button not working, the monkey will abandon his attempts to get bananas by pressing the button. Thus, the one-to-one reinforcement schedule is relatively easily learned and relatively easily broken.

The second type of reinforcement schedule is a set ratio. For example, our monkey's button may have to be pushed three times to produce a banana. However, three pushes always produces a banana. Thus, it will take a little bit longer for our monkey to learn to use the button to get a banana, but once he gets the hang of it, he will consistently push the button three times when he wants a banana. When we deactivate the button, he will push the button more times before he gives up, because he is used to it taking three pushes instead of just one. So, it takes a little longer to learn and a little longer to break. The larger the ratio between pushes and bananas, the longer it takes to learn and the longer it takes to break.

The third type of reinforcement schedule is intermittent, or variable ratio reinforcement. In this configuration, we insert a random ratio between button pushes and banana release. So, on the first time, it may take one push, on the second time three pushes, on the third time five pushes, on the fourth time two pushes, on the fifth time nine pushes, and only one push again on the sixth time. There is no predictable pattern to the changes in between reinforcement, only the knowledge that it will eventually come.

This can take more time for the monkey to learn, but it takes a tremendously long time for the association to break. After all, the monkey has learned that the reward may be just one more push away. When we unhook the connection between the button and the banana release, our poor little simian friend will go on pushing that button for a ridiculously long amount of time. This is especially true if we increase the reward so that a successful button push releases a whole bunch of bananas.

Slot machines are based upon this same principle of intermittent or variable ratio reinforcement. There is a random relationship between lever pulls and winning, but the rewards look, feel, and sound rather big when they come. Slot machines are even more effective at producing a desired behavior from humans (that is, giving up all our money) when you place them in long rows or large rooms with many other slot machines. That way, humans hear other slot machines going off around them, and even though their own machine has not reinforced them for emptying their wallets and purses into it, the fact that other machines are paying out raises the sense that the big win is just a few lever pulls away.

Casino operators further capitalize upon these same basic learning functions of the brain by taking advantage of an emotional slingshot effect. They wait until the player is at a state of emotional discouragement, just on the verge of giving up, before they apply some sort of reinforcement, which provides a significant emotional boost. By bringing the person to an emotional low spot before boosting their spirits, they can achieve two major objectives. First, they can make the person have a large emotional response, thus making the reinforcement more powerful. Second, they can receive a rather large reinforcement for a disproportionately small reward.

These same principles of operant conditioning are being used by a wide variety of sources—including marketing (Peter & Nord, 1982), social media (Deibert, 2019), video games (Anderson, 2017), conspiracy theory groups (Berkowitz, 2021), and more—to control human thoughts and behaviors. They have proven to be very effective in their purposes.

How does all of this apply to abuse? First, we must remember that at its core, all abuse is about power and control over another human being. Operant conditioning is all about exerting influence on the way a person thinks, feels, and acts through the manipulation of external stimuli. Therefore, operant conditioning is a tool that is highly compatible with the goals of an abusive person. Many abusers learn operant conditioning accidentally and often unconsciously, by trial and error, and use it regularly and instinctively. Some have seen it modeled in the families in which they grew up, and it just seems natural and normal to them. Some abusers learn it overtly and apply it with precise intentionality.

Abuse in the context of a family or romantic relationship is a complicated thing. The relationship involves things that the victim of abuse wants, like the potential for moments of experiencing things that feel like love, acceptance, support, and peace. An abuser is able to use these things as a form of reinforcement, either by adding them when what they desire from the other person is present (for example, a subservient attitude) or removing them when the person they are trying to control is not doing what the abuser wants them to do (for example, having an opinion of their own).

Similarly, the relationship also carries with it the potential to evoke pain through things like criticism, rejection, verbal aggression, physical aggression, alienation of other loved ones, and more. An abuser is able to insert these things into the relationship as a form of punishment for their victim. Combining the different types of reinforcements and punishments in the relationship gives ample opportunity for repetition and the crystallization of the conditioning on the victim.

It is especially important to note that many abusers come across as unpredictable in their emotional swings. As such, their reinforcement and punishment patterns tend to follow the intermittent, variable ratio reinforcement pattern, which is the most powerful of all of the reinforcement schedules in operant conditioning.

In domestic violence, danger and harm come from sources that should be expected to be safe and nurturing. Part of what can be so disorienting about abuse is that the victim's relationship with the abuser is usually not all bad; as much as there are harmful elements in the relationship, there are other parts of the relationship that can be at least neutral, and perhaps even positive, tender, and nurturing in some ways. However, these positive aspects of the relationship do not buffer the effects of the abuse. Rather, they tend to add to the emotional slingshot effect of the abuse and further add to feelings of confusion and fear.

This all serves to essentially hijack the victim's innate survival mechanisms in the brain in a way that they are subconsciously drawn—even compelled—to follow themself in their attitudes, beliefs, and behaviors that are more likely to result in reinforcements and less likely to result in punishments from the abuser. As a result, the feeling that the relationship could be loving and safe is always hanging just out of reach but still feels close enough for the victim to believe that if they just try a little harder the relationship will be good. At the same time, the specter of pain and the fear of being hurt in a variety of ways is always hanging over the victim's head. Furthermore, the idea of the victim standing up for themself or leaving the abusive relationship becomes heavily conditioned with expectations of pain, failure, and despair (Miller, Lund, & Weatherly, 2012). They are built upon an extremely unsteady foundation in the relationship, but the deep psychological effects of operant conditioning serve to make them feel as if they have no other choice.

This sense of powerlessness to change or leave the abusive situation—and thus determine the decision to stay in abusive relationships for long periods of time or permanently—can also be better understood in the light of another form of behavioral conditioning, namely learned helplessness. Social scientist Martin Seligman and his colleagues conducted a number of experiments on various animals that involved administering electrical shocks to the animals under a variety of conditions (Maier & Seligman, 1976; Seligman, 1972; Seligman & Beagley, 1975; Seligman, Rosellini, & Kozak, 1975). As a part of these experiments, he set up a test chamber in which electrical shocks would be administered, but the animals could stop the electrical shocks by activating a certain trigger within the test chamber. As would be expected, as the animals discovered how the trigger worked, they were quick to activate it when they received electrical shocks.

The researchers evolved the experiment by deactivating the switch. When the animals who had learned to use the switch to stop the shocks were placed in these new testing conditions, they immediately tried to use the trigger when the shocks began. When the trigger did not work, the animals would try again and again with visibly growing desperation but would eventually give up and consign themselves to suffer the shocks until they ceased. Eventually, as this procedure was repeated, the animals quit trying to use the trigger at all, and simply laid in helpless suffering and allowed the shocks to happen without resistance, no matter how long they lasted.

The animals had learned on a deep, biological level that there was nothing they could do to stop their suffering. Therefore, the survival instincts to resist the suffering or seek relief in any way were eventually overwhelmed and shut down. This remained the case even when the trigger was reactivated and there was actually a means for them to end the suffering.

This disturbing set of experiments was later used to understand a variety of human behaviors, including the experience of being a victim of abuse (Hiroto & Seligman, 1975; Petersen & Seligman, 1983). Quite frequently, the patterns in an abusive relationship quickly and thoroughly teach the victim that their efforts to curtail or end the abuse either yield no results or are actually met with an increase in the frequency and intensity of the abuse.

The social aspects of the abuse—including isolation and the abuser preemptively shaping other people's opinions about the victim—often create circumstances in which the victim's appeals to others for understanding and help are met by indifference, incredulity, minimization, or blame. The abuser may capitalize upon these experiences, using them to taunt the victim that nobody will believe them, that everybody knows the victim is a liar or crazy, that nobody will help the victim, and that nobody could ever possibly love the victim if they decide to leave.

This combination of experiences, with the abuser escalating abuse when the victim resists it and other people responding in incredulous and unhelpful ways, solidifies the sense that there is literally nothing that the victim can do to stop the suffering. This is further compounded when gospel doctrines are perverted to suggest that continuing to be abused is what God and the Church require of the victim. Hope is extinguished, all the way down to the biological level. God-given survival instincts are shut down. It is little wonder, then, that being a victim of abuse leads to a strongly elevated risk of suicide (Devries et al., 2011).

ABUSE CHANGES THE BODY

It is easy to picture the idea of abuse changing the body as being a matter of broken limbs, brain injuries, torn ligaments, scars, and long term mobility issues from physical trauma. It is true that these are all things that result from physical or sexual abuse. But, there are many other ways the body is changed by abuse that can be even more difficult to address and can be even more debilitating. And these other physical changes are not limited to physical assaults; they are caused by all forms of abuse including physical, sexual, verbal, emotional, social, and spiritual abuse.

Physical Symptoms. Medical research has found that a wide variety of physical symptoms and conditions are more common and/or more severe for adults who experienced abuse as children (Cesario, McFarlane, Nava, Gilroy, & Maddoux, 2014; Coker, Hopenhayn, DeSimone, Bush, & Crofford, 2009; Felitti et al., 1998; Fry, 1993; Leserman, Zhiming, Drossman, Toomey, Nachman, & Glogau, 1997; Loxton, Schofield, Hussain, & Mishra, 2006; McCauley et al., 1997; Springer, Sheridan, Kuo, & Carnes, 2003; Springs & Friedrich, 1992; Walker, Keegan, Gardner, Sullivan, Bernstein, & Katon, 1997). Some examples include:

- Nightmares
- Back pain.
- Frequent or severe headaches.
- Pain in the pelvic or genital area.
- Frequent fatigue.
- Difficulty sleeping.
- Abdominal or stomach pain.
- Vaginal discharge.
- Allergies.
- Breast pain.
- Loss of appetite.
- Choking sensations.
- Problems urinating.
- Diarrhea.
- Constipation.
- Vision problems.
- Hearing problems.
- Low iron.
- Asthma.

- Chest pain.
- Facial pain.
- Breathing problems.
- Fibromyalgia.
- Chronic fatigue syndrome.
- Irritable bowel syndrome.
- Cervical cancer.

Genetics and epigenetics. Science is still seeking to discover and more fully understand the mechanisms by which suffering abuse of all kinds results in these difficult physical symptoms. We have learned that the physical changes that can come from being subjected to abuse are due in part to the interplay between genetics and epigenetics.

In genetics, the actual structure of DNA that makes up a person's genetic patterns is known as their genotype. These genes contain the entirety of the genetic potential of the individual. However, not all of the genes within a person's DNA are activated or expressed, and various combinations of genes can be activated in a certain way that changes how those genes are expressed in a person physically. The current activation and physical and psychological expressions of a person's genes are known as their phenotype. Phenotype expressions can be things like height, hair color, cognitive functioning, heart disease, depression, or schizophrenia. All of the individual's current physical and psychological structures and functions are a part of their phenotype (Morrange, 2002; Morris, 2001).

The epigenome of an individual consists of a series of chemical tags that interact with that person's DNA. Epigenetics refers to the process by which physical changes surrounding our genes utilizing these chemical tags have the ability to turn certain expressions of a person's genes "on" or "off," so to speak. Epigenetic factors can change phenotypes. Genetic potential for both health and illness within a person can be activated or suppressed based on epigenetic mechanisms. Epigenetics have been found to be an important contributing factor to a variety of health issues, including obesity (Herrerra, Keildsen, & Lindgren, 2011), autoimmune diseases like Hashimoto's disease (Hewagama & Richardson, 2009), cancer (You & Jones, 2012), rheumatoid arthritis (Viatte, Plant, & Raychaudhuri, 2013), inflammatory bowel disease

(Annese, 2020), major psychiatric disorders such as schizophrenia (Abdolmaleky, Thiagalingam, & Wilcox, 2005), and many more.

These epigenetic factors inside of us are triggered by our exposure to different substances and experiences in our environment, including emotional experiences and relationship dynamics. The unique interplay of genetic and epigenetic factors within each individual determines how those experiences activate or deactivate specific phenotypic expressions of that person's genes. Stress and trauma are known to be extremely powerful environmental contributors to epigenetic mechanisms (Kanherkar, Bhatia-Dey, & Csoka, 2014).

It is also important to note that there are certain developmental periods in which exposure to negative environmental factors has a more powerful influence on epigenetic mechanisms. For example, children who have suffered abuse in early or middle childhood were found to experience a more profound impact on their epigenetic aging than children who were not in those same highly influential developmental periods when trauma occurred (Marini et al., 2020). This powerfully contradicts the justification given by many abusers, claiming that children of that age were "too young to remember" the abuse and therefore "can't have been affected by it." Indeed, the research on this topic strongly concludes that these early, formative years are some of the most impactful when it comes to producing epigenetic alterations of phenotype that result in long term negative physical and mental health outcomes (Howard, 2022; Pilkay, 2017; Yehuda & Lehrner, 2017).

No one is too young to remember being abused themselves or witnessing someone they love being abused. While it is true that children younger than a certain age do not keep coherent, chronological memories that are accessible to them in later life the same way they do with memories formed later in childhood, the body still stores all of these early memories in somatic memory. The person may not remember the events connected with these memories visually, but they remember the emotional and physical sensations associated with them, and these sensations are connected to the stimuli that were present when the memories were formed. The person's body then responds to those or similar stimuli in the future by activating those same physical and emotional sensations. For that reason, a person who was abused as a young child may not have a specific visual memory or chronological narrative of an abusive event, but they may have feelings of fear and distrust toward their abuser that are equivalent to what they would have if they had a visual memory. Indeed, the entire field of psychology began with an investigation of how early childhood experiences that were not consciously remembered impacted people throughout their entire lives (Edgcumbe, 2000; Samuels, 2003; Scharff, 1996; Thurshwell, 2009). As the renowned trauma specialist Bessel Van der Kolk (1994) states it, "the body keeps the score."

Polyvagal theory. Scientist Stephen Porges (2009, 2011, 2017; 2018) sheds further light on how the trauma of abuse leads to higher rates of chronic medical conditions and mental health struggles. When people experience things like trauma, chronic stress (like living in an abusive relationship), and adverse childhood experiences (like being abused or witnessing abuse), this can lead to dysregulation of the nervous system. This affects all aspects of the nervous system. Porges' polyvagal theory focuses on the impact of trauma on the autonomic nervous system (ANS).

The ANS is the portion of the nervous system that is responsible for the body's automatic functions, like heartbeat, breathing, body temperature, digestion, and so forth. It is also in charge of regulating the body's survival responses, in particular the fight/flight/freeze reactions that people experience in response to danger. As such, the ANS is constantly monitoring a person's senses to detect stimuli that would indicate conditions of safety as well as stimuli that indicate a threat to wellbeing and survival. All of these functions happen automatically, without any conscious thought on the part of the individual. In these environmental monitoring and automatic response functions, the ANS has three basic states:

- **Safe State**: When the ANS is functioning on this level, an individual feels relaxed and calm. In this state a person is able to feel connected to the people around them and develop deeper, meaningful relationships.
- **Mobilized State**: When active to a small degree, the mobilized state makes us alert, aware, curious, and interested. When some form of danger is detected, the ANS activates the

mobilized state at a higher level and deploys physical responses that may be necessary for survival. Heart rate and breathing increase. Pupils dilate for greater visual awareness. Adrenaline and cortisol are released to provide added strength and speed. The body undergoes a number of other changes to prepare itself to either overpower or outrun a threat and to reduce the risk of death should an injury occur. At this level, the ANS has prepared the individual for the "fight" and "flight" options. The parts of the brain that are designed to bond with others are essentially inactive as the priority of the ANS switches from connection to protection.

- **Immobilized State**: When activated to a small degree, the immobilized state places the body in a state of rest and recovery. However, it can also become activated to a high degree in response to danger. If the ANS senses that the magnitude of danger is such that neither fighting nor fleeing will be successful, it reduces the individual's heart rate, body temperature, and blood pressure to reduce the rate of bleeding from injuries in order to increase the chances of survival after being hurt. Pain numbing endorphins are released throughout the body as the ANS prepares the person for what appears to be inevitable injury or even death. This helpless, desperate "freeze" state can be accompanied by a mental state of dissociation, of being partially or even completely disconnected from one's body and senses to the point that some people feel like they are helplessly watching themselves from outside of their own body.

While these states are most easily apparent in dangerous situations, they are utilized each day as people navigate their physical and social surroundings. When a person's ANS is functioning in a healthy way, it can easily move through its different states in a magnitude that is appropriate to the actual degree of safety and the threats that are encountered in the environment.

The ANS also combines these states in ways that are adaptive in different situations. For example, when a person is engaged in recreation with others, the mobilized and safe states are activated simultaneously. When a person is engaged in quiet connection and intimacy with loved ones, the immobilized and safe states are active simultaneously. In both of these cases, the ANS is prioritizing connection over protection because it is able to determine that the situation is safe. When the ANS is able to be flexible, switching between states regularly as appropriate, and experiences a healthy dose of experiences with the safe state activated, it creates emotional resilience in an individual and the ability to recover and grow from adversities (Polyvagal Institute, 2021).

On the other hand, constant experiences of threats, abuse, trauma, and stress can dysregulate the ANS, leaving it stuck with the safe state deactivated. The person becomes locked into automatic priorities of protection, and their body's functions of connection with others are greatly reduced. Because of the constant reality of experiencing abuse and harm the ANS begins to be more and more alert for potential danger, narrowing the threshold for triggering its fight, flight, and freeze responses and broadening the number of stimuli that activate these states. It becomes harder and harder for the ANS to activate its safe state because threats and harm are consistently coming from sources that should be safe (Porges, 2017). This makes things like approaching a bishop, therapist, or other potential ally feel threatening. Their body may recoil from the possibility of speaking with these people, because although there is an expectation that they should be safe, the ANS has learned that stimuli that should signal safety are untrustworthy and risky.

Polyvagal theory helps shed light on the fact that trauma is not simply a matter of events that happen to a person. Trauma is the internal response to the external experience of adverse events. It is what happens inside of us because of what is happening outside of us. Many abusers seek to minimize the impact of some of their abusive behavior, rationalizing that some of the specific actions on their part "weren't that bad." They try to state that the other person is exaggerating their feelings and response or even faking entirely. However, when a victim has experienced a pattern of abuse, each incident of abuse is simply a part of the larger pattern of mistreatment, and the ANS responds to it as such. It reacts to the totality of the threat that the abuser has presented, not just the danger posed by the abusive attitude or action manifested by the abuser in that moment (Polyvagal Institute, 2021). Abuse is not an event; it is the overall experience of abuse in the context of that person's life, especially in the context of their relationship with a specific abuser.

Having a constantly activated protection response from the ANS is exhausting both physically and mentally. This can be one of the reasons that people who have been abused or have witnessed abuse—particularly while they were children—may turn to mood changing elements to try to cope. As a result, children who experienced or witnessed abuse are at a higher risk of developing eating disorders, self-harm like cutting, addictions to drugs and alcohol, high risk sexual behaviors, and so forth (Holt, Buckley, & Whelan, 2008). Having an ANS stuck in protection mode also contributes to the development of the various physical and mental health issues that have been discussed throughout this chapter (Polyvagal Institute, 2021).

It is important to note that in stark contrast to the claims made by many abusers and those who enable them that young children will not remember abuse and therefore not be affected by it, research indicates that children are at a vulnerable developmental stage. Having prolonged and repeated adverse experiences including being abused, neglected, or witnessing abuse can have a profound mental and physical impact on children throughout their lives.

For example, a large research study of more than 17,000 patients conducted through a partnership between the Centers for Disease Control and Kaiser focused on experiences known as adverse childhood experiences, or ACEs (Felitti et al., 1998). This expansive study demonstrated a direct link between the number of ACEs a person experiences as a child, including abuse, neglect, parental addiction, and witnessing domestic violence in the home—and a wide variety of negative health outcomes.

In general, they found that experiencing ACEs led to higher rates of mental and physical health issues, and the more ACEs that were experienced, the higher the risk. For example, they found that when people had experienced four or more ACE's, they had much higher rates of things like heart disease (240 percent), cancer (190 percent), drug abuse (1,030 percent), stroke (240 percent), diabetes

(160 percent), major depressive disorder (240 percent), obesity (160 percent), and suicide attempts (1,120 percent) (Felitti et al., 2019). The horrifyingly elevated risk of self-harm and suicide as a result of being abused and/or witnessing abuse are of particular concern and should emphasize the crucial need to take abuse to and in the presence of children very seriously.

To further emphasize how damaging abuse is, science has also shown that these changes from an ANS locked in protect mode as a result of trauma and abuse can be so powerfully reinforced and entrenched that they activate epigenetic mechanisms. As a result, the physical and mental health effects of trauma can be passed down genetically for at least three generations (Bezo & Maggi, 2015; Collins & Roth, 2021; Conching & Thayer, 2019; Cunliffe, 2016; Hjort et al., 2021; Jawaid, Roszkowski, & Mansuy, 2018; Kellerman, 2013; Park, 2019; Polyvagal Institute, 2021; Stenz, Schechter, Serpa, & Paoloni-Giaconbino, 2018; Yehuda & Lerner, 2018; Yehuda et al. 2016). This is one of the reasons that preventing abuse, detecting it early when it happens, responding to stop it, and ensuring that victims of abuse are protected from further abuse in the future is so important; it is not just the victim in front of us that will suffer long-term effects of the abuse if it is left unaddressed. The impact of the sins of the fathers will literally be passed down on a genetic level from generation to generation unless corrective action is taken. The needs of the many call to us in the form of the one.

ABUSE AFFECTS THE MIND

It would be difficult to overstate the immense impact that suffering abuse or witnessing a loved one being abused can have on both short-term and long-term mental health. In general, people who have experienced or witnessed abuse in their home and family life develop significantly higher rates of a large number of mental health concerns as a result (Boyle, Jones, & Lloyd, 2006; Campbell, Sullivan, & Davidson, 1995; Jarvis, Gordon, & Novaco, 2005; Kavak, Aktürk, Özdemir, & Gültekin, 2018; Kimber et al., 2017; Marinovich, 2019; Merlin & Mohr, 2001; Oram, Trevillion, Feder, & Howard, 2013; Salcioglu, Urhan, Pirinccioglu, & Aydin, 2017; Sansone, Chu, &

Weiderman, 2007; Stiles, 2002). These issues include:

- Depression.
- Anxiety.
- Post-traumatic stress disorder.
- Eating disorders.
- Self-harm.
- Disrupted ability to feel safe.
- Suicide attempts and fatality by suicide.
- The development of an addiction as a means to cope.
- Disrupted attachment leading to the development of anxious and avoidant attachment styles and borderline personality disorder traits.
- Risky sexual behaviors by children.
- Behavioral issues and defiance by children.
- Social skill issues.
- School performance issues.
- Low self-esteem.
- Difficulty trusting other people.
- Increased risk of developing psychosis.
- Fighting, bullying, lying, and cheating by children.
- Regressive behaviors by children.
- Law-breaking behaviors by children.
- Higher rate of risk-taking behaviors resulting in higher rates of physical injuries for children.

When discussing the impact of experiencing or witnessing abuse, it is important to recognize that it has a tendency to rewrite a person's view of themselves, of other people, and of the way the world works in general. Experiencing abuse—especially from a spouse, parent, or other family member—is a world-shattering experience. It leads a person to question everything they thought they knew about relationships, love, trust, faith, and everything that serves as an anchor in their lives.

As the mind tries to make sense out of abuse coming from the people in their lives who should be the most loving, safe, and nurturing people to them, victims of abuse tend to develop narratives and beliefs that they use to try to understand what happened and to cope with its implications. These tend to crystalize into a number of constraining beliefs that become the person's new way of understanding the world. These beliefs are an attempt to cope, but often end up being an internalization of the abuse they suffered externally. As a result, the damage an abuser has done to a victim manages to repeat itself over and over again as these new thought patterns play out in all areas of their lives. As observed by world-renowned trauma therapist Francine Shapiro (1989, 2012, 2017), these thought patterns tend to fall into a few general themes:

Theme of Responsibility/Defectiveness. With all of the blame-shifting that is usually part of an abuser's tactics of minimization, deflection, and control, victims of abuse are constantly bombarded by the message that the abuse is actually their fault. This can be framed on multiple levels as being either due to things the victim supposedly does wrong ("If I just listen to him without asking questions, he won't get angry") or aspects of their personality and character that are defective ("I'm just too awkward and I always end up doing things that embarrass him. He has every right to lash out. I'm just such a burden"). When this external campaign of blame is internalized by the victim, their sense of cause and effect is warped in a way that serves the self-justifying narrative of the abuser.

One of the reasons that themes of responsibility tend to take root is that in an odd sort of way, they seem to provide some sort of hope. If the abuse is my fault because of things I do, the reasoning goes, then I have the power to stop the abuse by changing my attitudes and actions. If you are the abuser, that is true. If you are the victim, it is not. And yet, the idea that the abuse is because the victim is somehow responsible or broken is a lie that is repeated so frequently and forcefully in abuse that many victims find themselves completely believing it.

There is a large spectrum of negative cognitions that fit within this theme, ranging from things like, "I'm not good enough," to "I don't deserve love," to, "If I was more attractive, this wouldn't happen to me," and, "With the mistakes I've made, I don't have a right to expect any better" (Shaprio, 2012).

It is tragic that historically, when victims of abuse reach out for help, they often hear other people—even local Church leaders—mirror these same negative cognitions back to them. This often happens in the form of questions and insinuations such as:

- "What were you wearing?"
- "You know, this is why we have all of those lessons about modesty. It can be very hard when a man has such attractive daughters who aren't exactly following all of the Church's standards."
- "What did you say to him that got him so mad?"
- "Well, you have put on a few pounds since you got married. If you took better care of yourself and better care of your husband, this sort of thing wouldn't happen."
- "You must have done something to give him the impression that you wanted him to do that."
- "Did you say no? Well, maybe you didn't say no clearly enough or forcefully enough."
- "You must have done something to make them feel threatened."
- "You just attract way too much attention from other people. Of course he's jealous. You really should try to tone it down."
- "You know, a little bit of plastic surgery could fix this. Your husband can't be happy with a dumpy looking woman."
- "I've found it helps if you just phrase things in a way that doesn't make your husband feel like you are questioning his authority."
- "Well, you know, you are kind of awkward. You have a tendency to say the wrong thing."
- "Maybe you should try going to the temple more and praying a little more earnestly."
- "You should be careful about looking too accomplished. It can make a man feel insecure."
- "Perhaps if you tried saying things as questions rather than as statements you wouldn't come across as being too pushy."
- "Do you have any idea how many single people there are who wish they could be married? You have to take the bad with the good. I think what you really need is a dose of perspective and an attitude change."
- "Your expectations for marriage may not be very realistic."
- "Maybe you need to work on being more forgiving.

Remember, 'He that forgiveth not his brother's trespasses stands condemned before the Lord; for there remaineth in him the greater sin.'"

Both science and doctrine agree: abuse is not caused by the victim! Abuse is the choice of the abuser. There is no such thing as "reasonable provocation" for abuse. We should take great care never to say, do, or imply anything that would reinforce the idea that victims of abuse are somehow responsible for being abused. In doing so, we add to the psychological damage of abuse.

Theme of Safety/Vulnerability. Being abused in any way—especially by someone who is a close loved one and should be counted on for protection and comfort—shatters a person's sense of safety and creates a sense of nearly constant vulnerability. This sense of profound vulnerability is due in part to the damage that abuse from a trusted family member or loved one does to our first and most basic mechanism for emotional regulation: our connection to a safe and reliable attachment figure (Bowlby, 2008).

Infants rely entirely on the adults around them being aware of what they are experiencing and being responsive to their needs for their very survival. Not only that, but the people around infants are largely responsible for their mental stimulation and socialization, both of which have an enormous impact on their physical, mental, social, and emotional development.

As children continue to grow, they begin to venture out into the world bit by bit. In doing so, they experience a variety of things, both positive and negative. When they are overwhelmed or distressed, children seek out their attachment figures for comfort. If the attachment figures are present, accessible, and responsive, then contact with the attachment figure helps the child become regulated again and ready to continue to engage in experiences that help them learn and grow. When children have a parent or guardian who serves as this sort of a secure base, they are much more likely to be mentally, emotionally, and socially well balanced. This allows them to feel secure with themselves and to feel safe building relationships with others. It facilitates the development of emotional resilience (Bowlby, 2005; Holmes 2014; Terzi, 2013).

Even as we grow into adulthood, this need for secure bases of attachment remains with us (Goodwin, 2003; Mikulincer & Shaver, 2013; Pietromonaco & Beck, 2019). Even if an adult's life is filled with adversity, having a secure base of a reliable and responsive attachment figure provides a safe haven that allows them to weather the challenges and still thrive. It helps them build and maintain a healthy sense of self, and allows them to be able to identify and create healthy relationships (Johnson & Denton, 2002).

However, when someone who has been or should be that secure base acts out in an abusive way, that entire process of attachment is disrupted. This sends rippling effects through all of the mental, social, and emotional dynamics that are associated with core attachments. Self-concept and self-esteem are upended. Beliefs about relationships are overturned. The world at large becomes something that feels threatening and unpredictable. This kind of attachment injury is world-shattering. It is a phenomenon that is both mental and physical (Johnson, Mankinen, & Milikin, 2001). It's impact is difficult to overstate.

The internalized negative cognitions that accompany this theme may include things like, "I just can't trust anyone," or "I'm never safe," or, "Nobody cares and nobody is ever going to help me," or, "Eventually, everyone is going to hurt me," or, "It's not safe to show my emotions" (Shapiro, 2012). For the abused and traumatized, the world has become a place that seems like it is full of people who are either cruel or indifferent or both. The victim of abuse becomes keenly aware of anything that could be a threat of any kind or to any degree. This is one of the reasons victims of abuse are reluctant to speak up, to report abuse, and to ask for help. This also leads to victims of abuse feeling afraid to be vulnerable or open with those who are offering to provide help.

Theme of Power/Control. Since abuse is a sin of trying to exercise power and control over another individual through force, intimidation, manipulation, and other means, it should not be surprising that it tends to create complicated beliefs and feelings about power and control in the minds of the victims. The tricks that abuse plays on a victim's psyche can lead them to feel as if they lack the ability to make meaningful choices about things that matter to them in their lives, or that their own agency can and will always be overpowered by circumstances or the agency of other people.

This theme of power and control is closely related to the previous theme of safety. When a person feels like they have control over important aspects of their life, they feel relatively safe and secure, with the belief that they can make decisions to help the outcomes of those things turn out the way they would like them to. In the areas of their lives in which they recognize they do not have direct control, people feel a sense of comfort in believing that someone who cares about them has the ability to intercede. This is one of the reasons that the idea of a loving Heavenly Father who knows each person individually and cares about them can be such a source of comfort in the face of natural disasters, political strife, and societal calamities.

But consider what happens to a person when the idea that they have the power to make choices is attacked and toppled. Consider further what the effects can be of witnessing that the person who appears to actually be in control—the abuser—is someone who is angry, critical, contemptuous, manipulative, hypocritical, image-obsessed, and self-interested. These paralyzing effects can be compounded by the perversion of gospel doctrines to justify abuse. The damage can be further amplified if the victim experiences a non-supportive, skeptical, or even hostile response from local Church leaders, law enforcement officers, or other people who should be in a position to help. The result is that any sense of personal efficacy or trust in human or divine compassion, mercy, and assistance is demolished. Faith in one's own ability to make a positive difference in the situation evaporates. The victim may come to believe through agonizing experience that things like agency, mercy, support, and love are real for other people, but not for them.

In general, there is nothing that an abuser would like their victim to believe more than the idea that they are powerless to resist the abuser's will, and that to do so would be wrong. The malignant message is that the victim is not in control, will never be in control, and isn't fit to be in control. Surrendering to the control of the abuser is advertised as the only real option for the victim, and resistance to being controlled by the abuser is punished. Through repetition, these thoughts are so powerfully reinforced that the abuser reaches a point of being able to inspire fear without having to take any immediate, meaningful action; the mere potential of what they might do is enough.

The negative beliefs associated with this theme range from "I cannot trust my judgment," to "Nothing I do will change anything," to "I just have to be perfect and please everyone," to "I am just powerless and helpless" (Shapiro, 2012). We learn that the War in Heaven was fought about the issue of divinely appointed personal agency, with Satan seeking to overthrow the agency of the children of God. The adversary may have lost that battle, but he seeks to win it over and over again in microcosm, one victim of abuse at a time, by destroying their faith and belief in their ability to choose in any way that matters.

VICTIMS OF ABUSE NEED US

Keep in mind, there is far more that is known about the effects of abuse than can be contained in this book. However, this overview of the devastating, whole-person, intergenerational effects of abuse should serve to counteract any attempts to minimize, justify, or excuse abuse of any kind. It should emphasize the urgency of acting to prevent abuse and to stop it when it is occuring. It should illustrate the need for ongoing support and protection after the immediate crisis has passed.

When someone has been abused or has witnessed abuse in their home, the damage can be monumental, and the subsequent needs for healing are proportional to that damage. Trying to heal without adequate help and support is a tremendous uphill battle against profound biological and psychological factors that can have a crippling effect upon the abused person. For that reason, they need those of us who are in a position to help to prioritize their needs for safety and healing above any other factors in their situation.

CHAPTER 6

HEALING FROM ABUSE

THE PATH OF HEALING

Healing from abuse is a process. It takes time, but it requires more than merely the passage of days, weeks, and months. In many ways, healing from abuse is like trying to rebuild your life after a devastating fire has burned down not only your house but your whole neighborhood. Victims may find themselves having to sort through the ashes of their heart, trying to salvage anything that can be saved and taking account of what they will need to build anew. They themselves are burned, raw, wounded, and weary. The landscape around them is now a charred desolation. There is no clear view of where they may go to find relief. They often don't know who to trust anymore. Hope is longed for but also something that is frightening, because many victims of abuse have held on to hope for so long that it seems like it is now just a lie, a mere fable they have told themselves to get through the day. They feel no assurance that the worst is behind them. After all, they have been deeply conditioned to believe that challenging the abuse or leaving the abuse will only lead to greater suffering.

For many people, the path of healing is not a straight, clear, linear ascent out of the valley of sorrow. It is often accompanied by many starts and stops, times of progress and times of regression, and a variety of roadblocks, barricades, and pitfalls. And, like the abuse itself, the healing is a whole person experience. It requires attention to all of the various facets of the victim that have been bruised, broken, suppressed, crippled, or amputated. Some parts of healing are about rebuilding what was torn down, and some parts are about building what was never allowed to grow. Other parts of healing are about redeveloping things that were bulldozed into a path of submission and subservience in the service of the abuser's crusade for power and control. Healing includes the shedding of beliefs and concepts that served as the chains of shackles of the abuse cycle. It involves the development of a new, more accurate way of view the self, others, the world, and oftentimes even of God.

Each survivor of abuse will have their own unique set of needs for healing. Some of these needs will not emerge and become clear until earlier, more basic needs have been met. Some will go through times and seasons where they are active, and others in which they are dormant. Some will appear to heal, only to need further attention later after the person has had certain experiences that challenge them in new ways because they are trying things they could not have attempted while in the abusive situation. It can be difficult to predict exactly how healing will look for any one person. That being said, there are some common elements that help in the process of healing.

ESTABLISHING PHYSICAL SAFETY

Trying to help someone heal from the trauma of abuse while they are still in an abusive situation is like trying to administer CPR to someone who has drowned while they are still underwater or trying to bandage up the wounds of a burn victim while they are still on fire. Just as it would be necessary to put out the flames or remove the drowning victim from the water before trying to administer to their urgent and long-term recovery needs, those who are suffering from abuse need to have a change in their circumstances that shields them from ongoing abuse in order to begin a process of actual healing. To leave someone in an emotionally toxic and life-threatening situation and expect them to heal in those circumstances is highly irrational.

As emphasized by the Church's guidelines on abuse, victims of abuse or suspected abuse should never be encouraged to stay in a situation that is unsafe. As a result, many victims of abuse find themselves needing a safe place to stay. This may be a short-term need or it may become a long-term or permanent need, depending on the circumstances of the abuse. Frequently, there will be an urgent, time-sensitive need for safe shelter in physically or emotionally dangerous circumstances, with enough time and resources available to help victims of abuse determine what their next steps should be.

Keep in mind, the risk for suffering violence and homicide is considerably elevated during the time period between when a victim determines they need to leave temporarily or permanently and the time they are able to reach safe shelter (Zahn et al., 2003). Therefore, if it is determined that this step is necessary, it should be acted upon as quickly as possible, and some sort of safety plan should be in place to help reduce the risk of harm or death to the victim.

There may be circumstances in which staying with a friend, colleague, family member, or even a member of the same stake may be a viable option. When this is the case, great care should be taken to not disclose the location that the victim is using for shelter to the abuser. Failure to do so places the victim and anyone offering shelter to the victim in danger. In general, however, the greater the history or risk of violence, the more compelling the reasons for finding a location further away and/or completely unfamiliar to the abuser.

There are also legal options that are designed to allow the victim of abuse to stay in their established residence and require the abuser to move out. Restraining and protective orders include an option that would require the abuser to move out and to continue to pay for the mortgage/rent, utilities, and taxes on the property while the victim continues to live there. It does not matter if the abuser's name is on the mortgage or lease for the property and the victim's name is not. Once abuse is a part of the legal picture, the rights and legal obligations of the abuser change, and the victim is granted certain legal privileges and protections. A perpetrator of abuse has no right to move back into the property until the court orders it, nor do they have the right to simply stop paying for the property in an effort to force the victim out (O'Connor Family Law, 2020).

That being said, this option carries with it the additional risk because the abuser knows exactly where the victim is living. The only thing stopping the abuser from coming to the residence is a legal order, with the threat of police response and legal penalties if the order is violated. If this is unlikely to be a deterrent of further harassment, abuse, and violence for the person who has committed about—and particularly if the abuser has access to firearms or other weapons—then this option is a dangerous one and would not be advisable.

One excellent resource for helping to identify options for creating physical safety conditions is the National Domestic Violence Hotline, available at thehotline.org, 1-800-799-7223, and via text at by texting "START" to 88788. Their website also has an excellent guide to help create a robust safety plan at: https://www.thehotline.org/plan-for-safety/create-a-safety-plan/.

Local resources in many communities also include victim advocates who work as an auxiliary to police departments. They can be very helpful at identifying locations and funding for emergency shelter options. Many communities also have designated shelters for women and children. These resources can usually be quickly located by a simple search engine query using the name of the service (victim advocate) and your location as search terms. Additionally, a searchable list of shelters for women and children has been compiled at https://www.womenshelters.org/.

The victim needs a living condition in which they are able to genuinely feel safe and protected from further abuse and harassment. This is a necessary part of allowing their body to begin to exit its constant state of fight, flight, or freeze. Through the process of developing enough room to start to fulfill immediate needs for safety, the victim of abuse can begin to work on sorting out the confusing jumble in their mind and heart, begin to get the various kinds of assistance that they need, and work on getting to a state of greater mental clarity to begin making important and difficult decisions about their lives and their next steps forward.

If and when the time arrives that a victim of abuse is contemplating returning to sharing a living situation with the person who committed abuse against them, this decision should be made slowly, with great care, and in consultation with competent and qualified professionals. Moving back in with someone who abused them is a high-risk time for an escalation of violence toward the victim, including an elevated risk of being killed. This remains true even when multiple psychological services have been provided to try to reduce the risk of violence (McFarlane, Nava, Gilroy, & Maddoux, 2015).

For example, many abusers are assigned anger management classes, either by the court, a local bishop, or a therapist. Some people may consider the completion of an anger management course as a sign that the abuser is now capable of refraining from further violence and that the risk factors in the relationship have been greatly reduced or eliminated. However, research on anger management shows that the victims of abusers who have completed anger management courses report essentially no change in the amount of aggression, anger, and violence that they experience from the abuser after they have completed anger management treatment (Arce, Arias, Novo, & Fariña, 2020; Bennett & Williams, 2001; Breslin, 2005; Day, Chung, O'Leary, & Carson, 2009; Epstein, 1999; Feder & Wilson, 2005; Gilchrist, Munoz, & Easton, 2015; Rosenfeld, 1992). There are no simple boxes to check off that indicate that someone who has engaged in abuse previously is now safe for the person or people that they abused.

There should be ample, compelling, multifaceted, and sustained evidence of safety before any consideration is made of moving back in with the person who committed abuse. And regardless of what evidence there may appear to be to suggest it may be safe, if the victim does not feel safe moving back in with the abuser, then it should not be done. The perpetrator was the one to make the choice to commit abuse. It is the victim who gets to be the one to make the choice about the future of that relationship.

As previously stated and as supported by both science and doctrine, the choice to leave the abusive relationship permanently is an entirely acceptable—and often necessary—choice for the victim. As Elder Holland (2021) so emphatically stated, "Everyone has the right to be loved, to feel peaceful, and to find safety at home." If the actions and attitudes of one who has committed verbal, physical, emotional, or any other kind of abuse make living with that person and feeling at peace, loved, and safe impossible, then the victim of that abuse deserves to be able to live somewhere where they can feel those things.

TAKING CARE OF THE BODY

The mind and the body are so deeply connected that the distinction we have a tendency to make between them is most likely only a social construct we have created to describe two parts of one thing (Littrell, 2008). People who have been abused often find that their body is highly dysregulated. They have a hard time sleeping. Their eating patterns and nutrition have been disrupted. Their body is holding on to an enormous amount of tension and stress. Their muscles are often tight and stiff. They may find that their digestive system is in distress. They may be over-exerting themselves physically and experiencing various points of pain throughout their body as a result. Or, they may be deprived of movement and exercise. They may lack exposure to the outdoors and connection with the earth, and as such are cut off from vital nutrients taken from the sun and the way the rhythms of the day and night affect important aspects of the body, such as the circadian rhythm. They may feel despondent, hypervigilant, or a mixture of both. And this is even without accounting for any physical injuries they may have suffered. No matter what the details may be, their bodies are in distress.

In this distressed somatic state, it is very challenging to have enough emotional and cognitive bandwidth to even attempt to deal with and make progress regarding the mental and emotional fog, dissociation, flashbacks, and confusion that are a part of the experience of being abused. The mind is a part of the body, even if it is more than the sum of the body's parts. As such, it is difficult to make progress in the matters of the mind that victims of abuse suffer until progress is made with the tangible aspects of the body.

This is not to say that victims of abuse need to become health and fitness fanatics. It does mean, however, that people trying to recover from abuse benefit greatly from examining some of their basic physical needs, exploring to what degree those needs are being met, and then working gently, step by step, to help those needs be more fully addressed.

It bears great emphasis that this is not about the victim of abuse becoming more physically attractive or sexually appealing as a way to prevent further abuse. The abuse was never about how the victim looks, no matter how hard an abuser may try to blame it on that factor. Altering the physical attributes of the victim is never the solution. Abuse can only stop by alterations within the heart and psyche of the abuser or with strong boundaries protecting the victim from the abuser.

As a result, these acts of physical care should not be undertaken in an effort to look skinnier or more muscular or more conforming to a certain stereotype of beauty and attractiveness. In fact, doing so can keep the victim in the controlled mindset that was a part of the mental abuse in the relationship. It is that very way of thinking that they need to come to recognize as a weapon of abuse.

The purpose of these acts of physical care is to help the body begin to feel better physically by being less exhausted, less sore, less uncomfortable, less agitated, and so forth. By reducing the physical, visceral experience of these constant feelings of unwellness, the working memory in a person's brain begins to have enough spare room to begin working on the mental and emotional aspects of their circumstances.

The Most Basic Physical Needs. Two good places to begin this focus are sleep and eating. Regarding eating, most people experience emotional dysregulation simply by not having enough calories in their system (Fattorini et al., 2018; MacCormack & Lindquist, 2018). For many people trying to recover from abuse, simply making sure that they are consistently eating sufficient amounts of food spread out throughout the day can make a tremendous amount of difference in how they feel and their ability to begin to deal with the many emotional challenges of their situation. For those who struggle to eat enough or to eat throughout the day, simply starting by working toward eating multiple meals in one day is a good place to start. From there, other matters of nutrition can be addressed as the person has bandwidth to do so.

For those who struggle with emotional overeating, it is important to recognize that this is connected to the emotional turmoil they are experiencing (Giani, White, & Masheb, 2013). Physical care for them in this area does not look like going on a diet. Rather, it is beginning to recognize that much of what they experience as hunger cues are actually cues for other needs that have become disguised as hunger cues. They may be stressed, lonely, or tired. They are more likely to benefit from experimenting to try to find what has been masquerading as hunger cues and then working to try to find other ways to meet those needs. From there, they may try to experiment step by step with slowly transforming their eating habits into something that more closely matches their needs. But keep in mind that while some alterations in this area can be helpful to reduce physical distress, the beginning stages of recovering from abuse may not be the right time to try to fully tackle a binge eating problem.

Regarding sleep, it is difficult to overstate the tremendous impact it has on our physical and emotional well-being even under the best of circumstances (Luyster, Strollo, Zee, & Walsh, 2012). Negative outcomes of sleep deprivation include:

- Disrupted short-term memory.
- Disrupted long-term memory.
- Increased anxiety.
- Increased depression.
- Increased suicidal thoughts.
- Decreased impulse control.
- A weakened immune system, resulting in more instances of illness.
- Higher blood sugar levels and increased risk of type 2 diabetes.
- Decreased concentration.
- Decreased creativity.
- Impaired problem solving skills.
- Increased risk of physical accidents and injury.
- Increased blood pressure.
- Decreased growth hormone production.
- Weight gain.
- Increased risk of heart disease.
- Impaired balance.
- Increased risk of early death.

For many people who have suffered from abuse, sleep patterns have become highly disturbed (Gallegos, Trabold, Cerulli, & Pigeon, 2021). This is due in part to their disrupted sense of safety in their own home and in their own bed. After all, many victims of abuse are attempting to sleep next to the person who is abusing them. While sleep patterns may seem like the least of an abuse victim's worries, working to improve their experience with sleep can make an enormous impact on the process of recovery and healing.

Once a survivor of abuse has established a safe place to stay where the threat of ongoing abuse has been abated, he or she can begin working on developing habits that are conducive to good sleep. Some guidelines may include:

- Limiting or eliminating naps during the day and aligning their sleep schedule with the natural day and night cycle.
- Avoiding the use of computers, smart phones, and other screen-based technology for the last hour before bedtime. While these might seem like relaxing behaviors, they actually stimulate the brain in a way that is disruptive to sleep.
- Spending the last hour before bedtime doing activities that are physically relaxing and soothing for the body and mind. Good options include reading, taking a relaxing shower, stretching, or doing sleep yoga, meditating, and so forth.
- Going to bed at the same time each night.
- Waking up at the same time each morning.
- Taking time to journal and write down thoughts and worries from the day as a way to set them aside until morning.
- Exercise regularly but not in the last few hours before going to bed.
- Reduce caffeine consumption (Healthline, 2021a; Mayo Clinic, 2011).

Some survivors of abuse may find that their sleep patterns have been severely complicated and are hard to begin to regulate. In that case, it may be advisable for them to seek medical assistance to begin addressing this issue.

Time Outside. Another seemingly small and simple thing that can bring great things to pass in reregulating the body is exposure to the outdoors. Science has demonstrated that time spent outdoors helps the body become regulated in a variety of important areas, such as blood pressure, heart rate, and levels of the stress hormone cortisol. In fact, people who spend time outdoors regularly have significantly lower early mortality rates than people who do not have that exposure (Carpenter & Harper, 2015; Twohig-Bennett & Jones, 2018), and overall better health and functioning (Jacobs et al., 2008). This outdoor exposure also results in broad spectrum mental health benefits (Cox el al., 2017). While we are still learning to understand all of the connections, there is something about our relationship with this natural world that God has created for us that is healing and restorative.

To aid your body in becoming grounded and regulated again while establishing physical safety, consider developing some of the following habits.

- Regularly step outside to watch sunsets and/or sunrises.
- Give your body direct exposure to sunlight (not through a window) for at least twenty minutes in the early to mid morning.
- Take time to walk barefoot on grass, dirt, or any other natural footing that feels comfortable.
- Sit in the shade of a tree.
- Eat a meal outdoors.
- Find somewhere with natural running water, like a river, stream, or beach, and spend time listening to the sound of it.
- Walk in nature at a pace that feels comfortable to you.
- Touch the bark of trees and the leaves of plants and focus on the sensation of touching them. Be sure to make sure that you are touching something safe!
- Dig into dirt or sand with your fingers and/or toes.
- Take time to watch clouds.
- Stargaze.
- Sit by a campfire at night.

There are many other activities that help activate the connection between nature and your body in a way that helps your body reregulate itself. The most important part is to try to engage with nature in a way that you are not distracted with other stimuli (not listening to music or using a smartphone) and where you are focused on what each of your senses is experiencing while you are in nature.

Be Still and Breathe. After a person has been immersed in the constant stress of living in an abusive situation, they often find that the very way they breathe has altered. Oftentimes, their breathing has had a tendency to become more shallow, more rapid, and centered inside their rib cage with an up-and-down motion. This pattern of breathing is a response to stress, but it also creates sensations within the body that perpetuate stress and keep the person engaged in a fight/flight/

freeze response. For that reason, making a daily practice of training oneself to breathe differently can be helpful in assisting the body to transition to a non-distressed mode of functioning. The benefits of learning to breathe intentionally and mindfully are quite broad and well documented (Bing-Canar, Pizzuto, & Compton, 2016; Burg & Michalak, 2011; Colgan, Christopher, Michael, & Wahbeh, 2016; Cho, Ryu, Noh, & Lee, 2016; Feldman, Greeson, & Senville, 2010). They include:

- Reduction in PTSD symptoms.
- Reduction in anxiety.
- Reduction in depression.
- Calmer heart rate.
- Better management of chronic pain.
- Lowered blood pressure.
- Improvements in diabetic symptoms.
- Increased adaptive responses to stress and adversity.
- Increased stimulation of the lymphatic system to detoxify the body.
- Improved immune system functioning.
- Increased energy.
- Improved digestion.

There are many different types of breathing exercises that can be utilized to assist in this form of self-regulation. The most basic elements of breathing exercises include:

- Sitting with a posture that will allow the stomach to expand.
- Breathing from the diaphragm with a forward-and-back motion, rather than in the chest with an up and down motion.
- Breathing slowly, in through the nose and out through the mouth.
- Focusing on the sensations of breathing.

From these most basic steps, there are a wide variety of breathing techniques that can be learned and applied, such as rectangular breathing, 4-7-8 breathing, alternate nostril breathing, Sitali or Sheetari breath, diaphragmatic breathing, pursed lip breathing, and many more. Instructions and demonstrations for each of these techniques can be found using a search with an internet browser such as Google, Safari, or Firefox. All of these breathing techniques are most effective when they are practiced daily. They can be used as a direct response to experiencing negative symptoms of stress, anxiety, panic, dissociation, and depression, but also can and should be used when not actively feeling those forms of distress to help create greater peace and calm, to help regulate the body's functions, and to build resilience against stressful triggers.

Engage the Senses. The body reacts to trauma in a way that is designed to help enhance our ability to sense or anticipate threats. We reach a state where we are constantly keyed up, with our body subconsciously scanning our environment to assess the potential for harm. As a part of this, people experiencing trauma often experience the sensation that the past is present, with old sensations and memories playing themselves out as if they were happening now. Small pieces of our environment that bear some resemblance to the circumstances in which we have been abused can set our body into a full-fledged emergency response. These can be things as simple as the sound of a door opening unexpectedly, footsteps in a hallway, the sound of a car accelerating rapidly, the sound of an object falling and breaking, or the sight of someone with a physical feature reminiscent of the abuser. Any sensory experience that could be tied to abuse of the past can potentially serve as a trigger. In this way, trauma ties our present experience to the past as a tool in avoiding further harm. This automatic, subconscious attempt at coping often becomes quite crippling.

The trauma response also makes use of our imagination, trying to determine all of the potential futures that could spring from the situation we are in now and trying to engineer how it can steer us toward futures in which we are not being hurt, or at least are being hurt less. In this way, trauma ties us to a vast host of potential futures. The combination of these two states—the past being present and all potential futures intruding on the present—is often quite overwhelming. It makes it difficult for us to be where we are in the present, experiencing what is happening right now, and being able to feel safe when we are safe.

People trying to heal from abuse can benefit from a number of practices designed to help them calm their senses down and ground them in what they are actually experiencing in the moment, rather than constantly being keyed up by past traumas and potential future pain. Many of these practices fall into the category of mindfulness, which is the mental state that people achieve by focusing their attention intentionally on what they are experiencing in the present moment. As a part of mindfulness, the person practicing it calmly acknowledges and accepts each one of these sensations, rather than trying to explain them or change them. Mindfulness has been found to be a very effective tool in assisting the process of healing from trauma (Goodman & Caleron, 2012; Ortiz & Sibinga, 2017; Treleaven, 2018).

One example of a simple mindfulness exercise is a senses census. It consists of the following steps:

- Choose a comfortable place to sit. Allow yourself to breathe for just a few moments and settle into where you are. Prepare yourself to be fully present for the time being. Let go of worries about tomorrow, the next day, or any time in the future and past. Your task now is to sit where you are and be fully present in what you are about to do. You can open your eyes to read the instructions for each part of the exercise.
- Close your eyes. Focus on your sense of hearing. Start by listening to the sound of your own breathing. Then, let yourself pay attention to all the different sounds around you. Don't just take inventory of all the sounds by trying to identify them, but listen to them; notice everything you can about them. How loud are they? What do they sound like? How do they mix together? How does your body respond to the sounds?
- With your eyes closed, now pay attention to your sense of smell. Breathe deeply through your nose, slowly, over and over again. Once again, do not take inventory of all the things you are smelling. Just let yourself experience what you're smelling. What do you notice about the smells? How does your body react to the smells? Also notice if there are any taste sensations associated with the smells that you notice.
- With your eyes closed, pay attention to your sense of touch. Do not just pay attention to what your hands feel, but let

your attention move to all the different parts of your skin. Pay attention to what it feels like to sit where you are sitting. Pay attention to the sensations you have on the skin on your legs, your arms, and your face. Once again, do not take inventory of all the things you are feeling. Just allow yourself to feel them. What do they feel like? How does your body react to each sensation?

- Open your eyes and allow yourself to look around without turning your head to either side. Don't worry about putting names to everything you are seeing, but focus on noticing what they look like. What are the colors like? What are the textures like? What are the shadows and the light like? How does your body react to each sensation?

- Close your eyes. Now, pay attention to your emotions. How do you feel what you are feeling? What are the sensations of those emotions in your body like? Is it just one emotion, or are there more emotions? Allow yourself to sit with your emotions for a time. Do not try to change them. Just let them be and notice what they are. If the emotions are unpleasant, simply sit with them and let them be. Notice that you are capable of doing this. Notice that doing so reduces the power they have over you.

- Open your eyes. Now, just sit for a few minutes and allow yourself to be open to all of your senses. What do you notice?

Like the breathing exercises previously mentioned, mindfulness exercises work best if they are practiced regularly. They can be used as a response to stress and trauma symptoms, and can also be proactively practiced to help the body reduce its reactivity. There are a variety of other mindfulness exercises that can be helpful, including the body scan, raisin exercise, five senses or 5-4-3-2-1 exercise, mindful walking, lake meditation, leaves on the river, and many more. Instructions and tutorials for these and other mindfulness exercises can be found using a search with an internet browser for terms including "mindfulness exercises," "mindfulness exercises for anxiety," and "mindfulness exercises for trauma."

Release Stress from the Muscles. All of our emotions are experienced physically, within our body, as well as within our mind. The effects of stressful and negative emotions build up over time, and many people experience this buildup in their muscles. For some people, this is felt in their chest, for some it is in their back, and others experience it as tension in their neck, forehead, or other areas of their bodies. These physical sensations of the body literally holding on to stress in the muscles is a part of what creates the overwhelming emotional and somatic experiences of trauma.

A technique known as progressive muscle relaxation (PRM) has proven to be very effective in helping the body release this tension that it stored up in the muscles, which provides both physical and emotional relief (Fairbank, Degood, & Jenkins, 1981; Scotland-Coogan & Davis, 2016). In this technique, a person purposefully increases the muscle contraction in areas where there is tension to push the muscle past its threshold of being able to hold tension. This then triggers the muscle to release the tension being held in that area and relax.

In PRM, the person practicing it sits in a comfortable position and closes their eyes. It is important for them to continue to breathe throughout the exercise, rather than holding their breath while they activate their muscle groups. They focus on one portion of the body at a time, activating each muscle group for ten to fifteen seconds and then relaxing for five to ten seconds. During the relaxation phase, the person should focus on the sensation they are having in the area they just activated. The activation of each area is repeated one or three times before moving on to the next area. The path of PRM can follow several patterns but often proceeds in the following order:

- Forehead. There are two different ways to activate the forehead. For the first set, bring the eyebrows down and in, as if trying to make "angry eyebrows." When done correctly, your nose should crinkle up as well. For the second set, raise your eyebrows as high as you can.
- Jaw. The jaw also has two different ways of being activated. For the first set, clench the jaw tightly. For the second set, open the jaw as wide as you can.
- Neck. The neck has four different ways of being activated. The first is to tilt the head forward and attempt to touch your chin against your chest. The second is to tilt your head back

and point your chin upward (be sure to do this motion slowly to avoid straining your neck). The third is to tilt your head to the left while keeping your left shoulder level with the ground. The fourth is to tilt your head to the right while keeping your right shoulder level with the ground.

- Shoulders. The shoulders have two different ways of being activated. The first is to raise both shoulders as if you were trying to clench your head between them. The second is to move your arms backwards and pivot your shoulder blades backwards as if you were trying to get them to meet in the middle of your back.

- Arms. The arms have two different ways of being activated. The first is to hold your arms straight down at your sides and then raise your lower arms as if you were trying to squash your biceps between your upper arms and lower arms. The second is to have your arms straight down at your sides and then carefully extend your elbows back to engage your triceps.

- Hands. To activate the hands, start with an open palm. Then, clench your fists tightly.

- Stomach. To activate the stomach, clench your stomach muscles while engaging your chest muscles. When you are doing this correctly, it will feel as if you were pulling all of your abdominal muscles inwards towards your solar plexus region, right below the sternum.

- Buttocks. To activate the buttocks region, clench them inward.

- Upper legs. To activate the upper legs, while seated raise your lower legs to be as close to parallel with the floor as you can. This should activate your thigh muscles.

- Lower legs. There are two ways to activate the lower legs. For the first one, while seated, raise your feet about an inch off the ground. Then, point your toes upwards towards your nose. You should feel this activate your calves. For the second activation, keep your feet raised in front of you and pivot your foot to point your toes as far out in front of you as possible.

- Toes. To activate your toes and the sole of your foot, sit with your feet flat against the ground. Then, curl your toes up underneath your foot as if you were trying to dig them into sand.

Like the other exercises in this section, progressive muscle relaxation is most effective when practiced at least daily. Most people notice that the more often they do it, the faster their muscles respond to their efforts to relax them and release the tension within them.

Grounding. As previously mentioned, part of how trauma functions in the body is to keep it stranded in painful experiences of the past or paralyzed by all of the potential possibilities of pain in the future. Healing happens in the present, with what a person is experiencing in the here and now. Grounding techniques are designed to help a person root themselves in their present experience as a way to counteract the time travelling effects of trauma, such as flashbacks, nightmares, and intrusive thoughts.

A wide variety of grounding techniques can be effective in grounding us in the present. It can be helpful to experiment with several of them and have a few that you have found to be helpful ready to employ when needed. Some grounding exercises include (Covington, 2003; Living Well, 2015, Shapiro, 2012):

- Verbally orienting yourself. Find a place where you can speak out loud. Say what your name is and how old you are today. Describe your physical surroundings. Talk yourself through what you have done today. Talk yourself through the plans you have for the rest of the day. Talk to yourself about what is happening right now that means you are safe today.
- Take your shoes off and walk barefoot in some form of nature. Focus on the feelings you are having with your feet being directly connected to the ground.
- Splash your face with water. Notice the sensations associated with this. Focus on the sensation of individual drops of water as they roll down your skin.
- If you are in the presence of other people who are safe, mentally remind yourself about the experiences you have had with these people that let you know that you are safe with them. Then, focus on what they are saying and doing now.
- Pick an object in your environment. Trace its contour with your eyes several times.

- Rub your hands together. Focus on the growing sensation of warmth that results.
- Get your hands in some dirt or sand, whether that is simply playing with it or engaging in gardening.
- Play a game of catch with a soft, comfortable ball or object.

There are many grounding techniques that you can experiment with. You can find instructions and tutorials in grounding techniques by typing "grounding techniques" as a search term in an internet browser.

By Small and Simple Things. While these small acts of physical self-care and self-regulation may seem to have little to do with healing from abuse, they are the foundational steps toward helping the body and mind begin the process of stabilizing. As a survivor of abuse begins to attend more to his or her body's needs for care and maintenance and helps their body know that it is safe, then their body in turn becomes more and more capable of contributing to the process of their healing. What was previously a downward, debilitating cycle resulting from abuse can become an uplifting, virtuous cycle that contributes to recovery.

ATTENDING TO PRACTICAL NEEDS

Recovering from abuse often brings with it many radical changes to a person's life. Quite frequently, victims of abuse have been financially dependent on the person who abused them. They are often isolated from friends and other contacts. Many of them have not been able to complete a higher education or some form of technical training and thus have limited options for providing an income for themselves. While most, if not all, aspects of their own lives have been turned upside down, the world keeps moving forward, and its requirements and demands do not cease. It can be extremely overwhelming. In many ways, it can be hard to even know where to begin to deal with the basics of living.

There is no single path to sorting out practical needs. However, there are some guiding principles that can be useful for everyone in the early stages of recovering from abuse.

Simplify Where you Can. If you were physically carrying too much weight on your back while going on a long hike and trying to carry all of that weight for the full distance would result in physical injury, what would you do? One of the simplest, most logical, and most practical solutions would be to reduce the amount of weight on your back. If you are trying to recover from abuse—and especially if you are in the early days where your life is still very much in flux—this same principle applies.

You are not expected to be a superhero. No mortal has unlimited strength. Consider the wisdom the Lord shared in Mosiah 4:27: "And see that all these things are done in wisdom and order; for it is not requisite that a man should run faster than he has strength. And again, it is expedient that he should be diligent, that thereby he might win the prize; therefore, all things must be done in order."

Elder Jeffery R. Holland (2013) built upon this counsel when he shared the following: "In preventing illness whenever possible, watch for the stress indicators in yourself and in others you may be able to help. As with your automobile, be alert to rising temperatures, excessive speed, or a tank low on fuel. When you face 'depletion depression,' make the requisite adjustments. Fatigue is the common enemy of us all—so slow down, rest up, replenish, and refill. Physicians promise us that if we do not take time to be well, we most assuredly will take time later on to be ill."

Do not be afraid to evaluate things in your life and determine that, at least for the moment, that is a piece of weight that you are not able to carry right now. That may range from a semester at school to an extra obligation at work to various projects and chores in the home to a specific calling. There is no shame in recognizing that you need to temporarily put down some weight in order to deal with the enormous emotional burden of trying to put your own life back together. As your life begins to take form again, you will reach a point when you can pick many or all of these other things up again. But in the meantime, you must learn to be very honest with yourself about exactly how much you can carry.

Start with What Is Both Urgent and Important. Many things in your life are important, but not all of them are equally as urgent. While you are in the early stages of rebuilding your life, you may find that you need to start by prioritizing the things that are both important and urgent. That includes things like having a place to stay, having utility bills covered, and covering the basic physical necessities of survival. If, for a period of time, you find that this is all you can manage, that is entirely okay. You are most likely experiencing shock, grief, and post-traumatic symptoms. Under these circumstances, it is vital to recognize that you are currently quite literally in survival mode. You will need to work on moving out of that state with time, but it is important to recognize it for what it is.

If, for a time, you are just getting through the day, that is a totally acceptable victory for someone who has experienced what you have. You will get stronger. You will regain your capacity to do more. Do not punish yourself or shame yourself for having your body react to trauma and shock the way it was designed to. By not trying to push yourself beyond what is reasonable while you are in survival mode, your body will begin to recover. Pushing too hard in survival mode keeps you stuck in survival mode.

You may find that you need some help even sorting out what the most important and urgent things are and how to attend to them. It is a perfectly viable and wise option to accept the help of someone whose brain is not currently in fight/flight/freeze mode to help you sort this out, make initial plans, and make arrangements.

Practice Flexibility in Timing and Style. More than at almost any other time of life, people who are in the early stages of recovering from abuse and figuring out where their life is headed moving forward will find that they need to develop the ability to be flexible. There are a lot of ways to create flexibility, even when the demands of life are unyielding. You may find that you can work through things by being flexible about when things happen. Another form of flexibility can be created by altering how things are done. Sometimes it is necessary to develop flexibility in who does certain tasks. Perhaps you may find that in some areas, reordering priorities may be necessary.

Seek Peer Guidance. As someone in the early stages of recovering from abuse, you may feel terribly alone. That, however, could not be further than the truth. A very large number of people have walked the path that you are walking. They have faced similar pains, fears, and heartaches. They have experienced what it takes to rebuild their lives.

There is great value in being able to talk to other people who are experiencing and have experienced what you are going through.

There are numerous support groups for people who have experienced abuse. One easy way to find one near you is at thehotline.org. You have the ability to immediately chat with someone online who has experience with abuse and can be supportive. You can also find local support groups through that resource, or through using a search engine and inputting the terms "support groups for domestic violence near me." Other good online resources include Hope Recovery (https://www.hope4-recovery.org/group.html), Fort Refuge (http://www.fortrefuge.com/aboutus.html), and DomesticShelter.org (https://www.facebook.com/groups/domesticshelterscommunity).

While you are receiving support and guidance from others in these kinds of support groups, keep one thing in mind; they are able to provide perspectives, talk about experiences, and even make suggestions and recommendations, but ultimately you are the one who should make decisions for your life. They can and will provide you with many ideas and options, and this is good. But none of them should make choices for you. You can use their input to educate yourself about possibilities in preparation for receiving your own personal guidance and revelation from the Lord about what options will be best for you.

Ask for and Accept Help. Almost certainly, you will need to ask others for assistance while you are in the early days of trying to recover from abuse and charting a path forward for yourself. Now is the time to be open to asking for and accepting help, whether it is financial assistance, help with child care, aid with figuring out a budget, help securing a job or a scholarship, assistance with handling online accounts, or any other practical need where you feel overwhelmed, uncertain of what to do, or simply in need of assistance.

The Savior tasks His disciples with responding compassionately and generously to those who are in need. Right now, as one who has received deep wounds of the spirit and whose life has been uprooted, that is you. Allow the people around you to fulfill their discipleship by attending to your needs in the same way the Savior would do if He was with you physically. It does not matter if these people are members of the Church or not, or if they even believe in God. His Spirit has worked in the hearts of many to fill them with love and concern for those who need help. The things they have experienced in their life to create their desire to help you are a sign that God has prepared for your need long before it came into existence. Allow Him to bless you in the ways He has spent so much time preparing for. Allow those who are ready to help you to be blessed for fulfilling the righteous desires of their hearts. Allow yourself to be blessed with the deliverance the Lord has prepared for you.

Remember, at the Sermon on the Mount the Lord attended to the people's need for food before He tried to lift them to a higher and holier life. His intention is to do the same for you in all of the needs you have right now. He wants to help fulfill your immediate mortal needs, and also wants to show you a path He has prepared for you to a life that is safer, happier, and more peaceful than what you have had to suffer through.

LEGAL ASSISTANCE

Abuse is a sin against God and an attack against a beloved son or daughter of God. It is also a violation of the laws of the land. Just as much as good doctors and therapists are a part of what God has prepared to help people who have suffered abuse, the laws that prohibit and prosecute abuse are a part of what the Lord has prepared to help those who have been victimized. They are a tool that He intends us to use, as evidenced by the Church's policies that require local Church leaders to report abuse to civil authorities and that forbid local Church leaders from discouraging people to report abuse to law enforcement officials.

Consider the following principles taught in scripture:

We believe that governments were instituted of God for the benefit of man; and that he holds men accountable for their acts in relation to them, both in making laws and administering them, for the good and safety of society. . . . We believe that the commission of crime should be punished according to the nature of the offense; that murder, treason, robbery, theft, and the breach of the general peace, in all respects, should be punished according to their criminality and their tendency to evil among men, by the laws of that government in which the offense is committed; and for the public peace and tranquility all men should step forward and use their ability in bringing offenders against good laws to punishment. (D&C 134:1, 8)

The involvement of law enforcement and the justice system in response to abuse is not something to be avoided. It is a tool that has been provided and is often a necessary step in ending present abuse and preventing future abuse.

Document as Much as Possible. A court of law relies heavily upon evidence for it to draw conclusions and take action. Anything you can do to document what has happened will be helpful in creating impetus for the court to provide help for you. There are a variety of ways that you can gather evidence:

- Take photographs of any injuries: bumps, bruises, scrapes, and so on.
- Take photographs of property damage: holes punched in walls, furniture that has been thrown, and so on.
- Gather together any medical records that are related to any injuries.
- Write down notes about abusive incidents. Include place, time, who was directly involved, who was nearby and may have heard or seen something, and so forth. Write down direct quotes about what was said, to the best of your ability to remember them. Include as many details about what was said, done, and what you felt as possible. This documentation can be used to demonstrate all kinds of abuse: physical, verbal, emotional, sexual, and so forth.
- Write down as much contact information (names, addresses, phone numbers, email addresses) as you can gather about people who may have witnessed the abuse directly or indirectly. That includes people who might have observed the physical or emotional aftermath for those who were abused.

It is a wise idea to gather and store this information in a way that is not easily destroyed. For example, create a personal Google account and upload these things to a personal Google Drive (as well as share that drive with other trusted individuals so there is a backup of all of the information). For safety reasons, it is also highly advisable to try to not let the abuser know that you are creating or storing documentation.

Act Sooner Rather than Later. A general rule of thumb is that the fresher your information is and the more recent the incidents of abuse are when you go to the legal system for help, the more likely you are to have the system respond in some sort of helpful way. The legal system acts best when there is a sense of urgency and immediacy in the need for protection and relief. Conversely, even if you have accrued a very large amount of evidence, if a significant amount of time has passed since the last incident, you are much more likely to encounter reluctance, hesitation, partial measures, or a complete lack of action from the legal system. This is one of the reasons that the policy of the Church is to report abuse immediately when concerns of abuse have been raised.

Secure Legal Advice, Representation, and Aide. The legal system can be complicated, with a vast and complex set of rules, procedures, and an entire language all of its own. While the justice system is designed to protect the innocent and hold the guilty accountable, its dynamics also make it possible for guilty parties to maneuver in such a way as to avoid accountability and even turn the tables on their victims once again. What is intended to be an instrument of aid, healing, and justice can be twisted to be just another weapon in the abuser's arsenal.

Victims of abuse are already under a tremendous amount of stress just by surviving the abuse and going through the harrowing process of seeking to establish safety. Adding the task of trying to figure out laws and legal resources and navigate documents replete with legalese and unfamiliar professional jargon can be overwhelming under the best of circumstances. It is highly advisable to not try to navigate it alone and to find allies and services that are familiar with the process who can talk you through your options, help you put things into place, and help the justice system work in the favor of the innocent as it is intended to do.

For initial reports of abuse, a victim advocate can help a survivor of abuse navigate the process of reporting abuse to the police and securing protective orders, if needed. If the reports of abuse turn into a criminal case, someone associated with the district attorney's office will be in charge of pursuing that legal case. The services of the victim advocate and the district attorney's office are typically free.

Outside of that, however, there are many choices that a survivor of abuse many need to consider that have legal implications and details. This is particularly true in matters of separation, divorce, and child custody matters. For these issues, it is heavily recommended that the survivor of abuse obtains a lawyer of their own.

In general, the services of lawyers are expensive. However, there is no substitute for a lawyer when one is needed. Do not let financial concerns keep you from getting a lawyer if you need one. Keep in mind that abusers are fully capable of trying to use lawyers and the legal system as a weapon to harass their victims and try to regain or maintain power and control. Abusers typically have more financial means than their victims, and in legal situations where one person has a lawyer and the other does not, the person without a lawyer is at a profound disadvantage, regardless of what the facts of the situation are.

Fortunately, there are a number of free and low-cost options for legal representation and advice for people who cannot afford typical lawyer fees. For instance, the American Bar Association strongly urges all lawyers to do fifty hours of work per year without charging for it. They have resources to help connect victims of abuse with *pro bono* (free) legal advice and financial aid to help pay for legal representation. Their resources can be accessed here: https://www.americanbar. org/groups/legal_services/flh-home/flh-free-legal-help/.

There are also organizations that are dedicated to providing free or low-cost legal services for victims of abuse, such as https://www. lawhelp.org/resource/legal-aid-and-other-low-cost-legal-help.

Another organization, WomensLaw.org, offers a registry of organizations that provide legal services for victims of abuse, with a focus on services for women. This can be found at https://www.womenslaw. org/find-help/finding-lawyer.

There are Federally funded legal aid programs for those with economic necessity. They can be researched and applied to here: https:// www.usa.gov/legal-aid.

The National Legal Aid and Defender Association offers a similar set of resources, which can be accessed here: https://www.nlada.org/

tools-and-technical-assistance/civil-legal-aid-resources/what-legal-aid.

Many lawyers also offer free initial legal consultations. These typically last from ten to sixty minutes. This is not the same as having a lawyer represent you in a case, but it can be useful to answer some initial legal questions and point you in the right direction for the first steps you need to take to get legal help. In addition, many law schools offer free legal clinics.

Even if you do not feel certain that you need legal help, advice, and representation, there is great wisdom in seeking out consultation, representation, and legal resources. It can make an enormous difference for the options available to you for protecting yourself and others who are in danger and in rebuilding your life.

If Children Are Involved, Ask for a Guardian ad Litem. When there are legal questions or disputes about the custody of children—which is very common in cases of separation or divorce, especially in cases in which one spouse and/or the children have been abused—the lawyers for each party work to promote the interests and position of the adults that they are representing. They generally do not even meet with any children who might be involved. As such, the lawyers for both sides only know what their respective clients present to them regarding the children.

What often results is that both the abusive spouse and the non-abusive spouse attempt to represent what they see as the thoughts, feelings, desires, and needs of the children with whatever evidence they believe backs up their perspective. This can become very convoluted, since it is very common for the abuser to minimize, justify, redefine, obfuscate, and generally manipulate information about the abuse and about the children.

The commissioner, judge, and other members of the court who are hearing the case may feel that they do not have the information they require to make a clear judgment about custody issues. This can lead to the court ordering default custody arrangements that do not take into account the harm done by the abuse and the physical and emotional needs of children who have witnessed a parent being abused, suffered abuse themselves, or both.

What is often needed is someone whose role it is to investigate, evaluate, and legally represent the children directly, without being beholden to either of the parents in any way. That is the function of a guardian ad litem, to "review the facts and recommend steps that are in the best interests of the individual [child] before the court" (Moore & Hobbes, 2017). Most judges place a great deal of weight on the evaluations and recommendations of guardians ad litem.

A guardian ad litem must be appointed by the legal decision maker, which is most often the judge assigned to the case. You cannot simply hire one on your own. However, there are a number of ways to try to get a guardian ad litem involved to represent the interests of the children:

- A lawyer can file a motion to appoint a guardian ad litem with the court. This does not automatically mean that one will be appointed. Once the motion is filed, the judge will determine if the involvement of a guardian ad litem is appropriate.
- A guardian ad litem can be appointed as a part of a protective order. Typically, this must be explicitly requested as a part of the application for a protective order.
- In some states, guardians ad litem are automatically appointed if there have been allegations of abuse or neglect.

A guardian ad litem can be the deciding factor in making the voice of the children heard by the court directly, rather than being filtered second-hand, argued over, or hijacked by the abuser's preferred method of portraying the children in a self-justifying, self-serving way.

Guardians ad litem can come from a variety of backgrounds. Some of them are lawyers, some are therapists, some are clergy members, and some are even laypeople. There is a diversity of skill sets, perspectives, experience, and even priorities and biases amongst guardians ad litem. In some cases, a judge will assign a specific guardian ad litem. In other cases, the judge will ask the legal representation of both sides to try to come to an agreement on the appointment of a specific guardian ad litem, with the caveat that if they cannot come to some kind of agreement, a guardian ad litem will be appointed at random based on a rotation list of available guardians.

The selection of the right guardian ad litem can make a vast difference in outcomes. As a result, it is wise to ask your lawyer which guardians ad litem they know and have seen behave in a way that is based on sound methods and principles, especially where abuse is concerned. In general, it is best to have your lawyer work on the negotiations until they can come to an agreement on a guardian ad litem they have confidence in. Similarly, it may not be wise to simply agree to a guardian ad litem that the abuser's legal counsel is proposing to use, since they may be making that suggestion based on their knowledge that the guardian ad litem in question has a tendency to be biased in a way that does not adequately take abuse and neglect into consideration.

What may result is a sort of a standoff, with both lawyers stating they are unwilling to budge on opposing and mutually exclusive guardian ad litem recommendations while the clock ticks down to the deadline at which a random guardian ad litem will be appointed. This can be nerve wracking, since neither side is interested in having an unknown guardian ad litem appointed because it introduces a degree of uncertainty into the situation.

If this is the case for you, consult with your lawyer on their recommended course. While you consider their recommendation, also consider the following principle. While both sides in a custody dispute have reason to be worried about a random guardian ad litem being appointed, the risk of that random appointment is not equal. In general, the abusive spouse/parent is at a higher risk. Whereas some guardians ad litem have a motivational bias toward maintaining as many parental rights of abusive parents as possible in the interest of "preserving families" or "defending paternal rights," there is research to suggest that there are more guardians ad litem who are primarily motivated to insure that children are protected (Cooley, Thomson, & Colvin, 2019). Therefore, the abusive spouse/parent is at greater risk of having a guardian ad litem appointed who will not lean in their direction in the course of a random drawing or rotation.

As a result, in a standoff decision like the one described above, there may be some wisdom in trying to wait as long as possible for the deadline to approach before making a decision. In that particular game of chicken, the lawyer for the abusive party is more likely to acquiesce first, preferring to work with a known factor rather than having to brace for an unknown appointment that could be even more staunchly positioned against abuse than the guardians ad litem that your lawyer is proposing.

When a guardian ad litem is appointed, be sure to cooperate fully and promptly with all of their requests. This will likely include granting them access to all mental and physical health records, school transcripts, and even things like texts and emails. Give them access to everything they need to gain a full and well-rounded understanding of what has happened. Do not be alarmed when they ask to have access to the children without you present. Their role is to represent the children, not you. This is exactly what you want in this situation; for the court to know that they are hearing from the children without them being filtered or influenced by you or by the abusive spouse/parent.

SOCIAL SUPPORT AND CONNECTIONS

Since one of the key tactics of abuse is to place a wedge between the victim and other people, healing from abuse requires re-establishing meaningful and safe connections with others. This is not a simple matter, since abuse frequently deals critical damage to a victim's self-respect and sense of self-worth. He or she may deeply struggle to believe that he or she has anything to offer to other people. His or her faith that others will care and respond in loving ways has been deeply eroded. While safe and open connection to others is something victims of abuse have been starved of and desperately need, it is also a source of anxiety. As such, it is not uncommon for them to feel ambivalent about trying to build relationships and connections.

Remember, people who have suffered abuse—especially when it has been prolonged—have been physiologically locked in their fight/flight/freeze mode, and their autonomic nervous system (ANS) is now operating on overdrive trying to scan for actual and potential threats in their environment and in their interactions with other people. As a result, in the early stages of trying to reach out and make social connections, their neurological warning system is likely going to be set off again and again, even in situations where they are totally safe and socially accepted.

This is to be expected and is not a sign of weakness, nor is it the result of the person being overdramatic, paranoid, or neurotic. It is a natural survival response to having been abused. It takes repeated exposure in safe environments to cues that used to be threatening (like the presence of another person who has some physical resemblance to the abuser, experiencing some degree of difference in opinion from another person, the existence of a certain degree of noise and social bustle, and so on) for the ANS to begin to register that no threat is present and to begin to accurately identify emotionally and socially safe situations.

There are many things that survivors of abuse can do to help them navigate these challenges in rebuilding social connections. For example, practicing the physical self-care techniques like breathing exercises, grounding techniques, and progressive muscle relaxation before entering social situations is helpful in proactively calming the ANS down and helping it begin the process of learning to recognize social safety again. While in social situations, the survivor of abuse can work on actively monitoring his or her sensations of anxiety and fear. If they feel like they are escalating, it can be helpful to briefly excuse themselves from the social situation and practice one of these techniques to help their body calm down.

It can also be helpful for survivors of abuse to begin to visualize the alarm system inside of them as if it were a separate entity. This is a technique known as externalizing (White & Epston, 2004). The greater the detail in the externalizing, the more powerful a tool it can be. That includes going so far as to give it a name ("Spike"), draw out what it looks like, identify its tone of voice and favorite phrases and strategies, and generally anthropomorphize it (although it doesn't have to be in human form; any form that feels like it fits will do). These strategies can be very helpful in creating a sense of mental and emotional distance between the survivor of abuse and the overactive internal warning responses.

The survivor can then work on identifying when Spike is talking, examining what Spike is saying, noticing what Spike seems to be trying to get them to focus on, exploring what Spike wants to get them to ignore, and questioning and challenging what Spike is trying to force them to do. From there, they can work on exposing Spike for who he is, actively focusing on the things that Spike is trying to hide from them, and in general not cooperating with what Spike is trying to get them to do. The focus is on accumulating small victories in recognizing Spike, finding what Spike is trying to hide, reframing what Spike is trying to get the person to focus on, and learning to not let Spike determine the survivors behaviors. Each small victory lessens Spike's volume and control in the survivor's mind and body and makes them more capable of connecting in real and safe ways with others.

Others can help in a few general ways. First, there will be times when survivors of abuse feel the need to talk about the hurt they have experienced in the past and the challenges they are facing now. What they need from other people is for them to listen. Listening means opening one's heart and mind non-judgmentally and seeking to understand what the other person is experiencing and expressing. Listening is non-competitive and non-corrective and certainly never involves any degree of one-upmanship. Counterintuitively, it is not intended to change the speaker in any way. In fact, the goal of listening isn't even to make the other person feel better. That may sound strange, but listening is about receiving, holding, and honoring, not imparting. Listening is about joining, being present, being safe, and being loving. You don't have to know the right thing to say. All you have to be able to do is listen and be present and care.

In addition to listening, others can be a sounding board for survivors of abuse as they work on building confidence in their own perceptions, judgments, and abilities to make decisions. This is not the same as telling the survivor what to do, which should be avoided at all costs. In serving as a sounding board, there are several guiding principles that friends and supporters can rely on:

Validate Emotions. It is important to recognize that the survivor of abuse has a lot of reasons for feeling the way that they feel. Sometimes, these reasons are clear. Other times, they are confusing, mixed, or even hidden. Whatever the reasons, it is important to start by seeking to understand and validate their emotions. No emotions should be labeled as out-of-bounds, sinful, or unacceptable. The surivors of abuse may feel strong and even frightening emotions like anger and hatred. If these are a part of their emotional experience, then they must be acknowledged before they can eventually be resolved. Having any emotion is not wrong. Matters of right and wrong come into play in how we act upon those emotions.

It is not unusual to sometimes have emotions that seem completely contradictory simultaneously (Linehan, 1987). For example, they may feel both love and hatred, relief and sorrow, hope and dread, all at the same time. These are normal and rational emotional responses to having experienced harm and abuse from someone that they had a close relationship with.

There is great power in recognizing the emotion that someone else is feeling and validating those emotions (Lundberg, Lundberg, & Lundberg, 2000). Victims of abuse need to know that other people can handle their emotional realities and that others can understand that it is simply a part of surviving abuse and not something to be ashamed of.

Explore Current Perspectives. In conjunction with seeking to understand and validating a survivor's emotions, it is important to help them explore their perspective of their situation. What people perceive greatly shapes the options that they believe are available to them in dealing with their emotions, their relationships, and their circumstances. Keep in mind that perspective is also damaged by abuse, so there may be certain things that the survivor's overactive survival mechanisms have them focused upon because of past traumas, and there may be other things that are obscured or even completely hidden from the survivor at present. This is not a measure of intelligence or obstinance. It is a part of the impact of abuse.

While it may be true that on some topics survivors of abuse can have tunnel vision or still see reality in a distorted way that has been taught to them through abuse, it is always important to start by helping them explore what they can see and how they understand their situation. The simple process of having to talk it through and explore its facets verbally activates other parts of the brain that can help them create a more complete understanding of their experience.

It can be helpful to explore a few important aspects of their thought process with them, such as:

- What are you seeing right now that makes you think that?
- How did you arrive at that conclusion?
- Is that the only possible explanation, or do you see other possibilities?
- If that is true, how do you think we could know it?
- What about this feels similar to things you have experienced before?

- What do we actually know right now, and what is the evidence that is based on?
- We all make assumptions to help us make sense of our lives. What assumptions do you think you might be making in this situation? How could we test those assumptions?

If you are comfortable asking these kinds of questions, be sure to do so in a way that is not confrontational. Your attitude should be of mutually exploring the survivor's perceptions, without judgment or criticism. If you are not comfortable asking these kinds of probing questions, you can simply focus on having the other person explain to you their perceptions of the situation.

You may find that as the survivor of abuse shares their perspective that you have thoughts, perceptions, and ideas that may be helpful and that are beyond what they have told you. It is important for you to recognize that it is not your job, nor is it your place, to tell the survivor of abuse what to do. But, hearing other perspectives can be helpful. Before you share your thoughts, ask the survivor if they would like to hear them. It can be as simple as saying, "You know, while you've been talking, a few thoughts and ideas have occurred to me. I would be happy to share them, if you feel that might be helpful to you." Keep in mind that if the survivor says no, that is a completely acceptable answer.

If they do ask you to share your perspective, do not state your ideas authoritatively. You should avoid saying things like, "You should do x." Do not state things as absolute truths. You can share your ideas and what you are seeing that is leading you to draw the conclusions or consider the options that you are entertaining. Help them see what you are seeing and connect the dots between that and potential options. But keep in mind that your perspective also has its limitations. You can share your perspective, but do not seek to convert them to it.

In this process, always be humble and open to the need to learn more and to admit limitations to perceptions and opinions. Acknowledge the need for prayerfully seeking guidance about how to act.

Explore Options. Once options have been identified, it can be helpful to talk through the pros and cons of each option. As a part of this, it is important to consider the various ways each option could play out. It is also wise to consider who would be affected by each potential choice and in what ways. In this analysis, the truth that "not making a choice is making a choice" should also be fully examined. Consider what the likely outcomes of simply allowing the *status quo* to continue would be.

It can be helpful to examine what the various perceived obstacles to the identified options might be. Some of these obstacles may have ways to be worked through, and others may not. Every option will provide some sort of challenge to the survivor of abuse, and some of those challenges may seem more manageable than others.

In all of this, it is important to identify what the desired outcomes are, not just in the moment or with the present challenge, but in the long run. Some options may feel helpful in the short-term but would be counterproductive to their larger, longer lasting goals and desired outcomes.

Identify Resources and Assets. For some of the identified options to be viable, the survivor may need specific resources and help from other people. Examine what you yourself may be able to do to help, and research together what other people or organizations may be able to provide to help bridge the gap from what the survivor of abuse is able to do on their own to what would be needed to make certain options possible.

A good ally for survivors of abuse is someone who recognizes that the survivor will likely need help from a number of people and therefore doesn't try to overcommit themselves to things they aren't realistically able to do in the process of assisting. As someone trying to help a person who has been abused, you cannot provide everything they need all on your own. That's okay; you are not expected to be superhuman. And in fact, helping them make multiple supportive social contacts is vastly more healthy and helpful in the long run than trying to be their only source of support. Each new connection with a person who is willing to be loving and safe is another step in counteracting the isolation that has been a part of the abuse. So as a supporter, look for ways to facilitate additional safe social connections for the survivor, even in areas where you are fully capable of assisting them on your own.

Support Agency. Again, remember that it is ultimately the survivor of abuse who must be the one to make decisions. This is a part of helping them resuscitate their agency. Keep in mind, they may need to take a "baby steps" approach to making choices. Simply making a single small choice in the direction of exiting their traumatized *status quo* is a victory. Let them be in charge of their pacing. Quarter-steps and half-steps are all still movement and progress and these should be encouraged and celebrated.

CO-REGULATION: BEING A SAFE HARBOR

While there are times when survivors of abuse will need to talk about the traumas of the past, the fears of the future, and the challenges of the present, there are also times when they need to be able to put some distance between them and those things and simply work on what it means to be safe, have connections, and have a life. As simple as that may sound, it is actually quite challenging for many people in the early stages of healing from abuse.

As mentioned previously, the autonomic nervous system (ANS) of people who have been abused tends to be stuck in defense mode. As a part of its process of environmental threat scanning, each individual's ANS seeks to attune itself with the ANS of other people as a part of evaluating safety or danger. We see this process in all animals that are inherently social, whether it be herds of deer or flocks of birds. If one of these animals has its ANS alarms sounded, then all of the members of the flock or herd also go on alert. This increases the chances of survival of both the individual members and of the group.

Humans show the exact same group mechanics. Being in the presence of others who are stressed, angry, depressed, anxious, or hostile activates our ANS in threat mode, even if the anger and hostility is not aimed at us. Seeing another person be attacked, mocked, or otherwise abused has the same effect, even if we are not the target.

Conversely, being with people who are regulated, calm, and have their ANS in a safe and connecting mode can help ease a survivor of abuse out of having an alerted ANS into one that is functioning in modes of safety and connection. When other people can be present, attuned, and safe for victims of abuse, being in their presence is inherently biologically healing for those who have been abused (Polyvagal Institute, 2021).

A variety of other activities tend to help the ANS become regulated again. And each of these activities are enhanced when they can be shared with someone who is able to be present, regulated, safe, and supportive (Polyvagal Institute, 2021). These include:

- Engaging in artistic creativity.
- Singing, humming, or playing an instrument.
- Dancing.
- Engaging in physical forms of play.
- Spending time in nature.
- Feeling and expressing gratitude.
- Having experiences that evoke a feeling of awe.
- Helping another person.
- Practicing yoga or tai chi.

As a supporter, friend, and ally of a survivor of abuse, you do not have to know all the right things to say. You do not have to be capable of doing more than what you are already capable of doing. You do not have to be able to fix everything. Your ability to be present, to be loving, to be kind, to be accepting, to support their agency, and to be emotionally regulated is already a powerful and valuable resource you can offer to assist them in their process of healing.

SPECIALIZED PSYCHOLOGICAL SUPPORT

Abuse affects both the body and the mind. Just as you should make it a priority to get medical attention for any physical injuries that you have suffered, the Lord wants you to receive proper mental health treatment for the psychological wounds that have been inflicted upon you. Elder Jeffery R. Holland (2013) counseled, "Seek the advice of reputable people with certified training, professional skills, and good values. Be honest with them about your history and your struggles. Prayerfully and responsibly consider the counsel they give and the solutions they prescribe. If you had appendicitis, God would expect you to seek a priesthood blessing and get the best medical care available. So too with emotional disorders. Our Father in Heaven expects us to use all of the marvelous gifts He has provided in this glorious dispensation."

As you seek out a mental health provider, keep in mind that virtually all mental health providers are trained first as generalists, dealing with the most common mental health concerns like anxiety and depression. From there, many mental health providers develop specialties through additional training, degrees, and/or certifications in specific areas of mental health, such as autism or eating disorders. Trauma—especially complex post-traumatic stress disorder from prolonged abuse and neglect—is a complicated mental health issue. To work with it effectively, mental health providers need specialized training beyond their basic training as a generalist.

Just as you would not seek out a family medicine doctor to treat your cancer, you should not seek out a mental health provider who does not have specialized training in trauma. You need to make sure that you are getting state-of-the-art treatment that follows research-supported best practices. No matter what the skill level is of a therapist or counselor, and no matter how good their intentions may be, if they are not trained in the specialized skills that are effective at addressing trauma, then they are most likely not going to be the right choice for attending to your mental health needs.

While there are a variety of specialized modalities for treating trauma, I would strongly recommend that adults and teenagers seek out a therapist who has been trained and certified in Eye Movement Desensitization and Reprocessing (EMDR) (Shapiro, 1989). This research-supported treatment modality has proven to be highly effective with even very complex trauma. Furthermore, it is able to provide greater amounts of relief more quickly than many other methods of treating trauma, and is usually less difficult and stressful on the person going through treatment than many other methods (Davidson & Parker, 2001). You can use the following link to find an EMDR trained therapist in your area: https://www.emdria.org/find-a-therapist/.

While EMDR can be used on younger children, as well, play therapy can be very effective for children (Axline, 1969; Landreth, 2012). Play therapy engages children on their mental and emotional level, and uses the medium of play as a way for children to access their emotions and work through them, the same way that adults use words to deal with their emotions. You can find a certified play therapist at the

Association for Play Therapy's website at https://a4pt.site-ym.com/page/TherapistDirectory.

For many people, specialized medications may also be an important—even necessary—part of attending to their mental health needs after suffering from abuse. Again, rather than seeking out a family practice doctor or OBGYN or other medical providers with only basic training in psychiatric medicines, it is highly recommended to seek out assistance from a psychiatrist or psychiatric nurse practitioner. These professionals have had extensive training in prescribing medications to help with mental health concerns, including trauma.

A number of other treatments can help address the symptoms and underlying biopsychosocial-spiritual dynamics of trauma. These include but are not limited to biofeedback (Lande et al., 2010), neurofeedback (Van der Kolk et al., 2016), personalized repetitive transcranial stimulation (prTMS) (Cocchi & Zaleski, 2018), yoga (Rhodes, Spinazolla, & Van der Kolk, 2016), mindfulness based stress reduction (Polunsky et al., 2015), exposure response prevention (Foa & McLean, 2016), and even acupuncture (Kim et al., 2013).

The Lord does not want money to stand between you and the help that you need to heal. Be aware that fast offering funds are authorized to be spent to provide the specialized therapy needed by those who have been abused. Needs like yours are the reasons we collect these funds. Your need for financial support for appropriate therapy is just as legitimate as the need you may have for food from the bishop's storehouse.

One other thing to consider in psychological healing from abuse is the victim's need to rebuild their paradigm or worldview. Experiencing abuse tends to alter a victim's perception of themselves and the world, and in essence it writes for them a series of new, oppressive commandments, written "not with ink" but by the hand of pain and fear "not in tables of stone, but in fleshy tables of the heart" (2 Corinthians 3:3). There are many forms these corrupted commandments can take, but they may include things like:

- Do not share your opinion.
- Anything you say to a man/adult must be stated as a question.
- Never appear to have accomplished more than the abuser.
- Do not try to make friends. Nobody will like you, anyway.

- Do not have a good opinion of yourself.
- Don't try to do anything difficult. You will only fail and make yourself look like a fool.
- You are only a good person if you keep the abuser happy.
- You do not matter as much as other people.
- You have a very limited role in this life and should never try to reach beyond it.
- Your feelings don't matter.
- Your preferences are annoying and should be kept to yourself.
- Appearing righteous and happy is the most important thing. Preserve appearance at all costs. Put on a smile and act happy no matter how you are feeling.
- You are not that important to God.
- You don't make a difference and you can't make a difference.
- Nobody ever misses you when you are not around.
- You are pretty stupid.
- You can't take care of yourself.
- You can't expect anybody to treat you well.

Many people who have been abused have these beliefs etched deep into their souls, and they have developed a whole way of perceiving the world and a whole lifestyle which has contracted itself in order to obey these commandments. To heal, survivors of abuse must begin to recognize these false commandments and oppressive beliefs for what they are. And from there, they must begin a path of learning to disobey these false commandments.

The process of doing so can be incredibly frightening. After all, each of these commandments has been written and reinforced by the repeated infliction of pain. But until the survivor of abuse has found a way to begin to extract these poisoned daggers of the mind that are a part of the psychological effects of abuse, they continue to suffer the abuse in the present, even if they have been delivered out of the presence of the abuser.

Fortunately, this is not a battle that needs to be won all at once. Even small steps and nascent efforts are a part of healing. It can be difficult to know where to begin. However, the following concepts may prove useful.

- First, work to identify what corrupt commandments you have internalized. You may find that you need the help of someone you can trust who knows you well to help you identify these.
- Second, for each corrupt commandment that you recognize has made its way inside your mind, identify what you do to obey that corrupt commandment. You may need assistance from a trusted friend, family member, or therapist to help you see this clearly. Seek a trusted outside perspective.
- Third, rate these corrupt commandments in the order of how hard you feel it would be to start breaking them.
- Fourth, select the corrupt commandment that you believe will be easiest to start to break. Develop a plan with small steps you will take to challenge and disobey this corrupt commandment.
- Fifth, experiment with breaking that corrupt commandment on a daily basis.
- Sixth, keep a record of what you experience as you try to do this, including:
  - What seems to work.
  - What obstacles you encounter.
  - How it feels when you work to break the corrupt commandment.
  - How it feels when you are successful at breaking the corrupt commandment.
  - Questions and concerns that come up for you as you experiment.
  - Plans for applying what you learn as you experiment.

Do not expect this to be a smooth or easy process. But, it will become a rewarding one. As you progress through this quest of challenging the false ideas that abuse has implanted in your mind and then discarding them and the behaviors that maintain them, you open yourself up to a much more liberating and inviting world in which you are free to be defined as who you really are and what you really can be, rather than what the abuser tried to teach you that you are.

SPIRITUAL SUPPORT

Quite simply put, being abused can shake a person's faith in themselves, in humanity, in local Church leaders, in the Church as a whole, and even in God. This is especially true if spiritual abuse is a part of what the victim has suffered, with the twisting and perversion of doctrines and practices of the Church in the service of the abuse. Just as abusers try to make victims question and doubt their own perception and judgment and try to cut them off from other people, they also have a tendency to try to make victims feel that they are incapable of receiving or understanding personal revelation.

This can leave the victim feeling deeply spiritually unworthy and distant from God, or even worse, unimportant to God. This is amplified if they have experienced other members of the Church—especially those in leadership positions—responding in ways that have felt dismissive of the abuse or even supportive of it. They may struggle with what has been called in philosophy the problem of evil (Hickson, 2013), with its heartbreaking question, "If there really is a God, and He really knows everything, and He really is all powerful, and He really loves me, then why did this happen to me?"

In many ways, just as the world as a whole fell into a time of universal spiritual confusion, misinformation, and partial truths during the period of the Great Apostasy, those who have suffered spiritual abuse have also passed through the experience of a false, scattered, and misshapen form of the gospel being preached to them as if it were true. And just as false ideas about religion have been used as an instrument of violence and oppression over many nations and peoples, these distorted presentations of the gospel have been used as a weapon and a tool to hold victims of spiritual abuse in darkness and pain in subjection to the unrighteous dominion and control of the abuser.

And just as a Restoration was needed to deliver the world from this state into a place of greater light, knowledge, understanding, and opportunity, those who have suffered spiritual abuse need to be led out of the darkness and into the light, where gospel principles and doctrines are taught in their true nature and where the corrupted versions of these ideas that they have been taught are exposed and dispelled.

As a survivor of abuse, it can be difficult for you to discern where and how gospel principles have been perverted and misapplied to you and internalized by you. You may have reached a point where you lack confidence in your own ability to learn the truth. But, if you are willing to engage in a process of personal searching and learning and if you turn for assistance to those who can help you in your process of spiritual clarification, you will find that you are fully capable of knowing the truth.

Take time to study the scriptures. It can be helpful to do this as a general study, to simply give yourself time and opportunities to feel the spirit outside of the suffocating confines of an abusive relationship. It can also be helpful to revisit different teachings and doctrines that have been used against you or have been cited to support the abuse. Learn more about them in the Topical Guide, the Gospel Topics Essays, general conference talks, and the Church magazines. Pray for understanding and discernment, deliverance from false teachings, and a true understanding of the doctrines that have previously been misused to hurt you. Discuss these with trusted members of the Church. Record what you are learning in a form that you can review later.

If you are endowed, take time to go to the temple. Visit the temple with new eyes, as if you were seeing it and experiencing it all for the first time. Pay special attention to details such as what covenants you are making and with whom you are making them. Notice what is taught about your individual relationship with God. Learn more about the sealing ordinance and how it actually works. Notice the patterns in the narratives that are present. Explore what is taught about the relationship between men and women and adults and children. Ask yourself, "If the Lord is presenting to me a story in the temple about being abused and then being delivered and healing from abuse, where does that story show up? How is it taught? What specifically is taught as a part of it?"

Above all, remember that anything that you have been taught to believe that does not harmonize with the idea that God loves you, that you are worthy of being treated with dignity, respect, and love, and that your life and your happiness are important is not of God. As you progress through this process of having the doctrines of the gospel delivered from their mangled, abusive manipulation and restored to their true form in your understanding, you will feel moved upon to echo the words of Isaiah when He spoke of the deliverance of the Lord: "The people that walked in darkness have seen a great light: they that dwell in the land of the shadow of death, upon them hath the light shined" (Isaiah 9:2).

CHAPTER 7

REPENTING OF ABUSE

A FOCUS ON THE ABUSER

Most of this book is dedicated to examining the experience of victims of abuse, their needs, and the path for moving forward and healing. However, understanding some aspects of the way forward for people who have fallen into the sin of committing abuse is also necessary, both for the sake of the abuser trying to repent and change, but also to help victims of abuse think through their relationship with the abuser.

Victims of abuse have some very difficult decisions to make about what the future of their relationship with the abuser is going to be. A number of important questions need to be answered as a part of contemplating possibilities for the future. These include:

- What is it about this person that has led them to choose abuse? (Remember, abuse is about the abuser, not about the victim.)
- Has the abuser changed, or are they in the process of changing in a way that is meaningful and sustainable?
- What indication is there that the abuse will cease?
- What potential is there for building a relationship that is positive and healthy?
- What was the foundation of our relationship in the first place? What do we have to build upon?
- What would it take for me to not only feel safe, but loved and respected in this relationship?
- Is this the relationship I want to have with the person I want to have it with?

In building an understanding that will help answer these questions, there are some important points to be aware of. Remember that abuse is a manifestation of struggles, challenges, and maladaptive aspects of the person committing abuse. Their task is not merely to cease the abusive behaviors. Their task is to work on changing the things that led them to the choice of abuse in the first place. Doing anything less tends to simply lead to another prolonged calm stage in the build-up toward another incident of abuse.

Perhaps one of the most clear guides is a quote mentioned earlier from the Church's website about abuse. It is worth examining in greater detail to explore how it can guide decision making about whether or not—and to what degree—to work on reconciling and reunifying with the abuser.

"If another one of your family members is the offender, you may need to consider removing him or her from the home. While this may feel like the family is being torn apart, the separation is an important step that can lead to the eventual healing of everyone involved. In some situations, family reunification may eventually be possible through help from civil authorities and professional counselors. In other situations, family reunification may not be advised."

Let's examine the elements of this statement in greater detail:

- **"You may need to consider removing him or her from the home."** This policy is in favor of the person who has committed the abuse being removed from the home, rather than displacing the victims. That may not always be possible or safe, but it is clear that the victim's needs are prioritized. Church leaders and other helpers should not be afraid to support a course of action in which the accused abuser is removed from the primary household. This is not a violation of their rights. This is an accurate acknowledgement that their actions have made the home and family unsafe.

- **"The separation is an important step that can lead to the eventual healing of everyone involved."** It is clear that removing someone who has committed abuse from the family's residence is not considered "breaking up the family," even though arguing that it is often an abusive person's attempted defense against the move. Rather, this restructuring is establishing safety. Also, it is clear that the expectation is not for the healing process to be rapid, but rather that healing and wholeness will come "eventually." The separation is likely to not be brief, and may in fact last for a long period of time.

- **"In some situations, family reunification may eventually be possible."** The wording here is very precise. It is not claiming that reunification is possible in most situations. The word *some* does not even necessarily imply a majority of situations. Reunification is not automatically a goal after a separation has occurred. There are some situations in which it makes sense as a goal, and other situations in which it does not. Also note the use of the word *eventually*, which again supports the idea that the time of separation is not intended to be brief or short-term.

- **"Reunification may eventually be possible through help from civil authorities and professional counselors."** Notice how this talks about intervention by both the legal system and by trained, qualified, and expert mental health practitioners as being precursors to potential, eventual reunification. The abuser is not sheltered from legal consequences. The mental health needs of the victims are attended to. The mental health contributors of the abuser's poor choices are addressed.

- Keep in mind that mental and emotional issues do not form overnight. They are created over a long time, through multiple contributing factors. Similarly, their healing and improvement take time and are not the result of simply taking a few classes and engaging in some therapy sessions. Change is real, hard work, both inside of therapy and outside of it. It does not simply happen by having checked off the boxes of going to an anger management class and meeting with a bishop.

- **"In other situations, family reunification may not be advised."** Not only is reconciliation and reunification with an abuser not always the goal, sometimes it is counterproductive to the primary goals of helping the victims heal and move forward with a happier, better life. The abuser does not get to dictate whether or not this is the case. It is determined by the emotional realities of those who have been abused.

What can we learn from this? First of all, there should be no hesitation to remove an abuser from a household or have the victims leave if abuse has occured. Second, there should be no rush and no pressure toward reconciliation and reunification. Third, if reconciliation and reunification are to be considered, there is a great deal of work to be done, both legally and from a mental health perspective. These things should be given time to fully play out.

Fourth, reunification should not be attempted if there is reason to believe that there is still a potential for further abuse. Even then, the ability of the victims to feel safe and open to the idea of contact with the abuser is the more important factor, and should be the primary consideration. Fifth, in many situations attempting reunification would be unwise and should therefore be avoided. Families in this situation should be fully supported.

In addition to understanding the courses of action suggested by the Church's policy, developing a greater understanding of what leads to someone committing abuse can help you develop greater confidence in evaluating the degree to which they are changing. As we explore these factors further, keep in mind that the ultimate deciding factor in whether or not to attempt reunification is not whether or not the abuser has changed—after all, it is difficult to fully predict what their actions will be after reunification even if someone appears to have made substantial improvements. Rather, the deciding factor is whether or not the victims of abuse can feel safe with that person.

You do not have to psychoanalyze the abuser and predict their future and base your decision upon that. There is no line of evidence of potential change on the abuser's part that, once crossed, obligates or compels you to return to them. There is no degree of contrition on the part of the abuser that will transform your choice not to return into a sin. The sin of abuse on their part has created for them the need to repent. What it has created for you is a choice of what to do about it. And it is a choice. You may choose to leave, you may find that you feel safer and happier away, and you may choose never to come back. That is your choice to make, a choice created by the abuser's use of their own agency, and it is not made wrong by repentance on the part of the abuser.

PRECURSORS OF ABUSE

For the abuser, abuse does not begin in the moment they first commit an act of verbal, emotional, physical, or sexual abuse. Various dynamics that have contributed to them developing their tendency toward coercion and violence have been in motion long before the first act of abuse takes place. While there is no single psychological profile of someone who commits domestic violence, there is a common thread of multiple contributing factors that can add up in a variety of ways that lead someone to the choice of committing abuse (Azhagar, Chinnakkaruppan, Hassan, & Ashan, 2018).

That being said, it bears great emphasis that there is nothing that forces a person to become an abuser. There is no disease, mental health diagnosis, or personal tragedy that makes someone powerless to choose some path besides committing abuse (Ganley, 1995). No one is fated to become an abuser. No one can force or coerce someone else to behave abusively. People who commit abuse often want to blame the abuse on their victims, on their circumstances, on their levels of stress, and so forth. But the truth is that there are many, many other people in similar circumstances with similar stressors facing similar challenges who do not turn to abuse as a way to try to manage their situation.

Psychosocial Risk Factors for Abusers. A number of psychological circumstances have been found to be more common in people who commit abuse. They include but are not limited to the following:

- **Low emotional intelligence.** Emotional intelligence is defined as "a set of skills hypothesized to contribute to the accurate appraisal and expression of emotion in oneself and in others, the effective regulation of emotion in self and others, and the use of feelings to motivate, plan, and achieve in one's life" (Salovey & Mayer, 1990). Emotional intelligence includes the ability to understand what is contributing to one's own emotions and a tendency to work to regulate these emotions in a healthy way. It also includes the ability to accurately perceive the humanity and feelings of other people, to experience empathy, and to act on that empathy.

It should be noted that emotional intelligence is not a static trait. It can be developed and learned (Serrat, 2017). Similarly, like any paradigm or skill, it can also be neglected and will erode over time if not exercised and applied.

People with lower levels of emotional intelligence have been found to be significantly more likely to abuse other people (Winters, Clift, & Dutton, 2004). They struggle to accurately understand their own emotional contributors. They often have unhealthy methods of trying to deal with unpleasant emotional states, such as lashing out, avoidance, blaming others, and seeking to numb or distract themselves with substances or other high-stimulus experiences. They tend to be wrapped up in their own emotional states in a way that overpowers their sense of empathy for other people. They often feel that the emotions of others—especially those that would require an exercise of compassion, patience, or sacrifice from them—are a burden.

People with lower levels of emotional intelligence are much more likely to experience and feel motivated by an emotional state known in psychology as schadenfreude, which is the feeling of taking enjoyment or satisfaction in seeing another person experience misfortune, pain, or discomfort (Dashborough & Hardy, 2017). As such, people who develop and cultivate a mindset in which they take pleasure in causing other people discomfort, humiliating other people, embarrassing other people, scaring other people, and so forth are actually reducing their degree of emotional intelligence.

What can be deceptive is that people are entirely capable of having low levels of emotional intelligence and yet simultaneously presenting themselves as charming, charismatic, and adept at leading other people to form a positive opinion of them. Keep in mind that many people with low emotional intelligence have found a way to put up a public persona, but their real challenges with emotional regulation are often pent up and building up pressure until they are in a private situation. That is where they most often become plainly and abundantly manifested.

- **Narcissistic personality traits**. Narcissistic personality traits include an inflated and grandiose sense of one's own importance, abilities, entitlements, rights, and virtues. As such, people with narcissistic personality traits often exhibit an exaggerated need for praise, attention, and admiration. In addition, people with narcissistic traits tend to be profoundly lacking in their empathy for other people. These traits can become pervasive enough to become the core organizing structure of a person's personality (American Psychiatric Association, 2013).

  They tend to build up a personal narrative about themselves as being exceptional. They see themselves as constantly being the best or superlative in some way. They cannot tolerate the idea that they have faults and failures, or that anyone would see them as anything less than the way they prefer to see themselves. They value other people as a means to validation of their preferred way of being seen. If someone or something challenges their preferred way of being seen, they tend to consider that thing or person a threat and work to undermine or destroy it. For these reasons, people with narcissistic personality traits tend to have a great deal of difficulty with intimate relationships such as marriage and are at an elevated risk of being abusive (Coleman, 1994; Rosen, 1991). However, they are often fully capable of presenting a public image that is charismatic, charming, and even popular.

- **Borderline personality traits**. Borderline personality traits can be difficult to identify because they often get mixed up in a swirl of emotional swings of depression, anxiety, and other intense states. It is defined as a pervasive instability in self-image, emotions, and relationships. This instability is caused by a deep and abiding fear of abandonment and a hypersensitivity to things that could be perceived as abandonment (American Psychiatric Association, 2013). They often feel profoundly empty inside and are desperately looking to fill that emptiness. They may feel fundamentally broken in some way or unlovable and are looking for someone or something to fix that about them.

This often leads to relationships that have an intense "push-pull" dynamic to them, with a high amount of emotional reactivity both in the positive and the negative. In particular, their experience and expression of anger is often quite intense, disproportionate to their circumstances, and often entirely inappropriate.

The person with these personality traits alternately idolizes the person they are in a relationship with and then devalues them, based on where they are in their cycle of fear. When they are in their devaluation state, they are often devastatingly adept at tearing the other person apart emotionally. They also have a tendency to be rather impulsive with things like spending, reckless driving habits, eating habits, body alterations, self-harm, and so forth.

A person with borderline personality traits may enter a relationship with someone else viewing that person as a savior who can fix what is wrong with them and help them finally feel whole. When the romantic partner fails to accomplish this, the person with borderline personality traits often takes this as a form of abandonment or betrayal, and acts in various ways to punish the other person, often with abusive results (Coleman, 1994; Goodman & New, 2000).

- **Antisocial personality traits.** The term *antisocial* is often used colloquially to refer to someone who is introverted or who prefers to spend time alone rather than socializing with other people. That is not, however, the way the term *antisocial* is used in psychology. When speaking of antisocial personality traits from a clinical perspective, it refers to a condition sometimes known as sociopathy. People with these traits consistently show no regard for the concepts of right or wrong. As a result, their behavior toward other people can present along a spectrum ranging from cold and disinterested to actively contemptuous and antagonistic (American Psychiatric Association, 2013).

As a result, people with antisocial personality traits have a tendency to lie, behave violently, and use drugs. They frequently find themselves gravitating toward criminal activity. They tend to feel no remorse and no empathy for pain they cause other people. Their tendency to not care what other people think may sometimes seem attractive and compelling to other people. However, they typically do not feel or act upon any sense of loyalty. When they do form relationships, they tend to be jealous, vengeful, intentionally cruel, and violent. The most common feeling they have about other people is contempt. They also tend to feel bored and listless, and enjoy conflict as a means of stimulation (Spidel, Vincent, Huss, Winters, Thomas, & Dutton, 2017).

Unfortunately, antisocial personality disorder is notoriously difficult to treat (Mayo Clinic, 2021). When people with these traits go to therapy, they typically use what they learn in therapy to simply become more effective at manipulating and hurting other people. For that reason, seeking to form or repair a relationship with someone with antisocial personality traits—especially if they are fully crystalized into antisocial personality disorder—is dangerous and unlikely to be successful.

- **Impulsivity**. People who struggle with impulse control, delayed gratification, a greater focus on immediate emotional states, and less thoughtfulness and regard for the consequences of their actions are more likely to commit abuse (Snoyman & Aicken, 2011). There are a number of effective means through which people who struggle with impulse control issues can learn to grow, adapt, and develop impulse control, which can help to reduce the risks associated with impulsivity.

- **Substance use.** People who use drugs or alcohol or who misuse prescription drugs are at a substantially high risk of engaging in abuse of all forms (Humphreys, Regan, River, & Thiara, 2005). The risk for violence and abuse is not only higher while the abuser is actively intoxicated, but it is also generally elevated. Part of what is problematic is that drugs tend to interact with the parts of the brain that regulate feelings of attachment to other people. Substance users create an attachment to their drugs that is not only similar to their attachment with other people but is in competition with their relationships. When the needs of another person pose a threat or inconvenience to the abuser's access to using drugs, the attachment to the drugs tends to win and can do so in ways that involve many types of abuse. The continued use of drugs also tends to create maladaptive attachment strategies in those who use them, further compounding the problem (Fairbairn, Briley, Kang, Fraley, Hankin, & Ariss, 2018).

- **Pornography use.** People who use pornography have been found to be more likely to see women as objects rather than as human beings. Their pornography use contributes to a desensitization to sexual violence and violence in general. It contributes to the development of a willingness to engage in dangerous and risky behaviors. It directly contributes to both sexual aggression and general aggression (Manning, 2009). In all of these ways, the developmental impact of pornography use increases the risk factors of that person who uses pornography becoming abusive.

- **Learned behavior and reinforcement.** People who commit abuse against others may have learned those behaviors in a variety of ways (Ganley, 1995). Some were exposed to verbal and physical abuse in their family of origin. Some may have been actively reinforced for being verbally caustic and physically aggressive by family members. Others may have had family cultures that embraced or enabled any of the risk factors mentioned to this point, such as encouraging narcissistic attitudes, excusing or minimizing abusive language or emotional manipulation, and so forth.

For victims of abuse who are contemplating if they want some kind of ongoing relationship with the person that abused them, one of the most important things they need to be able to determine is if it is safe to do so, both for themselves and for the other people who will be affected by their decision to try to carry on some kind of a relationship. In general, the more of these psychosocial risk factors that are present and the greater the intensity of each factor, the less likelihood there is of being able to carry on some form of contact without a recurrence or even an escalation of abuse. As previously noted, trying to maintain a relationship with someone who has antisocial personality traits is particularly dangerous.

The answer to the question of whether or not a relationship is possible is not necessarily all-or-nothing. For example, a young adult who grew up with an abusive parent may find that certain ways of relating are able to feel sufficiently safe. They may be able to establish certain boundaries that provide the necessary structure to protect themselves while still furnishing an avenue of connection that serves a beneficial emotional purpose for them. What this looks like may evolve over time, with some periods of expansion and other periods of contraction and withdrawal. What is possible depends a great deal on their ability to hold a boundary, the abusive parent's willingness to abide by that boundary, and their ability to recognize when they are starting to get sucked into old, damaging patterns.

That being said, great care and consideration should always be taken for those who are the most vulnerable in the situation and those who have the least power to make the decisions that would greatly affect their lives. The guiding principle should be that if an effort to maintain a relationship with someone who has committed abuse would do harm to a vulnerable person, then that action should not be taken. Consider, for example, a case in which a father systematically and regularly sexually abused all of his daughters throughout their childhood years. The abuse stopped when one of the daughters made the courageous move of speaking up, which led to her father's incarceration.

The children's heartbroken mother was faced with some incredibly difficult choices, with many people that she trusted telling her that she needed to stay married to her husband and try to work to keep him as involved with the family as possible. They often quoted church teachings against divorce. In all of this, though, important truths were being forgotten. For example, while speaking out against divorce, President David O. McKay also noted that there are things that are much graver than divorce that in fact can make divorce necessary. He went on to delineate that these things included sexual infidelity, addiction such as alcoholism, long imprisonment, violence, and other "calamities in the realm of marriage" (See Day, 2013).

In this case, the question that needed to be answered in determining what kind of relationship—if any—should be continued with the abusive father was how it would affect the daughters that he had so thoroughly and consistently betrayed and hurt to have their mother return to their abuser, embrace him, and then try to have an ongoing relationship with the daughters. In answering this question, it was important to acknowledge that any claim the father thought he had to the daughters by virtue of them being born in the covenant and sealed to him had been forfeited by him breaking the very covenant in question.

What these girls ultimately needed was the ability to say they did not feel safe being put in a position of vulnerability with him again and to have people understand that asking them to try to trust him again could only lead them to feel that others did not understand or care about the depth of the damage he had done to them. From there, what they needed was to have those who were in a position to make decisions act in a way that honored their needs for protection. Victims of abuse should never be compelled to do something in relation to their abuser that does not feel safe to them.

SIMILARITIES BETWEEN ABUSE AND ADDICTION

While addiction can be a contributor to abuse, there are also significant parallels between what makes someone vulnerable to developing an addiction and what makes someone at risk for becoming an abuser. Similarly, there are powerful analogs between what it takes to recover from an addiction and what it takes to truly change and cease to engage in abusive patterns. A full examination of the parallels between these two phenomena is beyond the scope of this book. However, there are key points that are worth including.

No quick fixes. As is true of the process of becoming an addict, a person does not quickly become an abuser. It develops slowly, insidiously over time. This fact directs us to a second important truth: just as there is no quick fix for addiction, there is no quick fix for overcoming the challenge of having become a person who abuses others (Washton & Boundy, 1989).

Accepting this is a challenge for many abusers. After all, abuse is an attempt at a fast-acting, problem-solving mechanism. It channels unpleasant emotions and difficult work into attitudes and actions that are much more impulse-gratifying and much more immediate than actual healthy coping. The very first thing that someone who abuses others must accept is that this very expectation—that things should be relatively fast and easy—is part of their problem and one of the first things they need to be willing to change.

Ownership of the problem. Just as an addict loves to have other people and other circumstances to blame for their addictive behaviors, someone who abuses others feels a desperate need—even an entitlement—to have other people and external circumstances be responsible for the abuse. The problem with these excuses is that they are just that: excuses. Research has shown that abuse is not caused by relationships. It isn't caused by the behavior or traits of the people they abuse. It isn't caused by stress. It isn't caused by exposure to domestic violence in their childhood. It isn't even caused by anger. After all, there are many people who experience anger and do not behave abusively.

What it is caused by is the relationship the abusive person has created with all of these factors and more. What are their expectations around these things? What meaning do they make out of these things? What is their pattern of responding to these things? How has this shaped their personality over time (Ruddle, Pina, & Vasquez, 2017)?

The cause of abuse, like the causes of addiction, are found inside the abuser. It has its roots in a combination of unhealthy beliefs, a misdirected personality, inadequate coping skills, unmet psychosocial-spiritual needs, and a lack of adaptive social support (Washton & Boundy, 1989). If someone who has abused others wishes to change, and if he or she wishes these changes to be sustainable, he or she must be willing to work on this inner level of causes for their abusive patterns. If they cannot accept that they are the cause of their abusive behaviors and continue to seek to blame others, their chances of recovery and change are very poor.

Choosing abuse has shaped you. Every choice we make shapes us, quite literally. As stimuli come into our brains, we process those stimuli and then make decisions based on the way we have processed those stimuli. As we do so, the brain makes actual physical connections made of neurons. These connections, when repeated and reinforced over time, become the structure through which we perceive the world and by which we reflexively respond to it. Our choices shape our brains. Our brains determine our perception. Our perception defines our options. Our options lead to our choices. Our choices continue to shape our brains. And so the cycle continues (Butler, 2010).

When we shape ourselves in this way, it is difficult to discern that we are doing so. Why? Because it is our brain that we are shaping, the very organ that we rely on to perceive and discern. Other people are often more capable of perceiving it than we are. We are too close to it. It's literally like trying to look at your own eyes without using any kind of reflection.

The truth of the matter is that if you have chosen a pattern that has led to you abusing others, you are a different person in many ways than you would be if you had chosen otherwise and shaped yourself differently through that repeated pattern of choices. This has become a form of maladaptive development for you. If you are to truly repent and change, you must embrace the challenge of actively and intentionally developing yourself differently, in a more adaptive and healthy fashion.

Otherwise, you are most likely consigning yourself to become the equivalent of what has become known in 12-Step circles as a "dry drunk" (Ranganatha, 1985). In drug abuse, a "dry drunk" is someone who is not drinking but still exhibits all of the emotional and relational patterns that they were engaged in while they were consuming alcohol. They may think that they are sober, but that is because they are narrowly defining their addiction as the consumption of alcohol, rather than recognizing it for the much larger psychosocial phenomenon that it is.

In terms of abuse, someone who is a "dry drunk" has typically focused on one specific type of abusive behavior that they have determined constitutes their abuse. They are technically not engaging in the specific targeted behavior (yelling, hitting, and so on), but besides that they are still exhibiting the same mindset and attitudes that have been a part of their abusive cycles all along. Like the "dry drunk" alcoholic, part of the problem they are facing is that the definition of abuse they are accepting and targeting in their efforts is too narrow to accurately reflect the totality of their abusive dynamics.

Refraining from abuse is the beginning of recovery, not the end. Another major parallel between addiction and abuse is understanding the scope of recovery. In addiction, total abstinence from the addictive substance or activity is just the beginning of recovery. It is "a prerequisite for recovery, not its endpoint" (Washton & Boundy, 1989).

In addiction, simply abstaining from using often begins with a process of "white knuckling," which is exerting willpower to resist urges to use. This is necessary but not sustainable as a long-term strategy. Ultimately, the recovering addict must make changes within themselves that address what fuels the urges to use in the first place.

The same is true of recovering from and repenting of abuse. It may begin with "white knuckling" through impulses, urges, and anger. It may mean learning to bite your tongue and practice basic anger management. But as we examined previously, abuse is not caused by anger, since most people are able to be angry without being abusive. And therefore, managing anger and the way we feel and express it by itself is not enough to cease committing patterns of abuse.

As someone seeking to change from being abusive, you must be willing to delve deeper. You must be willing to explore the contributors to your choice to be focused on power and control of other people. You must learn the functions this plays in your life. And you must learn to fulfil those functions in healthy, adaptive ways.

More than that, you must have a change of heart toward the people you have hurt. You must stop blaming them and trying to make them responsible for the abuse. You must stop feeling like you are their victim for them being hurt and putting up boundaries to protect themselves. You must cease any efforts to require them to be the source of what makes you feel better. You must accept the fact that they owe you nothing, that you are the one in their debt. You are the one who shattered the relationship, and therefore they are the ones who get to decide what kind of future they want that relationship to have. You must surrender any efforts to control them. Otherwise, you are just continuing to be a "dry drunk."

Beware of counterfeits for change. The road to true repentance can be littered with obstacles. One category of such obstacles is counterfeits to true change. For example, the path of repentance involves learning to feel true sorrow for one's sins and for how one has hurt other people. Many people experience self-pity along the path of repentance and mistake it for godly sorrow. Whereas true sorrow and empathy for others is transformative, self-pity is corrosive. It feeds one's sense of victimhood for being held accountable and breeds resentment for those whom they have hurt. It is a path back to the very state of heart from which the abuse was spawned. As taught in the Bible, the result is that this "sorrow of the world worketh death" (2 Corinthians 7:10).

Other counterfeits include but are not limited to:

- Bottling up one's emotions rather than learning to resolve them in a healthy way.
- Offering excuses in the guise of building understanding.
- Self-aggrandizement and pride disguised as a need for validation.
- Seeking to fulfill one's own emotional preferences in the name of doing what is best for the victims.
- Demanding that people dissolve their feelings by claiming that God demands that the victims forgive the abuser and never mention the sin again.
- Invalidating the real harm they have done by misapplying the doctrine of how the Atonement of Christ can heal all wounds.
- Seeking to remove the victim's agency by appealing to the sacredness of temple covenants.
- Claiming to take accountability while also demanding absolution misconstrued as repentance.

Be aware of anything that seems quick or easy, as they are most likely counterfeits. Be wary of anything that suggests that surface level changes are all that is needed. Shun anything that would tempt you to feel like you are entitled to the victims owning some responsibility for your abuse. Recognize the lies in the concept that committing abuse merely creates a series of boxes that one needs to check off, which then grants them the right to never have anyone have any lasting hurt about their actions and negates everyone's right to bring up the abuse ever again.

Adaptive re-development. At its core, repentance from abuse must be deeper than external behaviors. It is more comprehensive and more complete than learning not to yell or purposefully and mechanically adopting non-threatening body language or using "I feel" statements.

Learning to punch pillows instead of people is a superficial improvement that still leaves room for rage that has a myriad of causes that all need real solutions.

Court-ordered education and therapy usually just scratches the surface, offering Band-Aid-sized solutions for open heart surgery-sized problems. Indeed, anger management classes have been found to result in very little reduction in repeated instances of abuse. This is especially true when the measurement being taken is asking the survivors of the abuse about how much change the abuser's anger management class has made. From that perspective, the benefits of these anger management courses tend to measure at essentially nothing (Arce, Arias, Novo, & Fariña, 2020; Bennett & Williams, 2001; Breslin, 2005; Day, Chung, O'Leary, & Carson, 2009; Epstein, 1999; Feder & Wilson, 2005; Gilchrist, Munoz, & Easton, 2015; Rosenfeld, 1992). That is, in part, because they are not nearly comprehensive enough. As a result, the entire efficacy of anger management classes in reducing violence is in question. And yet, they remain a go-to intervention in our society in spite of their proven lack of meaningful results. They may serve as a place to start, but the research on the topic is very clear that completing them is certainly not where the journey ends. Otherwise, it all tends to serve as a revolving door filled with false assurances rather than a passage out of an abusive way of being.

Leaving abuse is about more than knowledge and techniques. A repenting abuser must be willing to accept that there are ways in which they have developed that are maladaptive and even harmful. Think, for a moment, of all of the ways a person develops as a child and adolescent. We develop beliefs, attitudes, patterns, strategies, motivations, fears, and ways of relating to people and the world. Our way of understanding the world and relating to it ultimately becomes our very personality through the process of repetition and reinforcement. All of this contributes to why a person chooses to abuse others. In many ways, learning to leave behind abuse requires engaging in a process of corrective re-development.

Again, this is an area with powerful parallels to the process of recovering from an addiction. Dr. Arnold Washton and Donna Boundy (1989) studied this re-development process in people who successfully recovered from addictions. Their findings are summarized below:

Each of these traits can be developed, either on the positive side or the negative side. Developing these traits positively will take time. The good news is that as a positive trait is developed and becomes more consistent, it makes the process of developing other positive traits more accessible.

As a word of warning, it can be very easy for a person who has committed abuse to fall into the trap of trying to develop the appearance of these positive traits without actually developing the substance of them, in the hope of proving to the victims that the abuser has changed and convincing them to trust him or her. You will notice that doing so is actually one of the maladaptive traits, namely an obsession with appearance. The person who has committed abuse must let go of their desire to try to convince everyone that they have changed and instead focus on the process of actually changing. When the change is real and sustainable, the believability of the change will take care of itself.

It should be noted that simply developing these positive traits in no way obligates the victims to reconcile or reconnect with the person who abused them. These developments help create circumstances of safety if the victims should choose to want a closer and more meaningful relationship at some point in time. Also, they help the abuser move forward and develop the ability to form non-abusive relationships with other people in their lives in the present and in the future. But if the goal of the person who has committed the abuse is to seek to make these changes in order to make the victims return and trust again, then they are still thinking with an abusive mindset. A truly non-abusive mindset is evidenced by a determination to make the needed developmental changes because they are the right thing to do to be reconciled with God, and allow the victims the freedom to make their choices about what feels safe to them.

DUTY TOWARD THOSE WHO WERE HURT

If you have abused someone, you have harmed them in a very deep way. If you are truly repentant, then your desire should be for their healing and well-being. In a truly repentant heart, this desire should be placed at a higher priority than things such as your desire for their forgiveness, your desire for their trust, your desire for them to think well of you, and your desire to carry on a close relationship with them. Those other things may or may not come, but they will be the prerogative of the person whom you abused. Abuse was your choice. These other items are theirs to choose.

They do not owe you anything; it is you who are in their debt. Your actions of repentance do not entitle you to anything from them. The fact that you have some kind of familial relationship does not obligate them to you; it only serves to make your betrayal of the safety that is required in such a relationship more damaging. If you are only repenting to try to get them to trust you, forgive you, think well of you, or return to you, then your repentance process is being hijacked by your continued desire to control someone else's thoughts, feelings, and actions. And it is that desire to control others that is at the root of what you are trying to repent of. ***You cannot fully repent of abuse while continuing a pattern of trying to control others***.

The eight, ninth, and tenth step of the 12-Step addiction recovery model can be instructive on how you should approach your interactions with those who have been hurt by your abusive actions.

Step 8: Made a list of all persons we had harmed, and became willing to make amends to them all. Taking a true, honest, and complete moral inventory of the effects of our actions is difficult for anyone. It is especially difficult for someone who has committed abuse. When a person strips away all of their excuses for their actions and ceases to blame their victims, they will experience pain. "The guilty taketh the truth to be hard, for it cutteth them to the very center" (1 Nephi 16:2). Nephi's words sound a bit like the guilty are going under the knife for surgery. And in reality, the process of repentance from abusive patterns is spiritual heart surgery. The heart of the abuser must be spiritually exposed, opened, examined, diagnosed, and repaired if they are to truly change and cease harming others. This is not a painless process.

Chances are, if a person has turned to abusive attitudes and actions, it is in part because they have not learned to deal with difficult emotions effectively. Certainly, they have not learned how to handle pain well. They have learned all sorts of unhealthy attempts at dealing with pain, including blaming others, numbing it out, and inflicting it on others as a way to attempt to download it out of themselves.

If a person is to go through the process of understanding how they have hurt others and becoming willing to make amends with no minimization, no strings attached, no sense of victimhood in the requirement to make amends, then they also have to become willing to accept the pain that comes with it. This pain includes a knowledge of what they have done, with no justification or rationalization to cloak it. It also includes a knowledge of what they have cost both the other person and themselves.

Becoming willing to make amends means becoming willing to change the things that led to the creation of the damage in the first place. It means to be willing to return control to the person or people that were hurt. It means being willing to accept all of the consequences that the abusive actions have caused, even if some of those consequences are long-term or permanent, like no longer being able to serve in certain callings or no longer having a specific desired relationship. It means learning to deal with pain through healthy means, with good psychological coping skills and real reliance on the Savior.

Becoming willing to make amends means the abuser also has to become honest enough and develop enough insight to understand and accept what has prevented them from being willing before. It means deciding to surrender those blockages, no matter how justified they may seem. It means becoming willing to be fully accountable.

And just what does becoming fully accountable mean? From years of clinical experience, my colleagues at Telos have developed a typology of accountability that I have found to be accurate and useful.

- **Level 0.** The person is highly defensive. They deny, excuse, blame, minimize, deflect, and seek to escape any degree of responsibility. Prominent emotions at this level may be contempt for those who were hurt and a sense of victimhood for being confronted.
- **The Wall.** Many people find it difficult to even desire to move beyond level 0. This wall can be made of many things, but a common element of this wall is fear. These fears can range from fear of getting into trouble, fear of loss of self-respect, fear of loss of respect and trust from others, and so forth.

- **Level 1.** At level 1, the person has been able to work through the wall of fear enough to own up to their actions and admit they were wrong.
- **Level 2.** In addition to confessing actions and admitting they were wrong, the person is willing to apologize sincerely for their actions to those who were affected. The person feels genuine remorse, as opposed to self-pity.
- **Level 3.** In addition to the parts listed in the first two levels, the person takes action to make restitution for the damage done by their actions.
- **Level 4.** In addition to the parts listed in the first three levels, the person willingly accepts the consequences of their actions without complaint. They recognize that these consequences are just. They do not resent or blame others for these consequences.
- **Level 5.** In addition to the parts listed in the first four levels, the person seeks to learn from their mistakes and grow as a person.

To truly and fully repent, the person will advance through all five levels of accountability. However, there is a caveat; there are those who believe they have worked through all five levels of accountability and then use that belief to say that now the victims owe them. Now, they state, the victims must forgive them, must think well of them, must let them have the relationship they prefer with the victims. Again, this is a return to the abuser mentality and reveals that the process of repentance is not complete.

Step 9: Made direct amends to such people wherever possible, except when to do so would injure them or others. Level 3 accountability makes reference to making amends, which is the main theme of step 9 of the 12 steps. It is important to note that step 9 contains a major and very important caveat. This step recognizes that sometimes the nature of the damage done is such that attempts to make direct amends with that person may in fact do more harm.

What kind of harm might be done in attempting to make amends? There are many ways that it actually can. Sometimes, victims have worked hard to heal, to create a new life for themselves, to move forward and put the past behind them—a daunting task for anyone who has been traumatized. That peace is built by degrees and is the result of tremendous exertion. It is precious, and for a very long time, it is fragile. As such, it is important to recognize that the victim's need for peace is a higher priority than the abuser's desire for closure.

An abuser might object, "But closure will bring them peace!" This is a rationalization. This is the abuser advocating for what they want by claiming that it will be good for the other person. The truth is, the victim's closure may look entirely different from the abuser's closure. And closure is not the same as being completely healed. The victim may already have closure. It may not have come in a single, dramatic event as is often portrayed in books and movies. Rather, they are finding it one day at a time, living outside the shadow of the threat of continued abuse. It abides with them as they see the door is closed to them being hurt again by the abuser. That is their closure, and for it to persist the door must remain closed.

The abuser may feel that healing will come from clearing the air, so to speak, and offering and receiving verbal absolutions. Deep down, what they may want to hear is that the victim does not blame them and what they did wasn't really all that bad. However, reinserting themselves back into the victim's life in the name of giving closure to the victim may actually be the thing that disrupts the victim's closure and leads to substantial emotional setbacks for them. And when that happens, it is the result of the abuser again putting their own desires ahead of the needs of those they have hurt. You can never heal someone by continuing to do the same kinds of things that hurt them. And putting one's own desires ahead of the well-being of others is the common factor of all abuse. Thus, the abuse is perpetuated in the name of closure.

That is not to say that there are circumstances in which a victim of abuse may wish to have the abuser apologize to them directly. They may even wish for some form of reconciliation. But it is their desires and their needs that determine the timing, speed, and scope of such things. To do otherwise is to do more harm.

Attempts to force the issue of making amends or reconciliation are not only retraumatizing to the victims, but they actually serve to undermine that abuser's desire to have a long-term relationship with family members that they have hurt. For example, studies show that in cases where a child is estranged from a parent because of abuse and then is forced against their will to engage in treatment with the goal of reconciliation, the child becomes further entrenched in their rejection of that parent. The majority of children required to participate in this kind of intervention resented it into their adulthood and saw it as a contributor to long-term estrangement from the rejected parent (Jaffe, Ashbourne, & Mamo, 2010; Johnston et al., 2009).

Children also tend to experience this involuntary participation in reconciliation-focused therapy as another trauma in and of itself. They demonstrate outcomes from those interventions of substantial increases in mental health issues, including depression, anxiety, PTSD, self-harm, and suicidality (Silberg, Dallam, and Samson, 2013). A meta-analysis of outcomes of such treatments demonstrated that they have significant potential to do long-lasting harm to children. Children who are forced into these interventions against their will show much higher long-term risk of depression, anxiety, and suicide. This is particularly true in cases in which the abusive parent claims that the emotional distance between them and their child is due to purposeful parental alienation by the other parent rather than being a natural consequence of the abuse they themselves perpetrated (Mercer, 2019).

If some sort of healing or reconciliation is desired, science has shown a better, safer, and much more effective method than forced reconciliation counseling. Research has demonstrated that giving the child the choice to engage or not engage in conjoint therapy has better outcomes. If the child is not yet willing to engage in conjoint therapy, they can be supported by individual therapy to help them address their trauma. During this time, the best approach is for the estranged parent to back off, respect the child's boundaries, and show that they are willing to let the child be in control of what feels safe to them. If the estranged parent is able to do this and gives the child time to mature and work through things emotionally, they are much more likely to find themselves reaching a stage where the child wants to try to reconnect. But, this must be done with respect for the child's autonomy and their need to have some control over distance, speed, and level of connection following a traumatic experience of abuse from a parent. Using this approach, the harmful effects of long-term depression, anxiety, and risk of suicide are not present (Johnson et al., 2009). And, in the extraordinarily rare cases where reports of child abuse were false and a child has still been separated or distanced from a parent, research shows that children most often reconcile with the formerly rejected parent on their own, without any intervention at all (Johnston & Goldman, 2010).

Therefore, the single more influential, scientifically supported key to an abuser finding reconciliation and a renewal of a meaningful relationship with a victim of their abuse—if it is to be found—is to respect the agency of the victim. In practice, this looks like honoring the boundaries that the victim puts in place, earnestly working on self-improvement, apologizing and making amends if and when the victim is ready for it, and following the victim's lead in steps forward without pressure or coercion of any kind.

Step 10: Continued to take personal inventory and when we were wrong promptly admitted it. Abuse is rarely ever an incident; it is often a process, a pattern, and even a lifestyle or way of being. Similarly, repentance from abuse and recovery from being an abusive person is a process that involves developing a new mindset and way of being. An indispensable part of that new way of being is humility.

The noteworthy philosophy professor Terry Warner (2001) has observed that one of the keys to practicing real virtue is to be constantly open and seeking to discover where our virtue is lacking. When we are self-assured in the fact that we are both right, righteous, and justified in our actions, we are most at risk of blindly and emphatically being none of them.

Consider for a moment the degree of rationalization, justification, and self-deception that must go into the process of abusing someone else and still feeling right. For abusers, these three mind-poisoning dynamics are well rehearsed and can be deployed with ease, even effortlessly and subconsciously. They become a part of the lens through which the abuser sees the world, or as Dr. Warner referred to it, a part of their self-justifying image (Warner, 2001). While people who have committed abuse are working on changing their hearts, they must also work on changing their lens.

One perniciously distorting facet of that lens is our preferred way of being seen by other people. Everyone has a way that they would prefer for other people to view them. Perhaps it is as someone who is smart, intelligent, admirable, responsible, temperate, or trustworthy. As a result, we can begin to deceive ourselves when we are being foolish, ignoble, irresponsible, impulsive, or untrustworthy. When we foster our pride, the way that others see us becomes intensely important to us. We want it to match up with our preferred way of being seen. When we are proud, we begin to care more about (and stand in fear of) others' judgment and opinions of us than we do about making our actions conform with our own sense of right and wrong and with God's laws in His plan of happiness for us.

We begin to care more about how we will appear than what we actually are, what we will become if we continue on our current course, or what the results of our actions will be on other people. Our self-image can become the idol before which we bow and for which we become willing to fight many bloody crusades, regardless of the costs and the casualties. When we are enveloped in pride, the sense that others do not see us the way we wish to be seen creates a particularly intense discomfort (Ferrel & Boyce, 2015). The abusive, narcissistic response is to attack or discredit anything that does not reinforce our preferred way of being seen.

Repentance and recovery requires the development of willingness and vigilance to try to see oneself in a true light. It requires a repentant abuser to be aware of his or her own desired self-image and to be on the lookout for when he or she is acting in the service of that self-image. It requires a willingness to admit that they are wrong. It includes developing a genuine desire for correction when they are off course.

This task never ends. It becomes a new lifestyle, a new way of being. This transformation is necessary for those who have been abusive to be converted into someone who no longer feels like they are a threat to the victims of their abuse.

REPENTANCE IS ABOUT MOVING FORWARD, NOT ABOUT REWINDING

People who are trying to recover from having been abusive can fall into a trap of believing that their quest—and also their reward—is to be able to have everything go back to the way things were before the abuse occurred. This desire is understandable, but it is also illusory for a number of reasons. For example:

- Defining what "before the abuse" actually is turns out to be quite difficult. As mentioned previously, the seeds of abusive behaviors are planted long before the first obvious incident of abuse occurs. Many of the things that were shattered by abuse were built on shaky ground to begin with, since the seeds of abuse were already planted and growing underneath their foundations.
- What the abuser fondly remembers as their definition of "before the abuse" frequently does not match up with what the victims experienced. It may be something the abuser wishes to return to, but the victims fervently hope will never happen again.
- The concept of the "good old days" before the abuse is often in part or in whole a mirage formed for the abuser by a combination of grief at what they have lost through their abuse combined with a well-practiced pattern of minimizing and hiding the truth of their actions from themselves.

Many people who have committed abuse and seek to repent of it may hope that they can repent and ultimately not have to suffer any loss. This is bitterly ironic, given the extended period of loss their victims have suffered long before they themselves ever felt the first sting of their actions and given the long and arduous road of healing ahead of the victims. To expect the victims to be the only ones to suffer any loss is to victimize them all over again.

As much as these grief-stricken wishes are understandable, they are also unprofitable. A person can waste their life and continue to inadvertently cause tremendous amounts of pain to themselves and to others by chasing these illusions. Rather, those who have abused others must recognize that the repentance process is not about turning back the clock, it is about moving forward into the future and allowing those you have hurt to do the same. They may choose to do so in a way that involves you to some degree. They may need to move forward without you to heal. But you must let them move forward in whatever way they need. Like Adam and Eve, you cannot return to Eden. But if your repentance is sincere and complete, you may yet find your way to Zion. Do not throw away what you might have in the future by refusing to release your grip on your perception of what you had in the past.

CHAPTER 8

HELPING THE ABUSED

FOR RELIGIOUS LEADERS

Those who accept callings of local leadership within the Church are all too familiar with how daunting the task of helping the abused feels. For most of them, the things that they are being asked to do as leaders fall well outside what their education and professional training has been focused on. When we read of Enoch feeling inadequate when he received his calling (see Moses 6:31), it is easy to relate to it.

Through our callings, we learn a great deal about what the Lord can do through us when we learn to rely on Him, rather than trying to solve things with our own strength and wisdom. It is true that God can give you revelation to do any task. After all, servants of God with no education in shipbuilding and seafaring have been instructed in these two complicated skills and have sailed across entire oceans. These types of events do indeed happen when the Lord deems them necessary for his purposes.

The more common pattern in working with His servants, however, is to help His servants work within a variety of means that He has prepared in anticipation of the needs. He does not expect you to pray and receive revelation about how to perform brain surgery on someone in your stewardship who has a malignant brain tumor. Nor does He follow a pattern of inspiring a bishop, Relief Society president, or elders quorum president untrained in chemistry with the formula for a medication that would ease the burden of a member of their congregation living with the rigors of a chronic disease. It is not His method to have bishops conduct treatment for schizophrenia, relying on the Spirit to guide them in their efforts.

In all of these things, His method is for bishops and other local leaders to respond to the pleas for help from those within their stewardship with compassion. From there, they help the members of their congregation connect with the people who have been trained in the skills that are needed to attend to the causes of their suffering. The Lord's servants can continue to support those who are in need as they work with the resources that have been provided for them. But God does not expect His willing servants to become experts in healing skills through prayer, faith, and the mantle of a calling.

Domestic violence and abuse of all kinds are complicated matters that involve many psychological, physiological, sociological, and legal complexities. Dealing with it and all of the needs it creates effectively often requires the skills of multiple professionals. There is no shame, no lack of faith, in recognizing that this is an issue that is bigger than you as a well-meaning lay clergy member are prepared to provide on your own. That being said, the part you can and should play is profoundly important, even indispensable.

Your role in your calling is to connect the people in need in your congregation with the people the Lord has already prepared to help them. You have the ability to provide emotional support. You have the ability to provide practical support and overcome a variety of barriers that they would otherwise face in finding and using these resources. While there are many things you can do to make a difference, the following are some key tasks to focus on.

Task #1: Believe reports of abuse. Your job as a Church leader is not to be a detective or a child protection services investigator. Your job is to exercise an abundance of caution in protecting people from abuse. As such, if someone confides in you with a report of abuse, or if you see a situation in which there is reasonable suspicion of abuse, the *only* proper response from anyone in your position is to act upon it as if it is true.

You may be afraid to do this, worried by the thought that the report of abuse may be false and that your actions may end up damaging an innocent person. That fear is understandable, and your desire to avoid hurting an innocent person is commendable. But you must remember that, as mentioned previously, false reports of abuse are exceedingly rare. What that means is that there is very little chance of you harming an innocent person by believing the report of abuse, and an overwhelmingly large chance that you will do harm to an innocent victim by questioning, doubting, discrediting, diminishing, or disregarding a report of abuse.

As a leader in your local church unit, you also have the ability to lead out among other members of your ward, branch, stake, or district in creating and supporting a proper understanding of abuse and the response the Church has directed for local leaders to follow. You can help others build an understanding of abuse and the emotional, spiritual, physical, and practical needs it creates. You can be a voice advocating for generosity in the use of the resources your local unit has to offer in the service of victims of abuse. And you can be an active, loving supporter of those within your ward who have experienced abuse and are in need of healing. Be an example of a believer, not just of Christ, but of people seeking help and relief from the suffering caused by abuse.

In addition, you must have a clear understanding and belief of an important truth: abuse is not the fault of the victims. They did not do something to bring it upon themselves. They do not need to repent of being victimized. The abuser is fully responsible for their abusive actions, and they are fully accountable for ceasing the abuse and any further harm to the victims. This is not a matter of the victims needing to meet the abuser halfway, nor is it an issue of stating that the victims share some responsibility for the abuse. While it is true that the abuse cycle involves the victims, the victims do not co-create the cycle with the abuser. Rather, the victims are caught up in its currents like someone being dragged out to sea by a riptide.

A related truth that you need to believe is that no degree of virtue, no positive qualities, no amount of providing for a family financially provides any degree of excuse or mitigation for the harm done by abuse. Abuse is a game changer in a relationship. It transforms a relationship into something harmful, no matter what else might be present in the relationship to make it superficially appear to be good. An abuser cannot "balance out the ledger" by doing a lot of positive-seeming things and thus negate the damage done by the abuse. So, no matter how impressive the abuser's public image may be, believe that what the victim of abuse has experienced is crushingly different than what is usually visible from outside of the relationship.

Do not minimize. Do not justify. Do not explain away. Do not criticize. Do not ignore. Do not delay. Believe people who say they have been or are being abused.

Task #2: Work to protect those who have been abused or are in danger of being abused. When the Anti-Nephi-Lehies fled from destruction at the hands of the Lamanites, they were met with open arms by the Nephite people. They were given lands in Jershon to make a new home, and the Nephites placed armies between them and their aggressors to protect them (see Alma 27). This scriptural example is an excellent analogy for the response we should have for those who have suffered abuse.

As mentioned previously, one of the most common reasons that local leaders may hesitate to take action in this way is that they fear the consequences it may create for the person who has been reported as an abuser. To be sure, having charges of abuse brought against a person can have a significant impact upon them in their careers, their church service, their general reputation, and so on. Well-intentioned local Church leaders may find themselves trying to reduce or eliminate the consequences that can occur for those who have been reported as abusers.

This type of thinking—which often can be made to seem compassionate—is actually profoundly myopic. It fails to take into account the huge consequences that the abuse has already had upon its victims. It does not recognize the continued compounding of that suffering, the life-altering, soul-shattering nature of it, and the exceeding difficulty in healing from it without help. It also does not acknowledge the heartbreaking truth that unless acted upon, abuse and trauma form a cycle that often is passed down from one generation to the next, causing expanding ripples of suffering and pain (Kwong, Bartholomew, Henderson, & Trinke, 2003; Isobel, Goodyear, Furness, & Foster, 2019; Lieberman, 2007; Oliver, 1993). Those who need our help are right before our eyes, and also in the generations yet to be born.

When we think of what victims of abuse have suffered at the hands of those who have abused them, can we hear the haunting words of the prophet Jacob? "Behold, ye have done greater iniquities than the Lamanites, our brethren. Ye have broken the hearts of your tender wives, and lost the confidence of your children, because of your bad examples before them; and the sobbings of their hearts ascend up to God against you. And because of the strictness of the word of God, which cometh down against you, many hearts died, pierced with deep wounds" (Jacob 2:35).

Responding to a report of abuse is not about causing suffering or trouble. It is about ending it for those who are suffering because someone else is misusing their agency in a way that is causing them great damage. Responding to abuse is also about acting to stop the abuser from harming themselves as well by continuing to perpetuate a grievous sin that puts them in stiff opposition to God's laws. The abuse the offender is perpetrating is not only estranging them from their victims, but also from God. That needs correction. Responding to reports of abuse does not cause any more trouble than is already there. All it does is open it up in a way that makes solutions for the trouble possible.

So, in your response to reports of abuse, the needs of those who have been abused or are at risk of abuse are your priority. All other concerns must be placed in a secondary position.

Task #3: Provide resources, opportunities, and connections for those trying to rebuild their lives after being abused. For many years, the Church discussed its mission as being three-fold: proclaim the gospel, perfect the Saints, and redeem the dead. In recent years, the Church has added a fourth piece to this central mission to clarify just how essential it is to practicing true discipleship. That fourth piece is caring for the poor and needy. This makes it clear that attending to the needs of those who find themselves in difficult situations is not just an appendix to the mission of the Church and the Savior: it *is* the mission. Victims of abuse are frequently facing significant financial difficulty, and they always have substantial and urgent needs. Their plight is where the rubber meets the road concerning our discipleship.

As much as victims of abuse need emotional support, they also have a wide variety of practical needs. They absolutely need you to pray for them, befriend them, fast for them, express your love for them, and express your faith that the Lord will provide for them what they need. Along with that, keep in mind the teaching of James: "If a brother or sister be naked, and destitute of daily food, And one of you say unto them, Depart in peace, be ye warmed and filled; notwithstanding ye give them not those things which are needful to the body; what doth it profit? Even so faith, if it hath not works, is dead, being alone" (James 2:15–17). Our emotional and spiritual support will be hollow—and in many senses dead—if it is not matched with real, practical, temporal assistance.

Victims of abuse will have many needs, ranging from food, safe shelter, job opportunities, connections, resources, financial assistance, legal advice, help with child care, educational opportunities, and more. As stewards and ministers, these are the needs the Lord expects us to do all in our power to help meet, through a combination of our own works and through connecting the victims of abuse with other useful organizations and resources.

When victims of abuse come to local Church leaders seeking assistance, they should not experience something akin to what many people face when trying to make a claim with a home insurance or health insurance company, with the people being asked to help trying to find every reason to disqualify the petitioner from receiving help or trying to give only the minimum amount they can give without being seen as defaulting on their contract. The way we give to help victims of abuse should match what the Savior taught: "Give, and it shall be given unto you; good measure, pressed down, and shaken together, and running over, shall men give into your bosom. For with the same measure that ye mete withal it shall be measured to you again" (Luke 6:38). Those who come to the Lord's servants for help after abuse should not feel like they are running into a closed door. Rather, they should experience it like coming to an open portal leading them through to a better, safer place.

Task #4: Recognize and honor the agency of victims of abuse. People who have suffered from abuse have all had two experiences in common. First, they have been on the receiving end of someone else misusing their agency in a way that has been harmful to them. Second, they have often had their own agency significantly curtailed and even crippled by the person abusing them. In that way, abuse tends to be a sin *of* agency *against* agency. As such, many victims of abuse face a great deal of uncertainty and anxiety in trying to make choices—especially choices regarding how to move forward from the abuse and trying to heal—the same way you or I might feel uncertainty in trying to place weight on a leg that has been broken.

Part of what makes decision making difficult for victims of abuse is that their brain is still in fight, flight, or freeze mode. Their working memory is essentially flooded with pain from the past, threats and dangers in the present, and uncertainties about the future. It is very difficult on a physical level to think in this state. It often feels like having been kicked in the head or having suffered from carbon monoxide poisoning, and then being asked to perform a tax audit in a foreign language. It often takes time and the relieving of some immediate pressures to help reduce the difficulty in organizing thought and making decisions.

Throughout this process, it is very important to attend to two things. First, do not make decisions for the person who has been abused. It may take them time to work through their feelings and thoughts. They may need to examine things from multiple angles. They may need to get professional help and guidance. They may vacillate between choices. It may seem like the details of what they are reporting shift or come across as incoherent and inconsistent. All of these are symptoms of the abuse. Do not see these as signs that the person is "flakey" or "dishonest." Their brain's mechanisms for taking in information, organizing it, making sense of it, and making decisions based upon it have been overwhelmed. Give them time, be a sounding board, and be supportive. Validate that the difficulty they are having with thinking decisively is very normal for someone who has experienced what they have. But do not try to take control away from them.

Second, be aware of the fact that the abuser may still continue to try to impinge upon the agency of their victims. For example, in one case a woman and her children moved out of the house with the husband and father of the family because of his regular, violent rages and intense emotional abuse. The husband ultimately decided that he didn't like the situation, and insisted on moving back in, even though the wife and children were not comfortable with where he was in his progress with working through his violent tendencies. This man was told by his bishop that he had every right to move back in because it was his family and his name on the lease. In very plain words, this should *never* happen, and certainly not with the endorsement of a Church leader. It is emboldening and enabling someone to continue to use their agency in an abusive fashion without regard for its impact on others and is further deepening an unhealthy imbalance of power.

The agency of victims of abuse must be honored. What they need to heal, what their levels of emotional safety are, and what they need to feel safe are the things that should be given top priority. The abuser—who has already violated the agency of the victims—should not be permitted to try to trump these needs of the victims. This is still true even if their local Church leader's personal feelings are that the risk of renewed emotional, verbal, or physical abuse is low. It is not the feelings of the local Church leader or of the abuser that should be the deciding factor; it is the feelings, needs, and agency of the victims. Your role as a leader in the Church is to restore, protect, and prioritize the agency of victims of abuse.

Repairing Unfairness. Some local Church leaders may worry that prioritizing the needs of the victims is somehow unfair to the abuser. They may feel that the desire of the abuser to preserve their reputation, their calling, their standing with their job, and other items that would potentially be tarnished or forfeit if their deeds are brought to light ought to be somehow "balanced" with the needs for safety and healing of the victims. As noble-hearted as these concerns may be, they demonstrate a lack of understanding of what fairness is.

Holding someone accountable for their actions is not unfair. Preventing someone from hurting someone else is not unfair. Having someone face the natural consequences of the choices they have made—on their relationships, on their standing in the church, on their standing with the law, on their careers—is not unfair. As members of the Church, we recognize the divinely endorsed connection between choice and accountability.

One cannot light their own house on fire and then complain that they are being treated unfairly when they have no place to live. One cannot lash out hurtfully at those around them and then blame others for the fact that nobody wants to spend time with them. One cannot spend all of their money wastefully and then feel that they are being treated harshly when they have nothing left to pay for necessities. One cannot embrace Christianity while denying the law of the harvest: "Be not deceived; God is not mocked: for whatsoever a man soweth, that shall he also reap. For he that soweth to his flesh shall of the flesh reap corruption; but he that soweth to the Spirit shall of the Spirit reap life everlasting." (Galatians 6:7–8).

Those who sow seeds of abuse have put into motion things that, once they are ripened, will yield a harvest of pain, tears, regret, and difficult consequences. Oftentimes, the victims of abuse eat from the bitter fruits of this corrupt sewing in great abundance for months, years, or decades before the law of the harvest is fulfilled for the abuser. There is nothing unfair about the abuser finally having to be honest about what his or her actions have created. There is nothing unfair about the abuser having to be the one to wade through the damage themselves and having to work on picking up the pieces to strive to repair what they have destroyed for the sake of those they have hurt rather than for their own benefit.

What is unfair is that the victims have been the ones paying the price for the abuser's misuse of agency. The victims have done so over and over again in a way that has eroded them physically, emotionally, mentally, and often spiritually. Fairness requires a restoration of what has been taken from them. Fairness insists that the agency of the victims be returned to them. Fairness requires that those who have been mistreated are shielded from further harm. Fairness dictates that the victims should be the ones in a position to make choices about the future of their interactions with the abuser.

Elder Dale G. Renlund observed that fairness does not always mean that everyone receives what might superficially be perceived as equal attention or resources. He shared an experience his wife had in her childhood that illustrates an important nuance in understanding fairness.

> One day Ruth learned that her mother was taking a younger sister, Merla, to buy new shoes. Ruth complained, "Mom, it's so unfair! Merla got the last new pair of shoes."
>
> Ruth's mother asked, "Ruth, do your shoes fit?"
>
> Ruth replied, "Well, yes."

Ruth's mother then said, "Merla's shoes no longer fit."

Ruth agreed that every child in the family should have shoes that fit. Although Ruth would have liked new shoes, her perception of being treated unfairly dissipated when she saw the circumstances through her mother's eyes (Renlund, 2021).

In this example from an admittedly much less complicated situation, fairness was not about both sisters getting shoes so it appeared equal. Rather, it was about making sure each sister had shoes, which ended up with one sister getting a new pair of shoes and the other receiving nothing at that time.

This principle has application to cases of abuse. The abuser has had power, control, and the ability to utilize his or her agency, oftentimes with a tremendous amount of latitude. They have misused this agency, and in so doing have hurt others and severely limited their victim's ability to exercise agency. To make the situation fair, the victims must be given power, control, and the ability to exercise their agency without constraint by the abuser and without having to lie about, diminish, or deny what the abuser has done in an effort to shelter the abuser from accountability.

Elder Renlund shared a second example that is applicable to responding to abuse:

Consider a family in which each child received a weekly monetary allowance for doing common household chores. One son, John, purchased candy; one daughter, Anna, saved her money. Eventually, Anna bought herself a bicycle. John thought it was totally unfair that Anna got a bike when he did not. But John's choices created the inequality, not parental actions. Anna's decision to forgo the immediate gratification of eating candy did not impose any unfairness on Jack, because he had the same opportunity as his sister.

Our decisions can likewise yield long-term advantages or disadvantages. As the Lord revealed, "If a person gains more knowledge and intelligence in this life through his diligence and obedience than another, he will have so much the advantage in the world to come" [D&C 130:19]. When others receive benefits because of their diligent choices, we cannot rightly conclude that we have been treated unfairly when we have had the same opportunity (Renlund, 2021).

People who have committed the sin of abuse often feel victimized by the results of their abuse on their relationships. They look at other parents whose children respect them and feel close to them and are filled with jealousy. They covet the ability to be seen as a good, loving, stable parent or spouse. They frequently feel put off at the fact that those they have hurt no longer trust them. They may feel that the victims of their abuse are somehow abusing them back by feeling a need for distance, for being unwilling to make themselves vulnerable, for feeling disconnected, for being hurt, and for wanting a life that is far more distant than the abuser feels like he or she deserves.

In facing these difficult facts, those who have committed abuse are not being treated unfairly. They have not done what it would require to create and invite these types of feelings from those they have hurt. They had the opportunity to do so but used their agency to do harm instead. They exhausted funds of goodwill and safety and spent them on impulsiveness, anger, selfishness, and unrighteous dominion. Their own actions are what has bankrupted their relationships. Learning this is painful but not unfair.   What is unfair is when abusers insist that they be treated by their victims as if the abuse had not happened. What is unfair is when abusers claim that they should be the ones to be able to determine how comfortable a victim *must* feel, what a victim *must* choose in their relationship in the future, and how the victim *must* see them.

Words of Caution. As a local leader in the Church, you need to be aware that the first way you will often learn of abuse will be an oblique attempt by the abuser to diffuse any accusations that may surface against them. The abuser may come to you before you ever hear anything from the victims. Rather than making some confession of abuse, the abuser may seek to win you over, either by their charisma or by struggles they present to you and talk about earnestly trying to overcome, like an addiction to pornography.

The nature of these interactions will be designed to lead you to develop a positive and/or sympathetic relationship with you and to cast a preemptive spin on anything the abused party or parties might say. In doing so, they may even present to you some part of an abusive action that they have committed. However, this story is often carefully curated and minimized to prevent you from understanding the frequency, intensity, and impact of their behaviors.

This may look and feel like repentance. However, it is actually a strategy of telling a partial truth to sell a much bigger lie. It is designed to sow seeds of doubt about the larger, more complete version of the story that the victim or victims may share in the future. This strategy often has the effect of allowing the abuser to maintain control over the narrative (hide the whole truth) and minimize or eliminate any consequences for themselves if and when the victim ever speaks with you. This kind of "preemptive strike" is something that many perpetrators of abuse excel at and something they practice in various contexts in their lives.

Another common tactic is for an abusive person to visit a bishop or branch president to ask for help, spinning a tale of the abused spouse as an unsupportive, unforgiving, emotionally unstable person that is causing problems for the abuser by not being sufficiently understanding and forgiving. If there is any admittance of any misbehavior on the abuser's part, it is again heavily minimized and blamed on the stresses that the personality flaws of the victim are causing for the abuser. The abuser may even tell relatively accurate stories about powerful emotional reactions the victims have had toward them, which might indeed sound unreasonable in light of the fact that the abuser leaves or or minimizes the fact that this was in response to them acting abusively toward the victim. Remember, the truth can be used to tell a lie when it is taken out of its full context.

Oftentimes, the abuser may express thoughts that the victim must have some kind of mental illness in order to preemptively invalidate anything the victim may say. These claims of underlying mental health issues serve as a smoke screen to try to give an alternative explanation for the mental and emotional symptoms the victim displays of having suffered psychological abuse.

Then, when the victim of abuse finally tries to speak up, the bishop, stake president, or other local Church leader has been carefully prepared to interpret the things they are seeing and hearing from the victim as a sign that the stories the abuser has been telling about their mental instability are true. This is a powerful decoy to lead those who might otherwise help away from a knowledge of the truth. The result is that to the untrained eye, the situation will likely appear as if there is no abuse occurring or that it is not as bad as the victim is reporting. But those who have been immersed in abuse—as professionals or as victims—have learned that this is actually evidence of the severity of the mental and social aspects of abuse in play. In other words, this should be a red flag of abuse, rather than a reassuring sign that no abuse is occuring.

Seek the Unheard Voices. All too often, perpetrators of abuse have historically been visiting with their Church leaders on a regular basis, but nothing has been done to stop the abuse. The bishop or branch president may be working with the perpetrator to help them repent from using pornography. The local Church leaders may be supporting the abusive person as they complain about their spouse being unhelpful and their children being disobedient. They may have been offering a hand of fellowship and a compassionate ear as the abuser struggles with Word of Wisdom issues. And in fact, they may be praising the abuser for their faithfulness and willingness to work with their priesthood leaders.

All the while, there are voices not being heard. These are the voices of the spouse and/or children, often hoping forlornly that the constant visits with Church leaders will someday lead to a change in the abusive behavior. These hopes languish in vain, since issues of abuse are not even being discussed. Sadly, far too frequently the victims at home are never asked to come in to visit the local Church leader, as well. They are too often not asked how they are doing.

Many opportunities to check in with the others at home to see how they are being treated, how they are experiencing things at home, or what help they feel they need. Many women have expressed how painful it is to watch their husband check in with the bishop before sacrament meeting, reporting on whether or not they slipped in their efforts to stop using pornography or whatever items they are working on together.

These women report watching as the bishop greets their husband warmly and either congratulates the husband or consoles them and expresses their faith that they will do better. These same women often report that the bishop may never even make eye contact with them, and almost certainly never ask how they are doing or what they need. And while they watch this scene play out week after week, these women are still stinging from the physical and/or emotional blows they have suffered at their husband's hands throughout the week. While the message may not have been intentionally sent by the local Church leader in question, the message these women receive is that they do not matter. The spouse who is hurting them is embraced, but they are ignored.

If you are visiting with someone in your stewardship to work on issues of repentance or counsel, seek out the other voices in their family. Ask the spouse to come in and visit with you as well. Visit with the children. Ask specifically how they are doing. Ask them how things are going at home and how they are feeling. Seek them out, always. Check in with them regularly. Bring their voices out of darkness and obscurity and into the light.

CHAPTER 9

HOPE FOR A BETTER LIFE AFTER ABUSE

To summarize what has been taught in doctrine and in the Church's 2019 policy updates, when abuse has occurred, a separation of the abuser from the abused is wise and prudent. With time, real repentance, and healing, there are some circumstances in which reconciliation with the abuser and the continuation of that relationship can eventually be accomplished, if it feels safe and is desired by the victims. However, there are other circumstances in which that type of reunification would be counterproductive to healing and even dangerous.

Reconciliation and reunification with the abuser is not the ultimate goal. Rather, the ultimate goal is the cessation of the abuse and the healing of those who have been victimized. In some cases that may involve reunification, and in many cases it may not.

In all cases, victims of abuse need to know that they have choices about what they want to do with their lives. They can choose to leave for whatever length of time is necessary, including permanently. They can choose to begin a new life for themselves. They can and should have the very real and tangible support of their local Church leaders as they make these choices. And they have every reason to believe that they can create a new life for themselves in which they are safe.

This can be hard to believe in, however, due to the psychological impact of abuse. It can help to hear the stories of other people who have had to face the same terrifying, heartbreaking decisions and to hear not only of their struggles and their process of making the choice to leave but also of their joyful discovery that they have a future ahead of them filled with greater peace, love, and connection than they had dared to hope for.

In these stories, you will hear about the experiences these survivors of abuse had with other people. Some of them will provide examples of local Church leaders and friends who serve as an excellent example of how to provide the right kinds of support. You will also hear experiences of other people, including local Church leaders, struggling with misconceptions, traditions, and prejudices. This sometimes results in a failure to help, and at other times it prolongs and amplifies the damage of the abuse.

In sharing these stories, there is no intention of criticizing the Church on a global or a local level, nor is there any intention of shaming individuals whose responses were unhelpful or even harmful. These stories seek to simply tell the truth, with all of the good and bad included, since all of these aspects can be helpful in developing an understanding of how to provide the support that God wants us to provide for His children who are seeking to step out of the darkness of abuse and into the light of healing.

JENNA'S STORY

All abuse is a mind game. What may be hard to understand for those who have never experienced it is just how absorbing, deceptive, and convincing that mental aspects of abuse can be. You might think that after you have experienced it once it wouldn't have the same kind of hypnotic and stupefying power over you if you encountered it again, the same way a magic trick loses its power to fool you once you know how the magician does it. From my experience of being abused by multiple people, I can say that isn't true. If anything, being abused repeatedly only amplifies the way it enters your mind and uses your own thoughts and feelings against you.

The first time I experienced abuse was before I was married. A man who lived near my home sexually assaulted me repeatedly. While he hurt my body, he also poisoned my mind, actively telling me that he was doing this to me because God wanted it to happen. Looking back on the situation I have come to realize that when someone hurts us in such a shocking way, it is as if our mind tries to grasp onto some sort of explanation for how something so horrific could have happened. It seems that many people who abuse others have developed a sense of how to plant suggestions into their victim's mind when it is in this vulnerable, suggestible state. That is what this man did to me, planting these pernicious concepts deep in my mind when my emotions were the most raw and ragged.

This thought, that somehow these sexual assaults were God's will, combined with the deep emotional sense that somehow it was all my own fault in a way, absolutely immobilized me. I felt doubly trapped. I was cornered on the outside by this man's proximity to my home, and I was cornered on the inside by the idea that I could not fight God's will and that my own inadequacies and imperfections were why God let this happen to me.

The repeated assaults by this man ended when he ran into other trouble with the law and was taken away. While he was no longer physically present, the mental and emotional weapons he used in his abuse were still lodged inside of me. I didn't know how to cope. I felt emotionally, spiritually, and socially marooned on a deserted island that nobody even knew existed. I had no hope of being found or rescued.

A short time later, I learned that I was pregnant. I felt a whirl-wind of mixed emotions about something I had always dreamed would be a happy development. But that was not where my life was. After I had announced my pregnancy, a close family friend named Alan reached out to me. After the emotional excoriation I had been through, seeing someone seek me out and offer comfort was like stumbling across an oasis in what seemed like an endless desert. While Alan was not an active member of the Church, he showed an interest in me that I was not experiencing anywhere else and which I had feared I would never find. My heart, so battered from what I had been through, surged at the thought that there was some hope for a brighter future for me. Even though he lived far away and most of our interaction was long-distance, Alan and I dated through my pregnancy, and I felt an emotion that had become a stranger to me: happiness. I thought I had been blessed with a bright dawn after the long, dark night of my soul's despair.

Perhaps it is because of those feelings that it was hard for me to acknowledge the red flags I was seeing in Alan shortly after my son was born. I became aware that Alan was abusing alcohol and drugs. It didn't take long for him to begin engaging in a variety of mentally and emotionally abusive behaviors toward me.

Even with the emergency of these highly distressing behaviors, I was moved with compassion toward Alan. I felt that I understood the roots of his addiction and his abusive behaviors. His father had been abusive to him and his whole family, and had cheated on his mother, which led to a divorce in the family. Alan had suffered the pain of infidelity himself when a previous girlfriend cheated on him. At the time, I thought that the right way to handle the situation was to help him deal with what appeared to be the roots of his abusive behavior and addiction.

I asked him to attend Alcoholics Anonymous meetings. He agreed but only attended once. I asked him to pour all of his alcohol down the drain. He did but bought more the next day. I sent him a 12-Step Recovery book, and he literally threw it into the fire and burned it. So, I called him and talked him through Step 1 and helped him set goals. He never followed through. I convinced him to see a counselor, but he only went to one session. I took him to church with me, read scriptures with him, bore my testimony to him, and tried to connect him to the Savior. He never seemed to connect with any of it.

Instead, he began to rack up several DUI charges. He also started growing marijuana in my infant son's room and tried to sell it to make money. Everything I did to try to help him address what seemed to be the roots of his problems not only fell flat, but it seemed to lead to the situation growing even worse.

He lived in another state and was not close enough most of the time to do anything to hurt me physically, but mental and emotional abuse are not limited by geographical distance. His assault on my thoughts and feelings had a physical impact on me; I developed painful stomach ulcers and was in constant pain. I could barely eat. I lost weight precipitously, withering down to a mere 98 pounds. He never even needed to touch me to hurt me physically. Eventually, I found the strength and courage to end my relationship with Alan.

A few months later, my friend Ben started showing interest in dating me. In contrast to Alan, Ben was an active member of the Church, and from what I could tell, he seemed to have a strong testimony. I found great comfort and inspiration in what appeared to be his deep, spiritual roots. This major contrast with Alan made me feel much more hopeful that this could be a good relationship. Ben represented all of the things I had been taught to seek after in a relationship: he attended church regularly, held the priesthood, held a temple recommend, and in general checked off all of the boxes I had been taught about in my experience in Young Women about what I should look for in a dating partner and potential spouse. This made me feel hopeful that Ben would be safe and that a relationship with him could be a way to overcome the hardships I had faced and that I could have a better, happier life.

In the beginning of the relationship, that is exactly how it felt, and I relished the sense of safety I found being connected to him. Unfortunately, the longer we were together, the more things there were about him that came to light, such as the degree of his addiction to pornography and how severely this impacted his attitudes and actions toward me. He began behaving mentally and emotionally abusive toward me, and then I found out that he was being unfaithful.

Similar to how I felt about Alan, I was filled with compassion for Ben and tried to understand what was driving his actions. He had been mentally and physically abused by both of his parents, who were divorced. He had been introduced to pornography when he was only ten years old, and he had struggled with it immensely since that tender age. He had also been cheated on by a former girlfriend and struggled with trust. So, just as I had done with Alan, I tried to help Ben address his problems. I paid for him to have pornography blocking filters on his smartphone. I attended 12-Step meetings with him. I kept his laptop at my house to help him not relapse. But he always found ways to circumvent these precautionary steps. His abuse escalated further and further. Then one day he told me that he wasn't sure if the Church was true, and confessed that he had cheated on me.

With both Alan and Ben, I learned through many heartbreaking experiences that you can offer a person all of the love, patience, and understanding in the world and every resource imaginable, and yet you cannot change them. You can testify of the Savior to them and of the power of His Atonement to heal us, but nothing will help if they themselves do not have a change of heart. Somehow, I felt it was my responsibility to change them and heal them. I learned I did not have that power. No one had the power to do so without their cooperation.

Being abused felt terrible. Being cheated on was utterly devastating. In spite of that, the idea of being alone felt terrifying. In that emotional vortex of pain and shock, I returned to my relationship with Alan. His abuse toward me only continued to escalate. The day arrived when I realized that I was in danger—real physical danger—that could potentially end my life. It was then that I decided to end my relationship with Alan permanently. He responded with an intense escalation of abuse and harassment, both toward me and my family. It seemed to become Alan's driving motivation in life to be cruel toward me in as many ways as possible to punish me for leaving. I ended up having to get law enforcement involved, change my phone number, and alter many of my contacts because he just kept on trying to find new and inventive ways to find me and hurt me.

Eventually, and with much effort, that tempest passed. I had survived, but I didn't feel like a survivor. Between the sexual assaults and the abusive relationships with Alan and Ben, I felt completely broken. I was a mere shell of a person. My heart was beating, but I didn't feel like I was alive.

The good news is, that isn't how I feel now. I am now married to a wonderful man who has never once acted abusively toward me in any way. I have found meaning and healing as I work to help other women who are also experiencing abuse. As empty, purposeless, and discarded as I once felt, I now feel loved, filled, and lovingly employed as an instrument in the Lord's hands.

When I share my story with others, sometimes people ask me why I did not leave these abusive relationships sooner. I knew as soon as the abuse started that I needed to leave if it continued. In my heart, I was willing to forgive and forget the hurtful things that both Ben and Alan did, but I did not want to live the lifestyle of someone who was constantly being belittled, hurt, emotionally blackmailed, and punished. More than that, I did not want my child to experience those things.

I don't think I was ever in denial of just how bad the abuse was. My challenge was that I just couldn't let go emotionally. Certainly, I tried to stand up for myself. I had boundaries for how I was willing to be treated, and I communicated those boundaries repeatedly. But something about the nature of the abuse made it so that I constantly found those boundaries being crossed by both Ben and Alan and I just felt frozen. I felt incapacitated by the fact that I genuinely loved both of them and that I had committed myself to them. I have been given the gift of being understanding, of being able to look beyond the hurt that others inflict and see the good in them. And I am a deeply loyal person. I recognize that I was being far more loyal to them than I was to myself. These strengths, these virtues on my part were turned against me and used as a weapon to perpetuate their abuse.

I have come to believe that this is true of many victims; they are targeted because they are patient, loyal, and forgiving. They are lashed out against because they are dedicated to seeing the good in other people. This makes them low-risk targets for abusers who want to have their cake and eat it, too, to lash out angrily and abusively but not lose their relationships.

When people who have been abused ask me what is wrong with them that led them to be a target of abuse, I feel compelled to tell them that they are a target not because of what is wrong with them but because someone else chose to take advantage of what is right with them. They are good, decent, faithful people, and they believe that to be true of others. And when other people act abusively, victims of abuse are willing to give them chance after chance to change. That doesn't mean that victims of abuse need to stop being kind, loving, and forgiving. It does mean that they need to learn to be discerning of how those can be misused against them.

Interestingly enough, as hard as leaving was, staying away was even harder. After I had distanced myself or even left, the most frightening behaviors would typically cool down. That is when the more subtle manipulation would really kick in, and I would find myself missing the good moments and dreaming about the good things that I knew were in Ben and Alan. Seeing those things made the thought of leaving unbearable. Furthermore, I was a single mother. Both of these men had a relationship with my son, and I somehow felt that I would be hurting my son if I cut off those relationships.

When someone has control over every aspect of your life, and when you know that you are in love with that person, what results is quite a bit more like an addiction than a relationship. You know it is destroying you—that it could even potentially kill you—and yet you just can't seem to step away from it. As painful and dangerous as staying in the abusive relationship clearly is, the thought of leaving feels even more devastating and undesirable. All you see is a world full of bleakness and misery as you contemplate leaving.

I struggled to untangle this web of emotions that kept me turning again and again back to those who were abusing me. But there was a day when the Lord spoke to me through a conference talk by Elder Holland (2018). There were specific words he spoke that resonated within my soul: "'I, the Lord, will forgive whom I will forgive, but of you it is required to forgive all men.' It is, however, important for some of you living in real anguish to note what He did not say. He did not say, 'You are not allowed to feel true pain or real sorrow from the shattering experiences you have had at the hand of another.' Nor did He say, 'In order to forgive fully, you have to reenter a toxic relationship or return to an abusive, destructive circumstance.'"

I know he was speaking to a worldwide audience, but it also felt like he was speaking directly to me, individually. It was a few months after this talk, with its words still echoing in my heart, that I left Alan for the first time. Interestingly enough, when I did, I encountered opposition from my mother. She criticized me for being un-Christlike for deciding not to date a man who was deep in the throes of multiple addictions and who had consistently been manipulative, hurtful, and abusive.

I will admit, I was very angry at my mother. I was floored by the audacity she demonstrated in suggesting that I was the one who was being un-Christlike for trying to protect myself from being hurt, when it was Alan's actions that deserved to be condemned as being antithetical to the teachings and spirit of the Savior. I worked to let go of my anger at my mother and reminded myself that Christ does not expect or want me to stay in an abusive relationship. I was fully capable of forgiving while walking away and keeping myself safe. The two tasks were in no way incompatible.

Through all of this, most of the other people who knew me and loved me expressed their concerns and counseled me to leave the abusive relationships. I know they were very well intentioned, but most of what was done to try to help me didn't actually help that much and in many cases made things harder. I know that this is due in part to the fact that I found myself deflecting their concerns. I would defend or downplay the abusive actions. The more my loved ones tried to help me see what was wrong and urged me to leave, the stronger I would fight back. I think it was a difficult paradox for everyone that was involved.

I think what might have helped me more is if they had listened and expressed love for me, but refrained from trying to give me advice about what to do. I think it would also have helped to have them try to understand why I was struggling and felt that I needed to stay. I couldn't hear anything that challenged my commitment to those relationships. That was just the mental state I was in; anything that anybody did to try to help me out of those abusive relationships only resulted in me being more adamant about staying in them.

When Alan found out that my family was expressing concerns to me about our relationship, he was outraged. He became even more abusive to punish me for talking to other people about our relationship and for letting other people say negative things about it. He felt even more justified in trying to isolate me from my family, stating that they were just trying to control me and tear us apart.

In retrospect, I don't think the fault was in the efforts of my family. It wasn't unhelpful because of what they did. It was my mindset that made it impossible for their efforts to help me to be fruitful in any way.

What have I experienced after I walked away from these abusive relationships? I can answer that in one word: happiness. I have learned what it feels like to be truly loved and respected by someone. My son has a father who is kind and a good example to him. We are blessedly safe, both physically and emotionally. In the absence of being constantly criticized, picked on, controlled, and humiliated, I have started to feel like myself again. I am loved for who I am, flaws and all. The effects of my trauma are siphoning away, and the depression and anxiety that once held center stage in my mind and heart have been greatly diminished. I have found healing. I have found that there is no need to accept anything less than safety in a relationship. I have found that the fear of being alone and unloved was merely an illusion.

I want people who have experienced repeat abusers—who have lost all sense of self and happiness, who feel lost, hurt, and afraid, who are stuck in a dangerous situation—to know that they are not alone. This is not your fault. You can get away and be happy. There is help. Whatever is keeping you from leaving can be overcome. And when you do, you will be better off. You may not see a path to getting there, but I assure you, God does.

If your safety is at risk, please involve law enforcement when you leave, and please work with an advocate to create a safety plan! There are so many resources in our communities designed to help people in these situations. Please don't feel like you have no other choice but to stay. You deserve happiness. You are not selfish for doing what is best for you and your children.

Trauma changes you, but it doesn't have to control or define you. There is nothing divine or holy or Christlike about letting someone abuse you. No matter what you have done in your life and no matter what anyone may say, you do not deserve to be abused. Leave the abuse behind, and embrace the happiness that God has been preparing for you.

ROSE'S STORY

In 2016 I sat in my bishop's office once again. It had been a teary and difficult conversation already. After an hour or so of joint counseling with my husband filled with a tumult of confessions and justifications, the bishop had asked to speak privately to me.

Our bishop had been called less than a month earlier. I knew very little about him, nor did he know much about me. I had served in the Young Women presidency and had been close to his daughters, but other than girls camp and parent pickups we had not really spoken. He was now in possession of the hardest secrets of my life.

In well over a decade of marriage, I had endured my husband's addiction to pornography, his violent temper, and almost complete isolation from anyone of whom he did not approve. I became aware of his pornography use after the first year of our marriage when he lost his job for losing his temper with children at work. Pornography become a rabbit hole. As his addiction continued through the years, he grew to need different materials for stimulus: rape fantasy, teenage girls, and orgies had become his standard browser history. Paralleling this addiction was a constantly brewing anger. This was a strategic loss of temper, carefully crafted within the bounds he thought would be defensible if I ever reported him. At the height of his temper, he would threaten to kill me and the kids. Once he even acted on this threat.

We were still together because a bishop had told me after that attempt to kill us that my husband was repentant, and it was my job as his wife and through my covenant to help him repent. That bishop claimed that if I left, my sealing to my children would be dissolved and my abusive husband would have them in the eternities. His precept was that the Atonement would heal and erase my husband's sins, but I would be punished if I did not stay.

Over the course of the years of my marriage, I received similar responses from a total of eight bishops. Each one of them eagerly wrapped my husband in the warm arms of compassion, fellowship, and encouragement but scarcely even acknowledged me. When they did speak with me, it ranged from telling me it was my duty to support my husband regardless of how he treated me and the children to informal church disciplinary actions against me when I had to leave for a period of time because the violence and anger had gotten so bad. I was treated like not living in the same home as my husband while he engaged in regular violent outbursts was a grave sin. I was not allowed to pray in church, comment during lessons, or participate in any way other than attending until I was again living in the same home as my husband. The message sent was very clear: that bishop considered me to be unworthy because I was taking action to protect myself and my children, but my husband and his violence were treated as understandable, permissible, and excusable without any sort of disciplinary action.

The result was, five years later, I was still afraid for myself and my children every day. Nothing had gotten any better. In fact, things had grown to be devastatingly worse.

As a result, sitting in that office with my brand-new bishop, I braced for the usual counsel that those years had taught me to expect. I was surprised when it did not come. The bishop looked me straight in the eye and asked, "Is *this* the eternal marriage you want?" As hard as it was to admit to myself, I knew instantly that there was only one true answer to that question: no. There was nothing celestial about this marriage, even if it had been solemnized in a sealing ceremony in the temple. However, I did not know how to make this answer square with what I had been taught about being sealed in the temple.

He then talked to me briefly about a relation who had been in an abusive marriage and how they had all stood by praying she would leave and get safe. He believed that he could not and would not counsel me to leave, but he wanted me to really think about whether this was what I wanted in the eternities. He then asked me to share my testimony of the Savior and my Heavenly Father.

I am a returned missionary. I have always had a strong belief and firm testimony of the gospel, but that evening it was different. As I spoke, the Relief Society mask slipped, and I had to stop mid-sentence and say what I really needed to say. "I don't know if God loves his daughters as much as his sons. My experiences have taught me that there is no relief to my suffering, but I must endure to the end or lose everything. My husband can wallow in sin and hurt us repeatedly, but he is still the elders quorum president. And I am always told I just have to try harder to keep him from losing his temper again. I am the one who bears the consequences of all of his actions. Does God love his daughters as much as his sons?"

With tears in his eyes, the bishop simply said, "Yes."

That was not what I had been told by any of the other bishops. They had all said, in deed if not in word, that my safety and my well-being were expendable in the face of having to hold my husband accountable for how he treated me and the children. They acted in a manner that implied that men were too fragile to be challenged and too precious to be held accountable. As a counterpoint, women were ostensibly created to carry the burden of the sins that men didn't want to give up. When you are taught that repeatedly over the course of years by those who are in a position of spiritual stewardship over you, it begins to penetrate your heart like a lance. You begin to believe it.

But this one word spoken by a tearful bishop was the one truth I had needed people to tell me, the one truth I needed people to treat as a reality. If it was true, then all of the counsel that I had been given to suffer over and over again for my husband's sins of abuse like some kind of understudy Messiah—even if it would eventually cost me my own life at his hands or as a result of my own shattered and unrecoverable mental health—was simply wrong.

There was little my bishop could do or say at that point. I went home and opened my scriptures with his question in my heart. I turned ironically to my least favorite part of the Book of Mormon, Nephi slaying Laban. This had always bothered me. Nephi slays an unconscious man in the street, steals his clothes, and impersonates him to rob his house and kidnap his servant. These were not the heroic actions of a prophet in my mind. This time as I read it, the Spirit changed my perception. It was just a small shift starting with a long-standing, frustrated mental question: why is this even in the Book of Mormon? What does it teach us today? And suddenly my mind was opened. Nephi wrestled against doing something he believed to be wrong, something he had been taught was wrong all his life—something so profoundly important as to be included as one of the Ten Commandments. But the Spirit tells him it was necessary to save his children spiritually, and many generations following. Without slaying Laban, Nephi could not preserve the teaching of the gospel for his descendants.

I realized with a warm, deep understanding that this scripture was exactly what I needed that day. I was not slaying a person in the street, but like Nephi, I needed to choose to act in a way that I had fought against because I had been taught it was wrong to leave a temple marriage.

So yes, God does love His daughters as much as he loves His sons. And no, I did not want a celestial marriage in which someone would think and feel that way about me and treat me with violence and disdain. It may have been a marriage performed in the temple, but it was not a celestial marriage. Those are clearly two different things.

I had not broken my temple covenants. My husband was continuously breaking his.

I was not born to carry the weight of my husband's unrepented sins.

I needed to divorce my husband to protect myself and my children. My stewardship was to them.

I needed to leave.

After making that decision, I knelt to pray. I had no degree. I had nowhere to go. I was sure this was a correct choice. The Spirit was radiant in its confirmation, but the vastness of leaving was intimidating. Peace was spoken quickly to my mind, and I slept.

The next morning someone called and asked if I needed a place to rent in a city far away from my residence at the time. I was stunned. I had told no one I was leaving my husband. This offered home was blocks from an affordable university, and I knew I would need to work to finish my bachelor's degree. It was a miracle, one of many small and simple miracles that would line my path away from abuse.

Over and over the Lord provided people, help, and understanding. Our new ward enveloped the kids and me. All the things I most feared were swallowed up in compassion from others, hard work, and completely relying on the Lord. We were happier than I thought possible.

I was certain I would never remarry. After enduring that level of physical and emotional abuse, I would not trust anyone easily and I never wanted pornography in my home again. Surprisingly, less than a year after my divorce was finalized, one of my dearest friends found himself single again after some tragedies in his own life. It was as if the Lord had prepared me to be there for him at that time. We supported each other in our personal grief and spent a lot of time together with our kids. Our separate families felt like they were knit together in love, nerdy fandoms, and the Spirit. The kids quietly mentioned they believed we were meant to be a family. We agreed.

It has been several years now. My home is a place of peace and happiness. My marriage is loving in a way I thought impossible. While I still struggle from PTSD, I have wonderful support. My husband is my best friend and the greatest blessing I could never have known how to ask for. When I made the frightening choice to leave an abusive relationship, I could never have imagined just how much God had prepared for me and my children.

The poetic and prophetic words found in Isaiah 54 describe what I have experienced:

For the mountains shall depart, and the hills be removed; but my kindness shall not depart from thee, neither shall the covenant of my peace be removed, saith the Lord that hath mercy on thee.

O thou afflicted, tossed with tempest, and not comforted, behold, I will lay thy stones with fair colours, and lay thy foundations with sapphires.

And I will make thy windows of agates, and thy gates of carbuncles, and all thy borders of pleasant stones.

And all thy children shall be taught of the Lord; and great shall be the peace of thy children.

In righteousness shalt thou be established: thou shalt be far from oppression; for thou shalt not fear: and from terror; for it shall not come near thee.

Behold, they shall surely gather together, but not by me: whosoever shall gather together against thee shall fall for thy sake.

Behold, I have created the smith that bloweth the coals in the fire, and that bringeth forth an instrument for his work; and I have created the waster to destroy.

No weapon that is formed against thee shall prosper; and every tongue that shall rise against thee in judgment thou shalt condemn. This is the heritage of the servants of the Lord, and their righteousness is of me, saith the Lord. (Isaiah 54:10–17)

IRENE'S STORY

I heard footsteps, my footsteps, crunching on the gravel of a parking lot like any other you might find in any Small Town, USA. In contrast to the regular percussion of my steps, my ears also registered the freeform song of a robin mingling with the unmistakable call of a blue jay. I approached my van, opened the door, and pulled myself up into a chair. The atmosphere inside was a little stuffy from the growing heat of the morning, and it had that sippy-cup-and-soggy-crackers smell known by countless mothers. I gagged a bit as the aroma saturated my senses. I started the engine and hand cranked the windows for much needed fresh air before pulling the gear shift into reverse.

My foot did not release the break. Rather, I hesitated as my eyes caught a glimpse of something, a sight that might have seemed ordinary but felt somehow very significant. It was a pinpoint of light from the sun reflecting off the steeple of the old church building where I attended. With so many other sensations competing for my attention, that single point of light drowned out all of the other stimuli and held me captivated for a moment.

My mind was buzzing from the recent conversation with Bishop Connors. My hand went almost reflexively to my face to wipe away the damp tears that lingered there. As my fingers swept away the droplets, I could feel the smile that was lingering on my lips. Tears and smiles together; that was not the response I was expecting. But what had I expected? Certainly not what had happened.

Two days ago, I had made the appointment to meet with Bishop Connors. It was time to share the answer that Heavenly Father had given me. The thought of doing so had been daunting. I wasn't sure how to put it into words. *Heck*, I thought, *I can't believe I told him everything*. As unbelievable as my full disclosure felt to me, what had occasioned it during Trek was even harder to believe had been real.

Trek was another pinpoint of light, like the one that had caught my attention on the steeple of the church. Our ward went on a four-day trek just a week and a half prior to my meeting with Bishop Connors. We had all returned sunburned and stiff, but many testimonies had been strengthened during our time at Martin's Cove, reenacting the Pioneers' experience there. I was no exception to either the physical aftereffects or the spiritual edification. However, the way in which my testimony was strengthened was not the way I had been expecting.

My mind replayed what had happened in the bishop's office. "Welcome, Sister Newton," said Bishop Connors, shaking my hand. I returned the handshake and sat down in the chair across from him. My eyes glanced up above his left shoulder to where a picture of Christ knocking at the door hung and then tracked to the right where the picture of the Ogden Temple was placed. My eyes shot away from the temple and back down to the desk. Gathering my thoughts, I looked back up into the waiting face of my bishop.

"Well, you wanted to see me," said Bishop Connors. "How can I help?" I took a big, hard swallow, trying to wet my suddenly dry throat. I squeaked out, "Yes. I need to share with you what happened on Trek." Bishop Connors nodded, encouraging me to continue. "I know you saw me have a breakdown." Suddenly I stopped and thought, *Who am I kidding? The whole congregation saw my meltdown!* I steadied myself with a breath and said, "You remember how I dropped the handcart with my children still inside, and then I ran out into the field screaming my head off?" It wasn't really the sort of thing you had to ask if somebody remembered. But, I saw that his expression held no judgment, only a willingness to listen. So, I continued.

"Do you know why I flipped out?" I asked. He shook his head earnestly. "Well," I swallowed hard again, "I lost my stuff because Rick was not supposed to be there." My bishop's head tilted slightly in an inquisitive expression, as if trying to understand how my husband's presence would provoke such a significant emotional response from me. I took a deep breath and slowly exhaled. Saying this wasn't easy. Every word was a hurdle to be overcome.

"Bishop, for the entire time I was planning on going to Trek, Rick had promised to come along and help me. But on Sunday, just eight hours before we were supposed to leave, Rick told me he couldn't go, that his business partner, Jack, needed him." I felt the bitter sting of acid rising in my throat. "We had been planning for six months to prepare for this trek. I scrimped to save what I could and borrowed equipment so that we could go with the ward to see the place my ancestors walked. I put in all of that effort and made all of those sacrifices trusting he would be there to help me. And eight hours before it was time to go, he just abandoned me!"

"I didn't know that happened," the bishop admitted.

"I know!" I shot back forcefully. I wasn't mad at the bishop, but the feelings inside of me carried a tremendous amount of force and pain. "No one knew but the group leaders we were assigned to go with." I could see that he was being kind and trying to understand. He wasn't taking offense or chiding me for the forcefulness of my words. I could see that he could relate to the disappointment of having a spouse bail out of a commitment, but he was still trying to understand the depth of my response during Trek.

He had been willing to listen so far. I ventured to try to explain further. "Do you want to know why I was screaming and shouting out in that field? Rick! After leaving me for three nights and four days, suddenly he dared to show up, sneak under the handrail of the cart, and pull the family. That's why I dropped the cart. He was not there. He broke his promise to me and left me out in the cold on my own. He let me do the majority of the work, and then bam! He was there! But the hard part was over. I had done all of the sacrificing. And yet, he was expecting me to forget how he had let me down and to treat him like a hero for showing up at the end. He got to play out this little fantasy in front of an audience, trying to make himself look sweet and thoughtful and romantic, when nobody knew the real story. And I was just supposed to go along with it. And I just couldn't. So, I ran out into the field to get as far away from him as I could." I swallowed hard. It hurt to talk about the public farce my husband had engineered to hide his private abandonment. "And that's why my cart held up the entire ward for about fifteen minutes while I screamed my anger, my hurt, my rage, and my pain out in the field."

My words hung in the air and lines of anger creased my face. Could the bishop understand? My emotions surged, and I said through gritted teeth, "How dare he abandon me and then just show up when it is convenient for him and act like the hero?" My bishop nodded his head. I hadn't lost him yet, so I pushed on. "I spent the time in the dirt camping and trying to help my autistic kids get through the new surroundings and experience. I did all of that on my own, without Rick's help. And I needed his help! But he wouldn't give it. I packed everything. I drove hundreds of miles to get there. I did with women's pull." Tears were flowing freely down my face now. "I did it without him! But it wasn't supposed to be that way. He abandoned me!"

I was afraid that at any moment he might tell me that I was over-reacting, but that never happened. Rather, Bishop Connors sat back in the chair, nodding his balding head as he listened. So, I pressed onward. Perhaps he could already sense that as disappointing as Trek had been, this was about much more than that. "Bishop, what hit me with such force was that Rick always abandons me." Some truths shake us to our very foundations when we speak them. This was one of those truths.

For nearly seven years of our nine-year marriage, Rick had prolifically broken his covenants and his duty to our family. He was lost in his pain from the past and used drugs and alcohol to numb out the specter of childhood sexual abuse that haunted him. But what was the trade-off? The substances trapped him. They made the good in him inaccessible and didn't really end the pain. Rather, they sent him running in search of further distractions. Drugs ignited his sexual desire, so the next step in his cycle was to watch hours of pornography or find women and sleep with them. The final stage in this crescendo of addiction and self-destruction was when I would get in the way of his rage and become the target of physical attacks. But this was not new information to my bishop. I had shared my husband's cycle of addiction and abuse with him in previous meetings.

"Abandoned!" I spat the word again and tried to erase the wet shame on my face, attempting to force a smile. The smile would not come.

The bishop lifted his gaze from where his hands were folded in his lap, his expression full of love. "Sister," he said, "what are you feeling now? How can I help you right now?" I was caught off guard by his question. I thought that he would give me some kind of counsel or share some scripture to read and pray about. I just blinked at him, trying to register what he had just said. He sat forward in his chair with his open arms on the desk, allowing me the time to take it in and consider his question. After a few moments, he said, "I suspect that something more happened to you on the trek."

Not only was his suspicion true, but it was an understatement! I was transformed out on the trail, but I didn't quite know how to encapsulate the experience. But since the bishop seemed to already be aware of it to some degree, I tried to find the right words. "Bishop Connors," I said tentatively, "I could feel my ancestors close to me out there. It was like I was walking with angels. I could feel . . . " I took in a sharp breath. Would he understand? "I could feel Helen—my fourth great-grandmother—right beside me, encouraging me not to quit."

"Not to quit? What do you mean?" the bishop inquired.

I unblinkingly met his gaze, "I've always kept my covenants," I replied. "Even with Rick doing all that he was doing to himself, to me, to the kids. My commitment to the truth—to my Heavenly Father, to my Savior, and to the covenants I made in the temple—never wavered." I almost laughed as I considered how absurd the option of faltering in my faith felt to me. "Why would I jump ship from the gospel of Jesus Christ when all around me a hurricane rages?" The ship was the only safety.

Bishop Connors held my gaze, nodding his comprehension. I mean, sure, it would have been very easy to stop following Heavenly Father and Christ because of Rick's choices. I could have felt betrayed by God for Rick's actions. But I knew they were Rick's doing, not God's. It would also be easy to mope about and drown in self-pity based on the hell I was living in. I could have sought solace in some addiction or other distraction like Rick. But I didn't. I remained temple worthy.

Staying faithful had taken a tremendous amount of commitment and effort. But I knew it was the right thing to do, and I was certain it was worth it. Trek emphasized that point down to my core. Heavenly Father inscribed that truth deep inside me. With each step into Martin's Cove, I learned that I could do hard things when I focused on Christ. I also had the clear sense that more complicated things were to come, and that I would need all of my strength and divine assistance for the true Trek that was yet to come for me.

While I was literally pulling my family in a handcart by myself, Heavenly Father opened my eyes through the Spirit and showed me that I could provide for and protect my family. He had proven it to me on the trail. In fact, He had also shown it to me by how I had been loving and protecting my children for the past four years. When Rick's business partner had taken our money and invested it into another property and left us broke, I figured out on my own, with no help from Rick, how to get disability from SSI. I was the one who went to the WIC offices and jumped through all the hoops just for cereal, milk, and tuna. I found shelter for us when Rick was wasted and incapable of helping in any way.

All of these efforts to provide for my family had never been enough to meet our needs, though. We were always living on a wing and a prayer, always on the brink of disaster, but we were still alive. For all this time I had been carrying the weight of it all by myself, including the added deadweight created by Rick's addictions and abuse, without realizing what that meant. It meant I could carry the needs of my family. And it also meant I was not by myself. God was helping me carry it.

The quiet of the cove had acted like a lens to focus all of those realizations in my mind. Amongst the quaking aspens shimmering in the Wyoming wind, I learned that I did not have to remain powerless. I discovered that I needed to take control of providing for my kids and me. After all, it was what I was doing already, while trying in vain to hold on to the illusion that Rick was helping. It was time for me to find a job and hide the money from him. That was something he had been doing our whole marriage. The difference was, he was doing it for selfish, impulsive, and poorly thought out purposes. I needed to do it in order to take care of my family and not be fully at the mercy of Rick's addictions and mismanagement. An image representing my marriage to Rick coalesced in my mind, covered in weeds and rust and broken in several places. How broken can a marriage be and still continue to be a marriage?

"Sister," the bishop said, pulling me out of my musings. "I feel impressed to ask you what your plan is." I looked at him and thought numbly, *What's my plan?* I was quiet for a moment. I could feel the pressure of the emotional dam about to break inside of me. I had never spoken these words before. I had barely dared to form the thoughts. To speak them into existence felt like a point of no return, a Rubicon that once crossed could not be turned back upon.

I looked back up at my Bishop, my thoughts racing with the speed and force of a hurricane. *What was my plan?* It wasn't mine. Heavenly Father had told me what to do. He had given me a plan on Trek. But this plan was not what I had ever expected. It's not the sort of thing they talk about in Relief Society lessons or Sunday School. But I knew it was from God just as clearly as I knew the gospel principles taught in Church were true. To be honest, the plan freaked me out and filled me with too many thoughts of *what if* and *how would that work*, but it was time to share it with the Bishop. It was time for this truth to be brought to light.

"Bishop, I need to move away from here and back to my in-laws' basement apartment." My throat caught on that word. How could I go back there? That basement was filled with echoes of abuse. But that was the clear impression that I had. "I will go to night school to get my master's degree in special education, and I will get a job teaching to provide for my family."

The bishop's mouth hung open a bit as he took in what I had just said, and I raced to finish expressing the plan. "I can no longer depend on Rick for anything. He has abused and then abandoned me . . . us . . . the whole family. He has done it so many times. I know it won't stop." I was aware of the salt of tears on my face again, and I realized I was biting down on the inside of my cheek. In the emotional intensity of the moment, the pain didn't even register. "In that moment, crying out loud in front of the whole ward at Martin's Cove on Trek, I realized it. I knew that if I am to survive and find a way to live again. I can't depend on Rick." There. I said it. That was what Heavenly Father had given me while I was in the cove: an absolute knowledge that I can't depend on Rick. My family needed me to stop acting as if I could.

I felt the sensation of light streaming from me as the last words fell from my lips. I looked at the bishop. His eyes were brimming with newly formed tears. The Spirit was confirming to him that what I said was true. So, Bishop Connors did not hesitate to add his witness to my answer. "That is right," he said. "But there will be more challenges coming . . . sooner than you think." That thought hung in the air ominously while I blew my nose. He continued, "You will be faced with a decision that will have eternal consequences." My head tilted, and my wet eyes narrowed a bit in confusion with his response, but I felt the truth of it. Then again, is there such a thing as a decision as a parent or as a spouse that doesn't have eternal consequences?

Following this meeting, Bishop Connors gave me a blessing. As he laid his hands on my head, I felt warmth, light, and an almost visceral hug from my Savior. Words from Heavenly Father poured over me like a warm shower cleansing my pain and strengthening me. All I had learned in Martin's Cove had been confirmed and reinforced in the meeting, and my life would never be the same after that.

I have shared one example of the seven different bishops I've had over nine years of marriage to Rick. Some bishops have been more formal, stiff, and perhaps more attuned to the letter of the law, so to speak. They weren't bad men or bad bishops, but I don't know that I ever received from them what I needed. On the other hand, other bishops have been very in tune with the Spirit and have given me incredible counsel. As a woman who lived in a nine-year marriage filled with mental, emotional, spiritual, financial, and at times physical abuse, I did all that I could to stay close to the gospel of Jesus Christ so that I would not lose my way. I relied heavily on my bishops as a source of counsel and support.

Through those nine challenging years of marriage to Rick, I learned the power of the greatest and most challenging gift from our Heavenly Father: the gift of agency. We are all given the agency to make choices in our lives, and our Heavenly Father permits us to mess up on a spectacular and even apocalyptic level. He will not interfere with our choices or the choices of others, but there is always a way to overcome our foolish decisions or the harmful exercise of agency by others. That is what the Savior does for us.

Being married to someone with a psychotic disorder who refused professional help, counseling, or medication taught me that abusers can fall into certain categories. People who abuse can be what I call hunters. These people actively and intentionally seek out their victims, lure them in, and hide the truth until they have them captured in their power and control. People who abuse can also be what I call caged animals. These people are trapped within substance abuse, mental health struggles, or both. They don't know if you are there to help them or hurt them. And so they respond in a predictable fashion: with abuse.

Rick fell into the second category. While I feel genuine compassion for his struggles, I have also come to understand that these challenges do not result in a free pass or an excuse for abuse. While we may understand what fuels someone's drive to act abusively, nothing makes abuse acceptable or permissible in any way.

Rick chose to do street drugs in a misguided effort to find relief from his mental health condition, instead of seeking professional help. Rick chose to consume pornography and sleep with other women to hide his pain and run from his mental condition. The important concept in both of these sentences is that Rick chose. He had other options available to him, but he did not choose them. When I would reach out to help, Rick would panic and strike back in a variety of ways. Some were verbal, some were emotional, and some were physical. All were painful, and all did lasting damage to me. Rick's choices put us in more and more physical, emotional, and financial danger as those substances and behaviors became more and more dominant in his life.

This meeting with Bishop Connors was just one of several influential meetings I had with Church leaders throughout my marriage to Rick. There are a few other of these meetings I would like to highlight to help show how the Lord led me through a variety of experiences to reach a point where I was able to understand and accept the change that I needed to make.

Six years prior to that meeting with Bishop Connors, Rick and I were seated in another bishop's office. After a brief conversation, Bishop Simon asked, "Is that all you have to tell me?" Rick nodded once, as if what had been disclosed was entirely comprehensive. His eyes never once looked in my direction. I blew my nose softly and shook my head. Was there more to say? Certainly, and lots of it, but I could not manage to express any more of it. This had already been hard enough.

My eyes, strained from crying, fell upon my husband. He slumped in the chair next to me, still clad in his construction clothes and surrounded by the stench of sweat. Somehow, that seemed appropriate given what we had just discussed with the bishop. Bishop Simpson contemplated us for what felt like a very long time. His gaze fixed on me, with my overgrown pixie hair cut, maternity shirt, and our third infant baby on my shoulder. It shifted back to Rick, who looked like he would rather be anywhere else in the world than where he was at that moment. We were poorer than church mice and had no apparent right to ask for help, especially if you based our request on our moral condition. Rick had just confessed to how distressingly lacking that was. It was one of those moments where you would be just as happy to have the world end as to have to live through it.

We both felt the pressure and the shame. Rick's hand began to twitch and get fidgety and his leg bounced anxiously, shaking a bit of the dust of the day onto the carpet below. I couldn't help but feel like we were like that construction grime, staining the floor of the church building. We were the lowest of the low. We felt our shame as thick and filthy as the mud on Rick's boots. What brought us here into Bishop Simpson's office? Why would anyone suffer such humiliation and abasement? I had asked the Relief Society president for a food order. She passed our request on to Bishop Simpson, and he had said he wanted to see us before granting the request. So here we were, in all our glory. I had thought it was better than starving, but the sense of shame I felt while we sat there soiling the bishop's office gnawed at my insides more sharply than hunger ever had.

The graphic and shocking nature of Rick's confession had caught me quite off guard, to the point that I found myself vomiting in my mouth. I tried to swallow it back, but the acid burned and made it even harder for me to speak. I had just come to get a food order so my family wouldn't go hungry. Instead, I was sucker punched by a shocking and previously unheard confession from a man I was married to. I had known about his drinking and about some of his drug use, but this was the first I had heard about his use of porn. From what he said, it was clear that his pornography habit had progressed and evolved for quite some time. All of his words were like the smears of mud and detritus all over my husband. I prayed that my third child, who nursed at my breast, would be protected from any comprehension of the depths of what Rick had just said.

Bishop Simpson then spoke to Rick. "I'll need your temple recommend." My heart sank in my chest at this request, but I knew that that was right. It was a hard truth to accept, but Rick was very far from being worthy to attend the temple. Tears welled in my eyes as I watched his clay-caked hand reach into the back pocket for his wallet, open the bifold, and pull out a sweat-stained recommend. He slid it across the desk to the bishop in an act of surrender

In that moment, with the heartbreaking tableau laid out in front of me, images of our engagement flashed across my memory. Rick had said that we would never falter as long as we always went to the temple. We had attended the temple two times a month for nearly two straight years. Even when two of our children were born, we still kept up that pace in our temple worship. And then it all stopped as suddenly as if we had slammed into a spiritual brick wall in September of 2000.

After so much time of trying to compartmentalize his life, with outward displays of religiosity on one hand and alcohol, drugs, and a party lifestyle on the other, Rick had snapped. He could no longer live the double life. I did not understand it at the time, but Rick's schizophrenia was also in full bloom at that time. His mind had created an alternate reality that he tried to explain to me, but that I didn't really understand. Step by step, our lives were being consumed by his mental health crisis and addictions, but I did not yet know how to make sense of what was happening. But I vowed to myself to always be worthy to attend the temple, even if Rick was not.

The bishop asked Rick to leave the room and wait for me. Rick got up and slunk out of the room, head hanging in disgrace. As the door softly closed behind Rick, Bishop Simpson asked me, "What is your plan?" I mustered my ability to speak and shared my plan to move the family to Idaho and out of my dad's house.

My father would help Rick get a job with a framing crew. I figured being away from his drug using friends might help put an end to his cycle of substance use. I thought that getting some space away from the in-laws might help Rick calm down. If we could just get away from our current situation, maybe Rick would remember his family and repent and return to the gospel. Bishop Simpson sat in silence. I think he was praying. In his situation, I certainly would be. He looked across the desk at me and nodded but did not smile. Neither did I.

That lack of a smile turned out to be more than a little prescient. It was a warning of what was to come. No geographical relocation can move a person far enough away from the troubles they carry within themselves. It was a hopeful thought, but I did not yet realize it was a naive one. I did not know what else to do. I felt completely whiplashed. I had entered the bishop's office looking for hope and anticipating feeling better leaving it. Instead, as I left that room, my life was even bleaker than when I had entered it. I felt like I had asked for a fish and received a serpent. I don't blame Bishop Simpson. He was just as blindsided by Rick's confession as I was. I still wonder what he was thinking when he looked at me but could not find it within himself to smile.

To be clear, none of the bishops I worked with told me to stay married to Rick, or even to try to help him back to the gospel. They were very supportive of me and never once gave me a "duty to the priesthood" speech or tried to tell me that "wives should submit to their husbands." For that I am extremely grateful. If anything, it seems to me that they were trying to help me find a way out of this marriage rather than stay, even though none of them seemed to feel that they could actively ask me about that as an option. I was never pressured by a bishop to stay, unlike many other women I have met. It was my choice to never leave Rick because of the covenant I had made. And from what I understood, leaving Rick meant breaking a covenant. That's something I simply would not do.

I did not have fairy tale delusions when I got married. I knew that all marriages have problems, but I genuinely thought that Rick and I would work through them together. I did not realize that he had schizophrenia. I knew that there was something mentally wrong with him. But each time I would try to get him help, he would just look at me like I was insane.

In all of my experiences in my crazy, upside-down marriage, Heavenly Father placed bishops in my path to help and guide me to find the correct answers. The answers didn't always come when I wanted them. Sometimes, I don't think I was ready for them, but they did come.

Our move to Idaho brought us under the stewardship of Bishop Xavier. He was a man filled with love. He led his congregation with love, he counseled with love, and he never stopped loving the ninety and nine while he went after the one. My experience with Bishop Xavier felt like a three-year experience when it was only for seven months.

We arrived in Idaho with the new job, three babies, and what I wanted to call a fresh start. The truth was, the drugs, alcohol, and sex issues with Rick had grown more frequent and severe. Nothing had changed the way I hoped it would. In reflection, maybe that was why Bishop Simpson never smiled as I left the office. Perhaps he knew that would be the case but couldn't bear to tell me. In those bleak circumstances, I sought to make my Idaho ward my family.

I was called to be the second counselor in the Relief Society presidency. I was able to experience ward counsels and serve others on a level that I had not experienced previously. It was a wonderful and enlightening experience. Unfortunately, this new light in my life was met by a deepend assault by darkness. Rick's physical abuse accelerated, and it left its marks upon me. Bishop Xavier took notice of my injuries. He was constantly asking if I was safe, and I would lie and say that I was. I felt that hiding the truth was a part of being committed to my marriage. Bishop Xavier tried to extend friendship to Rick and connect him to the light of the gospel. Rick would have none of it.

Things continued to get worse. Rick lost his job. Construction opportunities dried up, along with our food and shelter. And yet, Rick could always seem to afford alcohol and drugs, and the pattern of the abuse never slackened. It's amazing how accustomed a person can become to misery.

Bishop Xavier never gave up on Rick or our family. He did all he could do to protect us from the constant suffering that was a part of our life. He did the right thing by loving both of us, in spite of Rick's obvious flaws and failings. After six agonizingly long months of sheer craziness from Rick's mental instability, Bishop Xavier had to step in and take some decisive action.

I will never forget Bishop Xavier's tear-stained face as he told Rick that he was being disfellowshipped. Bishop Xavier shook Rick's hand with such firmness and love. He tried to encourage him to continue to find Christ and sought to impress upon him that our family depended on it. Even though Bishop Xavier presented the disfellowship as a path to repentance and healing for Rick, it also impressed upon me just how damaged our marriage was.

Five years passed, with life continuing as a variation on the themes of addiction, abuse, and hardship. It was now November, 2006, four months since Trek and my visit with Bishop Connors. I had been married to Rick for nine and a half years and had five children. We had moved. I now worked full-time as a teacher, and I was working on my master's degree.

Rick was there for Thanksgiving that year. He was stoned, as usual. But in some ways it was different for me this time. In my mind, I had accepted that this is who Rick is. I was no longer hoping that he would be who he seemed to be when we were first married. I was no longer relying on him to change as a path for things to get better for our family.

Working and going to school gave me perspective and hope for our family. How Rick acted didn't matter to me anymore. I had shifted my focus. I was convinced that I just needed to keep going and provide for my family. My life was not objectively any easier. Rick's drugs, alcohol, and sexual acting out were all still in full swing. And yet, my life had become easier to bear by the mere acceptance of the fact that Rick would not change, and therefore I had to do some things differently. Work and school gave me something to focus on.

As Thanksgiving had passed, I found myself slumbering on the couch on Sunday morning, basking in the lights of our small Christmas tree. I remember waking and focusing on the pinpoints of light from the tree. I reflected on how each one gave meaning to the season. I felt pulled and directed by each of these tiny lights as my eyes scanned over each one in turn. I became aware of a feeling growing within me which expanded until it overcame me. I sat in that feeling for a moment, frozen there, as time seemed to stand still. The silence in my mind served as an empty stage for what came next, which was life-changing. In that silent, timeless moment, I felt a voice say, "You are released from your calling," It reverberated within me, filling me with warmth. I blinked at the lights of the tree until they came into focus through my tears, connecting with my heart as a beacon of light. And in the moment, I just knew: it was time to go.

Later that morning as I partook of the sacrament at church I felt the same warmth and light flood my soul for a second time. The voice came to me again, with the same message. "You are released from your calling." I ate the bread with those words speaking in my mind and bowed my head in thanksgiving and prayer. I listened to the words as the water was blessed, and more light seemed to fall upon me. It filled my being completely.

I felt the power of the Savior spark within me an unquenchable energy and conviction. I felt His love around me, quieting my fears. I felt strength build within me as my mind reviewed my temple covenants. Each one of these sensations was accompanied by an almost tangible feeling of light.

Suddenly, in my mind's eye, the light pushed out the darkness. What remained was a clearly defined line between me and the children on one hand and Rick on the other. My world was now separated from Rick's, and this allowed there to be light in my world, whereas darkness reigned so long as our two worlds were combined. In this new world of light, there were no tangles or threads of darkness reaching out toward me from the shadowy field where Rick stood. The distinction between the light and the dark was razor sharp. Such an eloquent lesson taught through such a simple image. I took the water from the tray, and as I swallowed it, I felt the Savior's love envelop me even more powerfully. "You are released from your calling," the voice repeated a third time. I had heard, and I had understood.

I knew what I needed to do. Following sacrament meeting, I looked up from the pew and locked eyes with Bishop Lewis, who was up on the stand presiding over the congregation. He never broke eye contact with me as I traversed the distance from my pew to the stand.

Without prelude, I asked Bishop Lewis if I could meet with him. He held my gaze and replied, "Yes. Come into my office." As we stepped out of the chapel, a sister from the ward helped to shuttle my five children toward the Primary room. As I strode across the mauve carpet, I reflected on my first meeting with Bishop Lewis four months ago. I had shared with him all of the ups and downs of my marriage and even insisted that he connect with my previous bishop to learn the details of my background. I didn't have time to do that with work and everything else I was trying to hold together.

Bishop Lewis opened the door; I walked into the office and sat down opposite his desk. He quietly took his seat. With my eyes locked onto his, I blurted out the phrase, "I'm getting divorced." Wow! That was not the way I thought I was going to start this conversation. I guess it just burst right out of me. He looked at me and sat forward in his chair. We contemplated each other for a moment in silence. Then he said, "I will support you. How can I help?" It was that simple. There was no interrogation about whether I was sure about the decision. There was no admonition that I should pray about it more. There was no attempt to prescribe me prerequisite actions before I left. It was elegant, beautiful, and exactly the right thing to say.

His next words surprised me. "What is your plan?" I did a mental double take. There was that phrase yet again! He was right to ask that. My conviction to leave Rick was absolute. But how to leave? Well, I hadn't even thought about it.

"I would need to continue my night classes and to keep teaching, so I would need to remain close enough to work. Moving back to my parents' home is not an option," I reasoned. My financial options at present were highly limited. While I had a job, I did not have any credit to my name because we had filed for personal and business bankruptcy due to disastrous business decisions on the part of Rick's partner, Jack.

As I sat pondering in the office, many questions and ideas started to flow within me. I knew I could not get a house, so I figured I would stay where I was in the basement apartment until Christmas was over, but I would find an apartment and figure out a way to move during the month of December. That would give me three weeks to pull together a plan and put it in motion. That would be tight, but I thought I could make it work. My mind tried to fit together logistical considerations like pieces in a complicated jigsaw puzzle.

The bishop's mind was drawn to a different topic, however. "Does Rick know that you want a divorce?" His question acted like a speed bump to my train of thoughts.

"No," I answered. "I was planning on telling him after he sobers up this afternoon."

To me, this felt like a minor detail. It was clear that the bishop felt very differently. His gaze held concern and a warning. "Make sure you are not alone with him when you tell him," he said. "I know he hasn't laid a hand on you in months, but things can change."

"Okay," I said, feeling like the concerns he was bringing up were the least of my worries.

"Can I ask you what you are going to do for money?" he asked.

"Well, I'm teaching full-time, so we have that under control," I said.

"Yes, I understand," the bishop acknowledged. "Do you have a reliable vehicle? Do you have it gassed up?"

"Yes," I said. I was feeling increasingly confused about the points he seemed to be driving at. What exactly did he think I needed to prepare for?

"Do you have a few different hotels you could go to in case waiting for one month just gets, you know, too much to handle?" he asked.

Clearly, what he was envisioning happening when I told Rick that I was getting a divorce was quite a bit different than what I was thinking. "Well, I didn't think about that, Bishop. I just need to get through the next three weeks till break, and then I can move," I said.

I guess it sounded to the bishop like I was only thinking about things in terms of time and calendaring. His next question cut straight to the point. "What if you need to make a run for it? What will you do?"

Make a run for it? I thought. *Why would I need to do that? This was my life, not some Hollywood movie that involved an elaborate chase scene or daring escape!* My expression telegraphed my confusion, and I answered, trying to reassure the bishop that I had things under control. "Well, I'm not sure what you are getting at, but I have my bank account separate from his. He can't access it," I said. "The van is in my name as well." There. That ought to clear things up. There was nothing to worry about.

"That's good to hear," he said and then persisted with his concerns. "Do you have a bag or two packed just in case you feel like you need to sleep over somewhere else?" he asked. "Do you have friends and co-workers you can count on to give you support as you are going through this transition?"

"Yes, I think so," I replied.

"Are you going to stay in the ward boundaries or move away from here?" he asked.

"Well," I mused, "there are some apartments down by the school that I teach at, so I was going to start looking there."

By this time, I was waiting for him to suggest the Witness Relocation Program! I felt certain that the concerns he was expressing were disproportionate to the task in front of me. In my mind, it was pretty simple: I was going to tell Rick that we are going to get a divorce. Then I would apply for apartments, and I would take the two-week Christmas break to make the necessary arrangements and move out. I would keep the kids stable and in their familiar places as much as possible. I had some friends that I could go to for emotional support and for other assistance if needed.

His worries were not abated by my explanation. "I want to ask this again," he emphasized. "Will you promise me not to be alone when you tell Rick about the divorce?" I relented and told him I would wait until everyone was home from church. The in-laws would be present upstairs, where they could hear if anything went wrong.

Bishop Lewis held my gaze longer and spoke with great conviction. "I want you to know that this is the right thing. The Spirit has confirmed it to me. I will be here no matter where you are." My heart was full at this expression of commitment to me and my children. I stood up, feeling ready to go and put things in motion.

"Will you promise me one last thing?" he asked. "Take my card, and call me if you need anything. I'll be here." I took the card and promised that I would. I shook his hand, and as I approached the exit, I looked back into his eyes. They were wet but encouraging. I walked out the door, never to see him again.

In retrospect, I can testify that all of those questions that the bishop had asked were from Heavenly Father. He prompted me to prepare for what would be the most intense emotional, mental, and physical abuse that I had ever experienced in my marriage. Rick's reaction to the news of the divorce was beyond anything I had ever imagined, and each question of the bishop's counsel proved to be inspired to prepare me for what was coming. As dangerous and harmful as things had been within my marriage, I had never been in so much danger as when Rick learned that I had decided to leave. I have since learned that this is the truth quite often; that the choice to leave is often the most dangerous time for many victims of abuse.

After a horrendous and terrifying night, my children and I found ourselves homeless but alive, and Rick found himself in jail. Our escape had been narrow and harrowing. I called the bishop like he had counseled me to do, and he was able to help me pay for a few hotels. He even gave me the heads up when Rick was released from jail after his drug buddies had posted bail for him. That phone call came just in time, and I began a race against time to leave my night class, collect my children, and disappear. Rick was out for blood. If I hadn't known that he was free and looking for me, I don't think I would be here now.

I wish I could tell you that after escaping all was well. But it wasn't. It was just the beginning. I had not done my homework when it came to apartments. I hadn't considered the possibility of waiting lists or how credit scores would affect my ability to secure an apartment. The result was that the children and I were homeless for three weeks while we tried to figure out what to do. Somehow, through all of that, I never missed going to work, getting my children to school, or attending my night class.

My life has transformed completely since leaving abuse, and it has all been for the better. Those early, frightening days of loneliness and uncertainty are far behind me. As I look at how I got from there to here, my heart is full for Bishop Lewis, Bishop Connors, Bishop Simpson, and Bishop Xavier. Each of them were incredibly in tune with the Spirit. They knew what to say and how to help me. They offered spiritual guidance and practical assistance. They believed in me and in the Lord's desire to deliver me and my children from abuse.

However, I know that this is not the case for so many women who find themselves in abusive relationships. This sad truth breaks my heart. And so, I wish to take a few moments to speak directly to bishops, elders quorum presidents, Relief Society presidents, stake presidents, and other Church leaders who will find themselves sitting across a desk from someone who is being abused. There are seven things I would ask you to do for these people:

1. Listen to victims of abuse. Believe them. Pray about what they are saying to you and feel from the Spirit what needs to be said.

2. Know that while each situation of abuse is unique, they are all dangerous. Abuse damages families, oftentimes far more than a family being broken up. There is hope for every soul, but frequently in abuse both souls need to separate from each other in order to heal. Allow for it. Support victims of abuse in this separation when they choose it.

3. Be a steward of the victims' safety. Please take care of the immediate spiritual health and physical welfare of the victims by assisting them in finding a place where they are safe and cared for.

4. Never put a victim in a situation against their will. Remember, as they have suffered abuse they have had control taken away from them. Your calling is to help them restore their agency. If you attempt to pressure them or leverage them in any way, this will only make them more likely to push away from you and other potential help. The victim of abuse needs to be able to be the one to choose when to leave. Your calling is to be there for the victims as they consider each step and enact their choices. You can help them think things through. You can help them explore options. But do not try to make choices for

them. This means that sometimes, you may clearly see the need for an abused person to leave, but they may not be ready to make that decision yet. When that is the case, your role is to continue to connect with them and to assist them in building other supportive relationships. You can help them sort through their tangled thoughts and feelings. But remember, the decision is theirs. You cannot make it for them. The more they feel supported and connected, the more likely they will be able to make the choice to leave when it becomes necessary.

5. Seek to understand. Be humbly aware that you don't know the situation that the victim faces behind closed doors. Be wise enough to know that in most cases of abuse there is a fairly convincing public facade in place. Do not assume that you understand the situation. Never suggest that it is a woman's responsibility to stick with her husband through an addiction, whether he tries to recover from it or not. Be cautious about simply bearing testimony or sharing scriptures about eternal families or commenting on how husbands and wives should love and support one another. In some circumstances, this is an excellent practice. In cases of abuse, doing so can put a tremendous amount of pressure on victims and lead them to believe that their religious leader is counseling them to stay in an abusive situation.

6. Be extra aware of the women and children around you. Watch their body language. Notice how they connect or push away from others. Look for those who are in distress. Reach out to them and seek to know them better.

7. Be the first to respond when a victim of abuse asks for help. Rally others to assist. Let them know that your support of their safety and their right to be free of abuse is unconditional.

For anyone who is suffering from abuse, please know this; you are not alone. Many people are beside you and are only waiting to learn about your needs in order to encircle you in friendship, love, and help. We are your supporters. Others have faced what you now face, and we have found a path to deliverance. We are eager to help you find yours, as well.

CHAPTER 10

CLOSING THOUGHTS

Abuse is a great scourge upon this world. It is like a ravaging horde of pillaging raiders, invading the homes of people from all stations of life, but often striking stealthily, in great secrecy. Deep wounds of the body and spirit are hidden in plain sight as victims of abuse seek to carry on with their lives in a world where someone they should have been able to love and feel safe with has violated their trust at the deepest level possible. Families are trapped in intergenerational cycles of manipulation, control, and violence, and are often camouflaged with the trappings of happiness, righteousness, and respectability, like the whited sepulchres the Savior warned about. Many forms of abuse masquerade as elements of culture and tradition, and therefore are accepted and practiced without critical examination. And worse still, faithful people are deceived into thinking that submitting to this diabolical dynamic is somehow their religious responsibility. At present, members of the Church suffer from abuse at rates that are equal to or even greater than the population at large. These are sobering truths.

They bring to mind God's lamentation when Enoch witnessed Him weep.

> And he saw angels descending out of heaven; and he heard a loud voice saying: Wo, wo be unto the inhabitants of the earth.
>
> And he beheld Satan; and he had a great chain in his hand, and it veiled the whole face of the earth with darkness; and he looked up and laughed, and his angels rejoiced.

And Enoch beheld angels descending out of heaven, bearing testimony of the Father and Son; and the Holy Ghost fell on many, and they were caught up by the powers of heaven into Zion.

And it came to pass that the God of heaven looked upon the residue of the people, and he wept; and Enoch bore record of it, saying: How is it that the heavens weep, and shed forth their tears as the rain upon the mountains?

And Enoch said unto the Lord: How is it that thou canst weep, seeing thou art holy, and from all eternity to all eternity?

And were it possible that man could number the particles of the earth, yea, millions of earths like this, it would not be a beginning to the number of thy creations; and thy curtains are stretched out still; and yet thou art there, and thy bosom is there; and also thou art just; thou art merciful and kind forever;

And thou hast taken Zion to thine own bosom, from all thy creations, from all eternity to all eternity; and naught but peace, justice, and truth is the habitation of thy throne; and mercy shall go before thy face and have no end; how is it thou canst weep?

The Lord said unto Enoch: Behold these thy brethren; they are the workmanship of mine own hands, and I gave unto them their knowledge, in the day I created them; and in the Garden of Eden, gave I unto man his agency;

And unto thy brethren have I said, and also given commandment, that they should love one another, and that they should choose me, their Father; but behold, they are without affection, and they hate their own blood...

Wherefore should not the heavens weep, seeing these shall suffer? (Moses 7:25–33, 37).

There is far too much suffering caused by abuse! It is indeed, as this scripture suggests, a great chain with which the adversary has bound many people down in bondage from generation to generation. The good news is that this is not a plague that we are powerless to do something about. The updated policies from the Church about responding to abuse are a call to action for all of us. No matter what the attitudes, actions, and traditions of previous generations have been, we can and must do better.

For those of who serve in leadership callings in the Church, our greatest example of responding to abuse comes from the Savior Himself. Consider for a moment that at the formal beginning of His mortal ministry, the Savior stood in the synagogue and read from the Torah, citing from words that the prophet Isaiah had written about Him and declaring His Messiahship in a reference clearly understood by those present. He recited: "The Spirit of the Lord is upon me, because he hath anointed me to preach the gospel to the poor; he hath sent me to heal the brokenhearted, to preach deliverance to the captives, and recovering of sight to the blind, to set at liberty them that are bruised, To preach the acceptable year of the Lord" (Luke 4:18–19).

Of all the Messianic scriptures the Savior could have chosen to make His public announcement in the synagogue that day, I find it interesting that He chose this one, which seems tailor made to declaring that an important part of His role as the Savior is to deliver the abused from their situation and heal their broken hearts. As we learn of possible abuse, this should be our priority as well.

The science on this matter gives us every reason to expect that as we listen to and believe reports of abuse, as we offer emotional and practical support for victims of abuse, as we hold abusers accountable for their actions, and as we allow the emotional needs of those who have been abused to determine the path to be followed towards healing, abuse will become less common among us. Furthermore, those who have been abused will be more likely to heal and move forward with peaceful and happy lives.

This change is within our power. It is time for us to act upon it.

REFERENCES

Abdolmaleky, H. M., Thiagalingam, S., & Wilcox, M. (2005). Genetics and epigenetics in major psychiatric disorders. *American Journal of Pharmacogenomics*, 5(3), 149–160.

Abramson, K. (2014). Turning up the lights on gaslighting. *Philosophical perspectives*, *28*, 1–30.

Almış, B. H., Gümüştaş, F., & Kütük, E. K. (2020). Effects of Domestic Violence Against Women on Mental Health of Women and Children. *Psikiyatride Guncel Yaklasimlar*, *12*(2), 232–242.

American Psychiatric Association. (2013). *Diagnostic and statistical manual of mental disorders* (5th ed.)

Anderson, R. J. (2017). *Screen savvy: Creating balance in a digital world*. Springville, Utah: Cedar Fort.

Annese, V. (2020). Genetics and epigenetics of IBD. *Pharmacological Research*, 104892.

Arce, R., Arias, E., Novo, M., & Fariña, F. (2020). Are interventions with batterers effective? A meta-analytical review. *Psychosocial Intervention*, *29*(3), 153–164.

Axline, V. M. (1969). *Play therapy* (Vol. 125). Ballantine Books.

Azhagar, V. K., Chinnakkaruppan, D., Hassan, K. H., & Ashan, F. (2018, January). Domestic Violence: Psychological Profile of Abusers. In *National Conference on Research in Domestic Violence (28)* p. 46.

Bargai, N., Ben-Shakhar, G., & Shalev, A. Y. (2007). Posttraumatic stress disorder and depression in battered women: The mediating role of learned helplessness. *Journal of Family Violence, 22*(5), 267–275.

Bennett, L., & Williams, O. (2001). Controversies and recent studies of batterer intervention program effectiveness.

Berkowitz, R. (2021, May 11). QAnon resembles the games I design. But for believers, there is no winning. *Washington Post.* Retrieved June 2, 2021 from https://www.washingtonpost.com/outlook/qanon-game-plays-believers/2021/05/10/31d8ea46–928b-11eb-a74e-1f4cf89fd948_story.html

Bezo, B., & Maggi, S. (2015). Living in "survival mode:" Intergenerational transmission of trauma from the Holodomor genocide of 1932–1933 in Ukraine. *Social Science & Medicine, 134,* 87–94.

Bing-Canar, H., Pizzuto, J., & Compton, R. J. (2016). Mindfulness-of-breathing exercise modulates EEG alpha activity during cognitive performance. *Psychophysiology, 53*(9), 1366–1376.

Bohall, G., Bautista, M. J., & Musson, S. (2016). Intimate partner violence and the Duluth model: An examination of the model and recommendations for future research and practice. *Journal of Family Violence, 31*(8), 1029–1033.

Bowlby, J. (2005). *A secure base: Clinical applications of attachment theory* (Vol. 393). Taylor & Francis.

Bowlby, J. (2008). *A secure base: Parent-child attachment and healthy human development.* Basic books.

Boyle, A., Jones, P., & Lloyd, S. (2006). The association between domestic violence and self harm in emergency medicine patients. *Emergency Medicine Journal, 23*(8), 604–607.

Brassard, M. R., Hart, S. N., & Hardy, D. B. (2000). Psychological and emotional abuse of children. In *Case studies in family violence* (pp. 293–319). Springer, Boston, MA.

Breslin, J. H. (2005). *Effectiveness of a rural anger management program in preventing domestic violence recidivism* (Doctoral dissertation, Capella University).

Buel, S. M. (1999). Fifty obstacles to leaving, aka, why abuse victims stay. *Colorado Lawyer, 28*(10/19).

Butler, M. H. (2010). *Spiritual exodus: A latter-day saint guide to recovery from behavioral addiction.* Provo, Utah: BYU Academic.

Burg, J. M., & Michalak, J. (2011). The healthy quality of mindful breathing: Associations with rumination and depression. *Cognitive Therapy and Research, 35*(2), 179–185.

Campbell, R., Sullivan, C. M., & Davidson, W. S. (1995). Women who use domestic violence shelters: Changes in depression over time. *Psychology of Women Quarterly, 19*(2), 237–255.

Carpenter, C., & Harper, N. (2015). Health and wellbeing benefits of activities in the outdoors. *Routledge International Handbook of Outdoor Studies,* 59–69.

Cho, H., Ryu, S., Noh, J., & Lee, J. (2016). The effectiveness of daily mindful breathing practices on test anxiety of students. *PloS One, 11*(10), e0164822.

Coates, D. (2010). Impact of childhood abuse: Biopsychosocial pathways through which adult mental health is compromised. *Australian Social Work, 63*(4), 391–403.

Covington, S. (2003). Beyond trauma. *Center City, MN: Hazeldon.*

Cocchi, L., & Zalesky, A. (2018). Personalized transcranial magnetic stimulation in psychiatry. *Biological Psychiatry: Cognitive Neuroscience and Neuroimaging, 3*(9), 731–741.

Coker, A. L., Hopenhayn, C., DeSimone, C. P., Bush, H. M., & Crofford, L. (2009). Violence against women raises risk of cervical cancer. *Journal of Women's Health, 18*(8), 1179–1185.

Colgan, D. D., Christopher, M., Michael, P., & Wahbeh, H. (2016). The body scan and mindful breathing among veterans with PTSD: type of intervention moderates the relationship between changes in mindfulness and post-treatment depression. *Mindfulness, 7*(2), 372–383.

Coleman, V. 1994. Lesbian Battering: The relationship between personality and the perpetration of violence. *Violence and victims, 9*(2), 139–152.

Collins, N., & Roth, T. L. (2021). Intergenerational transmission of stress-related epigenetic regulation. In *Developmental Human Behavioral Epigenetics* (pp. 119–141). Academic Press.

Conching, A. K. S., & Thayer, Z. (2019). Biological pathways for historical trauma to affect health: A conceptual model focusing on epigenetic modifications. *Social Science & Medicine, 230*, 74–82.

Cesario, S. K., McFarlane, J., Nava, A., Gilroy, H., & Maddoux, J. (2014). Linking Cancer and Intimate Partner Violence. *Clinical Journal of Oncology Nursing, 18*(1).

Children's Bureau (2019). What is child abuse and neglect? Recognizing the signs and symptoms. Retrieved April 16, 2001 from https://www.childwelfare.gov/pubPDFs/whatiscan. pdf#page=3&view=What%20Are%20the%20Major%20 Types%20of%20Child%20Abuse%20and%20Neglect?

Cox, D. T., Shanahan, D. F., Hudson, H. L., Plummer, K. E., Siriwardena, G. M., Fuller, R. A., . . . & Gaston, K. J. (2017). Doses of neighborhood nature: the benefits for mental health of living with nature. *BioScience, 67*(2), 147–155.

Cooley, M. E., Thompson, H. M., & Colvin, M. L. (2019). A qualitative examination of recruitment and motivation to become a Guardian ad Litem in the child welfare system. *Children and Youth Services Review, 99*, 115–124.

Cunliffe, V. T. (2016). The epigenetic impacts of social stress: how does social adversity become biologically embedded?. *Epigenomics, 8*(12), 1653–1669.

Dallam, S. J., & Silberg, J. L. (2006). Myths that place children at risk during custody disputes. *Sexual Assault Report, 9*(3), 33–47. Retrieved from http://www.leadershipcouncil.org/1/res/ cust_myths.html

Davidson, P. R., & Parker, K. C. (2001). Eye movement desensitization and reprocessing (EMDR): a meta-analysis. *Journal of consulting and clinical psychology, 69*(2), 305.

Dasborough, M., & Harvey, P. (2017). Schadenfreude: The (not so) secret joy of another's misfortune. *Journal of Business Ethics, 141*(4), 693–707.

Day, T. L. (2013). Bones heal faster: Spousal abuse in the church of Jesus Christ of latter-day saints. *Dialogue: A Journal of Mormon Thought, 46*(1), 64–93.

Day, A., Chung, D., O'Leary, P., & Carson, E. (2009). Programs for men who perpetrate domestic violence: An examination of the issues underlying the effectiveness of intervention programs. *Journal of Family Violence, 24*(3), 203–212.

Deibert, R. J. (2019). The road to digital unfreedom: Three painful truths about social media. *Journal of Democracy, 30*(1), 25–39.

DeKeseredy, W., & Schwartz, M. (2009). *Dangerous exits: Escaping abusive relationships in rural America*. Rutgers University Press.

Devries, K., Watts, C., Yoshihama, M., Kiss, L., Schraiber, L. B., Deyessa, N., . . . & WHO Multi-Country Study Team. (2011). Violence against women is strongly associated with suicide attempts: evidence from the WHO multi-country study on women's health and domestic violence against women. *Social science & medicine, 73*(1), 79–86.

Dodaj, A. (2020). Children witnessing domestic violence. *Journal of Children's Services*.

Domestic Abuse Intervention Programs (2021). *The Duluth model*. Retrieved June 28, 2021 from https://www.theduluthmodel.org/

Edgcumbe, R. (2000). *Anna Freud: A view of development, disturbance and therapeutic techniques*. Psychology Press.

Epstein, D. (1999). Effective intervention in domestic violence cases: Rethinking the roles of prosecutors, judges, and the court system. *Yale JL & Feminism, 11*, 3.

Evans, I. E., Martyr, A., Collins, R., Brayne, C., & Clare, L. (2019). Social isolation and cognitive function in later life: a systematic review and meta-analysis. *Journal of Alzheimer's disease, 70*(s1), S119–S144.

Fairbairn, C. E., Briley, D. A., Kang, D., Fraley, R. C., Hankin, B. L., & Ariss, T. (2018). A meta-analysis of longitudinal associations between substance use and interpersonal attachment security. *Psychological bulletin, 144*(5), 532.

Fairbank, J. A., DeGood, D. E., & Jenkins, C. W. (1981). Behavioral treatment of a persistent post-traumatic startle response. *Journal of Behavior Therapy and Experimental Psychiatry, 12*(4), 321–324.

Fattorini, N., Brunetti, C., Baruzzi, C., Macchi, E., Pagliarella, M. C., Pallari, N., . . . & Ferretti, F. (2018). Being "hangry": food depletion and its cascading effects on social behaviour. *Biological Journal of the Linnean Society, 125*(3), 640–656.

Faust, J. E. (November, 1987). The great imitator. *Ensign.*

Feder, L., & Wilson, D. B. (2005). A meta-analytic review of court-mandated batterer intervention programs: Can courts affect abusers' behavior? *Journal of Experimental Criminology, 1*(2), 239–262.

Feldman, G., Greeson, J., & Senville, J. (2010). Differential effects of mindful breathing, progressive muscle relaxation, and loving-kindness meditation on decentering and negative reactions to repetitive thoughts. *Behaviour Research and Therapy, 48*(10), 1002–1011.

Felitti, V. J., Anda, R. F., Nordenberg, D., et al. (1998). Relationship of childhood abuse and household dysfunction to many of the leading causes of death in adults: the Adverse Childhood Experiences (ACE) Study. *Am J Prev Med. 14*:245–58.

Felitti, V. J., Anda, R. F., Nordenberg, D., Williamson, D. F., Spitz, A. M., Edwards, V., . . . & Marks, J. S. (2019). Relationship of childhood abuse and household dysfunction to many of the leading causes of death in adults: The adverse childhood experiences (ACE) study. *American Journal of Preventive Medicine.*

Ferrell, J., & Boyce, D. (2015). *The anatomy of peace: Resolving the heart of conflict.* Berrett-Koehler Publishers.

Flett, G. L., Druckman, T., Hewitt, P. L., & Wekerle, C. (2012). Perfectionism, coping, social support, and depression in maltreated adolescents. *Journal of Rational-Emotive & Cognitive-Behavior Therapy, 30*(2), 118–131.

Foa, E. B., & McLean, C. P. (2016). The efficacy of exposure therapy for anxiety-related disorders and its underlying mechanisms: The case of OCD and PTSD. *Annual Review of Clinical Psychology, 12*, 1–28.

Fry, R (1993). Adult physical illness and childhood sexual abuse. *J Psychosom Res. 37*:89–103

Gallegos, A. M., Trabold, N., Cerulli, C., & Pigeon, W. R. (2021). Sleep and interpersonal violence: a systematic review. *Trauma, Violence, & Abuse, 22*(2), 359–369.

Ganley, A. L. (1995). Understanding domestic violence. *Improving the health care response to domestic violence: A resource manual for health care providers*, 15–42.

George, E., & Engel, L. (1980). The clinical application of the biopsychosocial model. *American Journal of Psychiatry, 137*(5), 535–544.

Gianini, L. M., White, M. A., & Masheb, R. M. (2013). Eating pathology, emotion regulation, and emotional overeating in obese adults with binge eating disorder. *Eating Behaviors, 14*(3), 309–313.

Gilchrist, G., Munoz, J. T., & Easton, C. J. (2015). Should we reconsider anger management when addressing physical intimate partner violence perpetration by alcohol abusing males? A systematic review. *Aggression and violent behavior, 25*, 124–132.

Goodman, R., & Calderon, A. (2012). The use of mindfulness in trauma counseling. *Journal of Mental Health Counseling, 34*(3), 254–268.

Goodman, M., & New, A. (2000). Impulsive aggression in borderline personality disorder. *Current Psychiatry Reports, 2*(1), 56–61.

Goodwin, I. (2003). The relevance of attachment theory to the philosophy, organization, and practice of adult mental health care. *Clinical Psychology Review, 23*(1), 35–56.

Hamarman, S., & Bernet, W. (2000). Evaluating and reporting emotional abuse in children: Parent-based, action-based focus aids in clinical decision-making. *Journal-American Academy of Child and Adolescent Psychiatry, 39*(7), 928–930.

Healthline (2021). *What is verbal abuse?* Retrieved March 16, 2021 from https://www.healthline.com/health/mental-health/what-is-verbal-abuse

Healthline (2021a). *The effects of sleep deprivation on your body.* Retrieved June 15, 2021 from https://www.healthline.com/health/sleep-deprivation/effects-on-body

Herrera, B. M., Keildson, S., & Lindgren, C. M. (2011). Genetics and epigenetics of obesity. *Maturitas, 69*(1), 41–49.

Hewagama, A., & Richardson, B. (2009). The genetics and epigenetics of autoimmune diseases. *Journal of Autoimmunity, 33*(1), 3–11.

Hickson, M. W. (2013). A brief history of problems of evil. *The Blackwell Companion to the Problem of Evil,* 3–18.

Hiroto, D. S., & Seligman, M. E. (1975). Generality of learned helplessness in man. *Journal of Personality and Social Psychology, 31*(2), 311.

Hjort, L., Rushiti, F., Wang, S. J., Fransquet, P., P Krasniqi, S., I Çarkaxhiu, S., . . . & Ryan, J. (2021). Intergenerational effects of maternal post-traumatic stress disorder on offspring epigenetic patterns and cortisol levels. *Epigenomics,* (0).

Holland, J. R. (May, 2007). The tongue of angels. *Ensign.*

Holland, J. R. (October, 2003). How do I love thee? *The New Era.* Retrieved February 16, 2021 from: https://www.churchofjesuschrist.org/study/new-era/2003/10/how-do-i-love-thee?lang=eng

Holland, J. R. (November, 2013). Like a broken vessel. *Ensign.* Retrieved June 21, 2021 from https://www.churchofjesuschrist.org/study/general-conference/2013/10/like-a-broken-vessel?lang=eng

Holland, J. R. (November, 2018). The ministry of reconciliation. *Ensign.* Retrieved February 17, 2021 from: https://www.churchofjesuschrist.org/study/general-conference/2018/10/the-ministry-of-reconciliation?lang=eng

Holland, J. R. (May, 2021). Not as the world giveth. *General Conference Report.* Retrieved April 15, 2021, from https://www.churchofjesuschrist.org/study/general-conference/2021/04/23holland?lang=eng

Holmes, J. (2014). *The search for the secure base: Attachment theory and psychotherapy.* Routledge.

Holt, S., Buckley, H., & Whelan, S. (2008). The impact of exposure to domestic violence on children and young people: A review of the literature. *Child Abuse & Nglect, 32*(8), 797–810.

Howard, A. E. (2022). *Transgenerational effects of trauma through epigenetic mechanisms* (Doctoral dissertation, Azusa Pacific University

Imber-Black, E. (1992). *Families and larger systems: A family therapist's guide through the labyrinth.* Guilford Press.

Isobel, S., Goodyear, M., Furness, T., & Foster, K. (2019). Preventing intergenerational trauma transmission: A critical interpretive synthesis. *Journal of clinical nursing, 28*(7–8), 1100–1113.

Jacobs, J. M., Cohen, A., Hammerman-Rozenberg, R., Azoulay, D., Maaravi, Y., & Stessman, J. (2008). Going outdoors daily predicts long-term functional and health benefits among ambulatory older people. *Journal of Aging and Health, 20*(3), 259–272.

Jackson, K.P., & Hunt, R.D. (2011). Reprove, betimes, and sharpness in the vocabulary of Joseph Smith. *Religious Educator 6*(2), 97–104.

Jarvis, K. L., Gordon, E. E., & Novaco, R. W. (2005). Psychological distress of children and mothers in domestic violence emergency shelters. *Journal of Family Violence, 20*(6), 389–402.

Jaffe, P., Ashbourne, D., & Mamo, A. (2010). Early identification and prevention of parent– child alienation: A framework for balancing risks and benefits of intervention. *Family Court Review, 48*, 136–152. doi:10.1111/j.1744–1617.2009.01294.x

Jawaid, A., Roszkowski, M., & Mansuy, I. M. (2018). Transgenerational epigenetics of traumatic stress. *Progress in Molecular Biology and Translational Science, 158*, 273–298.

Johnson, S. M., & Denton, W. (2002). Emotionally focused couple therapy: Creating secure connections.

Johnson, S. M., Makinen, J. A., & Millikin, J. W. (2001). Attachment injuries in couple relationships: A new perspective on impasses in couples therapy. *Journal of Marital and Family Therapy, 27*(2), 145–155.

Johnston, J. R., & Goldman, J. R. (2010). Outcomes of family counseling interventions with children who resist visitation: An addendum to Friedlander and Walters (2010). *Family Court Review, 48,* 112–115. doi:10.1111/j.1744–1617.2009.01292.x

Johnston, J. R., Roseby, V., & Kuehnle, K. (2009). *In the name of the child: A developmental approach to understanding and helping children of conflicted and violent divorce* (2nd ed.). New York, NY: Springer.

Jones, M. (2021). *All in* [Audio podcast] Apple podcasts. https://podcasts.apple.com/us/podcast/sage-williams-sexual-abuse-prevention-healing-and-hope/id1439975046?i=1000521444911

Jones, D. P. H., & McGraw, J. M. (1987). Reliable and Fictitious Accounts of Sexual Abuse to Children. *Journal of Interpersonal Violence, 2,* 27–45, 1987.

Kanherkar, R. R., Bhatia-Dey, N., & Csoka, A. B. (2014). Epigenetics across the human lifespan. *Frontiers in Cell and Developmental Biology, 2,* 49.

Kavak, F., Aktürk, Ü., Özdemir, A., & Gültekin, A. (2018). The relationship between domestic violence against women and suicide risk. *Archives of psychiatric nursing, 32*(4), 574–579.

Kellermann, N. P. (2013). Epigenetic transmission of holocaust trauma: can nightmares be inherited. *The Israel Journal of Psychiatry and Related Sciences, 50*(1), 33–39.

Kim, Y. D., Heo, I., Shin, B. C., Crawford, C., Kang, H. W., & Lim, J. H. (2013). Acupuncture for posttraumatic stress disorder: a systematic review of randomized controlled trials and prospective clinical trials. *Evidence-Based Complementary and Alternative Medicine, 2013.*

Kimber, M., McTavish, J. R., Couturier, J., Boven, A., Gill, S., Dimitropoulos, G., & MacMillan, H. L. (2017). Consequences of child emotional abuse, emotional neglect and exposure to intimate partner violence for eating disorders: a systematic critical review. *BMC Psychology, 5*(1), 1–18.

Kwong, M. J., Bartholomew, K., Henderson, A. J., & Trinke, S. J. (2003). The intergenerational transmission of relationship violence. *Journal of family psychology, 17*(3), 288.

Kimball, S. W. *Teachings of Presidents of the Church—Spencer W. Kimball.* Salt Lake City: The Church of Jesus Christ of Latter-day Saints, 2006.

Kimball, S.W. (1977, October) in Conference Report. *Ensign.*

Kübler-Ross, E. (1969) *On death and dying.* Routledge, New York, NY.

Kübler-Ross, E. (2005) *On grief and grieving: Finding the meaning of grief through the five stages of loss.* Scribner, New York, NY.

Lande, R. G., Williams, L. B., Francis, J. L., Gragnani, C., & Morin, M. L. (2010). Efficacy of biofeedback for post-traumatic stress disorder. *Complementary Therapies in Medicine, 18*(6), 256–259.

Landreth, G. L. (2012). *Play therapy: The art of the relationship.* Routledge.

Landrigan, P. J. (2005). Children as a vulnerable population. *Human and Ecological Risk Assessment: An International Journal, 11*(1), 235–238.

Leigh-Hunt, N., Bagguley, D., Bash, K., Turner, V., Turnbull, S., Valtorta, N., & Caan, W. (2017). An overview of systematic reviews on the public health consequences of social isolation and loneliness. *Public Health, 152,* 157–171.

Leserman J., Zhiming L., Drossman D. A., Toomey T. C., Nachman G., & Glogau L. (1997). Impact of sexual and physical abuse dimensions on health status: development of an abuse severity measure. *Psychosom Med. 59*:152–60.

Lieberman, A. F. (2007). Ghosts and angels: Intergenerational patterns in the transmission and treatment of the traumatic sequelae of domestic violence. *Infant mental health journal, 28*(4), 422–439.

Linehan, M. M. (1987). Dialectical behavioral therapy: A cognitive behavioral approach to parasuicide. *Journal of Personality Disorders, 1*(4), 328–333.

Littrell, J. (2008). The mind-body connection: not just a theory anymore. *Social Work in Health Care, 46*(4), 17–37.

Living Well (2015). Grounding exercises. Retrieved June 30, 2021 from https://www.livingwell.org.au/well-being/mental-health/grounding-exercises/

Lundberg, G. B., Lundberg, J., & Lundberg, J. S. (2000). *I don't have to make everything all better*. Penguin.

Luyster, F. S., Strollo, P. J., Zee, P. C., & Walsh, J. K. (2012). Sleep: a health imperative. *Sleep, 35*(6), 727–734.

Loxton, D., Schofield, M., Hussain, R., & Mishra, G. (2006). History of domestic violence and physical health in midlife. *Violence against Women, 12*(8), 715–731.

Lloyd, M. (2018). Domestic violence and education: Examining the impact of domestic violence on young children, children, and young people and the potential role of schools. *Frontiers in Psychology, 9*, 2094.

Maier, S. F., & Seligman, M. E. (1976). Learned helplessness: theory and evidence. *Journal of Experimental Psychology: General, 105*(1), 3.

MacCormack, J. K., & Lindquist, K. A. (2018). Feeling Hangry. *When Hunger Is Conceptualized as Emotion.*

Malkesman, O., Pine, D. S., Tragon, T., Austin, D. R., Henter, I. D., Chen, G., & Manji, H. K. (2009). Animal models of suicide-trait-related behaviors. *Trends in pharmacological sciences, 30*(4), 165–173.

Manning, J.C. (2009). *What's the big deal about pornography?* Shadow Mountain.

Margolin, G. (1998). Effects of domestic violence on children.

Marini, S., Davis, K. A., Soare, T. W., Zhu, Y., Suderman, M. J., Simpkin, A. J., . . . & Dunn, E. C. (2020). Adversity exposure during sensitive periods predicts accelerated epigenetic aging in children. *Psychoneuroendocrinology, 113*, 104484.

Marinovich, S. A. (2019). *Effects of Trauma on Young Children's Social Competence* (Doctoral dissertation, The Chicago School of Professional Psychology).

Mayo Clinic (2011). *Sleep tips: 6 steps to better sleep.* Retrieved June 15, 2021 from https://www.mayoclinic.org/healthy-lifestyle/adult-health/in-depth/sleep/art-20048379

Mayo Clinic (2021). *Antisocial personality disorder.* Retrieved May 12, 2021 from https://www.mayoclinic.org/diseases-conditions/antisocial-personality-disorder/diagnosis-treatment/drc-20353934

Mcalinden, A. M. (2006). 'Setting'Em Up': Personal, familial and institutional grooming in the sexual abuse of children. *Social & Legal Studies, 15*(3), 339–362.

McCauley J, Kern DE, Kolodner K, et al. (1997). Clinical characteristics of women with a history of childhood abuse: unhealed wounds. *JAMA 277*:1362–8.

McDaniel, S. H., Hepworth, J., & Doherty, W. J. (1992). *Medical family therapy: A biopsychosocial approach to families with health problems.* Basic Books.

McFarlane, J., Nava, A., Gilroy, H., & Maddoux, J. (2015). Risk of behaviors associated with lethal violence and functional outcomes for abused women who do and do not return to the abuser following a community-based intervention. *Journal of Women's Health, 24*(4), 272–280.

McGoldrick, M., & Hardy, K. V. (Eds.). (2019). *Re-visioning family therapy.* Guilford Publications.

Meier, J. (2013, September). *Parental alienation syndrome and parental alienation: A research review.* Harrisburg, PA: VAWnet, A Project of the National Resource Center on Domestic Violence. Retrieved from http://www.vawnet.org/assoc_files_vawnet/ar_pasupdate.pdf.

Mertin, P., & Mohr, P. B. (2001). A follow-up study of posttraumatic stress disorder, anxiety, and depression in Australian victims of domestic violence. *Violence and Victims, 16*(6), 645.

Mikulincer, M., & Shaver, P. R. (2013). Adult attachment and happiness: Individual differences in the experience and consequences of positive emotions.

Miller, K. B., Lund, E., & Weatherly, J. (2012). Applying operant learning to the stay-leave decision in domestic violence. *Behavior and Social Issues, 21*(1), 135–151.

Millet, R. L., & Newell, L. D. (2001). Reproving with sharpness— when? *Religious Educator 2*(1), 83–93.

Moore, A. A. (March 13, 1999). Faith: it goes beyond the hurt. LDS priesthood leaders key to helping end abusive situations. *Deseret News.* Retrieved April 22, 2021 from https://www.deseret.com/1999/3/13/19434086/faith-it-goes-beyond-the-hurt-br-lds-priesthood-leaders-key-to-helping-end-abusive-situations

Moore, S., & Hobbs, A. (2017). Guardian Ad Litem. *The Encyclopedia of Juvenile Delinquency and Justice,* 1–3.

Morange, M. (2002). The relations between genetics and epigenetics: a historical point of view. *Annals of the New York Academy of Sciences, 981*(1), 50–60.

Morris, J. R. (2001). Genes, genetics, and epigenetics: a correspondence. *Science, 293*(5532), 1103–1105.

National Center for Injury Prevention & Centers for Disease Control and Prevention (2010). National intimate partner and and sexual violence survey: 2010 report. Retrieved on April 22, 2021 from https://www.cdc.gov/violenceprevention/pdf/nisvs_report2010-a.pdf

Oates, R. K., Jones, D. P., Denson, D., Sirotnak, A., Gary, N., & Krugman, R. D. (2000). Erroneous concerns about child sexual abuse. *Child Abuse & Neglect, 24*(1), 149–157.

O'Conner Family Law (2020, April 1). Suffering from domestic abuse? You can stay in your home and your abuser can be forced to leave. Retrieved June 15, 2021 from https://www.familylawma.com/blog/2020/april/suffering-from-domestic-abuse-you-can-stay-in-yo/

O'Donohue, W., Cummings, C., & Willis, B. (2018). The frequency of false allegations of child sexual abuse: A critical review. *Journal of child sexual abuse, 27*(5), 459–475.

Oliver, J. E. (1993). Intergenerational transmission of child abuse: rates, research, and clinical implications. *The American journal of psychiatry.*

Oram, S., Trevillion, K., Feder, G., & Howard, L. M. (2013). Prevalence of experiences of domestic violence among psychiatric patients: systematic review. *The British Journal of Psychiatry, 202*(2), 94–99.

Ortiz, R., & Sibinga, E. M. (2017). The role of mindfulness in reducing the adverse effects of childhood stress and trauma. *Children, 4*(3), 16.

Osofsky, Joy D. "Commentary: Understanding the impact of domestic violence on children, recognizing strengths, and promoting resilience: reflections on Harold and Sellers (2018)." *Journal of child psychology and psychiatry* 59, no. 4 (2018): 403–404.

Park, S. C. (2019). Role of Putative Epigenetic Mechanisms in the Intergenerational Transmission of Trauma Effects in "Comfort Women" Survivor Offspring. *Psychiatry Investigation, 16*(6), 475.

Pietromonaco, P. R., & Beck, L. A. (2019). Adult attachment and physical health. *Current Opinion in Psychology, 25*, 115–120.

Polusny, M. A., Erbes, C. R., Thuras, P., Moran, A., Lamberty, G. J., Collins, R. C., . . . & Lim, K. O. (2015). Mindfulness-based stress reduction for posttraumatic stress disorder among veterans: a randomized clinical trial. *JAMA, 314*(5), 456–465.

Polyvagal Institute (2021, March 10). *Trauma and the nervous system: A polyvagal perspective [Video].* YouTube. https://www.youtube.com/watch?v=uH5JQDAqA8E

Peter, J. P., & Nord, W. R. (1982). A clarification and extension of operant conditioning principles in marketing. *Journal of Marketing, 46*(3), 102–107.

Peterson, C., & Seligman, M. E. (1983). Learned helplessness and victimization. *Journal of Social Issues, 39*(2), 103–116.

Pilkay, S. R. (2017). Mediation and Moderation of Intergenerational Epigenetic Effects of Trauma.

Porges, S. W. (2009). The polyvagal theory: new insights into adaptive reactions of the autonomic nervous system. *Cleveland Clinic Journal of Medicine, 76*(Suppl 2), S86.

Porges, S. W. (2011). *The polyvagal theory: neurophysiological foundations of emotions, attachment, communication, and self-regulation (Norton Series on Interpersonal Neurobiology)*. WW Norton & Company.

Porges, S. W. (2017). *The pocket guide to the polyvagal theory: The transformative power of feeling safe*. WW Norton & Co.

Porges, S. W. (2018). Polyvagal theory: A primer. *Clinical applications of the polyvagal theory: The emergence of polyvagal-informed therapies*, 50–69.

Plunkett, A., O'Toole, B., Swanston, H., Oates, R. K., Shrimpton, S., & Parkinson, P. (2001). Suicide risk following child sexual abuse. Ambulatory Pediatrics, 1(5), 262–266.

Purssell, E., Gould, D., & Chudleigh, J. (2020). Impact of isolation on hospitalised patients who are infectious: systematic review with meta-analysis. *BMJ open, 10*(2).

Protecting children and youth (2019). Retrieved April 19, 2021 from https://www.churchofjesuschrist.org/callings/church-safety-and-health/protecting-children-and-youth?lang=eng

Racovek-Felser, Z (2014). Domestic violence and abuse in intimate relationships from a public health perspective. *Health Psychology Research, 2*(3). Retrieved April 23, 2021 from https://www.ncbi.nlm.nih.gov/pmc/articles/PMC4768593/

Ranganatha, S. (1985). Dry drunk syndrome in alcoholics. *Indian Journal of Psychological Medicine, 8*(1), 26–28.

Renlund, D. E. (May, 2021). Infuriating unfairness. *Liahona.*

Rhodes, A., Spinazzola, J., & van der Kolk, B. (2016). Yoga for adult women with chronic PTSD: A long-term follow-up study. *The Journal of Alternative and Complementary Medicine, 22*(3), 189–196.

Rosen, I. 1991. Self-esteem as a factor in social and domestic violence. *British Journal of Psychiatry,* 158, 18–23.

Rosenfeld, B. D. (1992). Court-ordered treatment of spouse abuse. *Clinical Psychology Review, 12*(2), 205–226.

Rothschild, B. (2000). *The body remembers: The psychophysiology of trauma and trauma treatment.* WW Norton & Company.

Salcioglu, E., Urhan, S., Pirinccioglu, T., & Aydin, S. (2017). Anticipatory fear and helplessness predict PTSD and depression in domestic violence survivors. *Psychological Trauma: Theory, Research, Practice, and Policy, 9*(1), 117.

Salovey, P., & Mayer, J. D. (1990). Emotional intelligence. *Imagination, cognition and personality, 9*(3), 185–211.

Samuels, A. (2003). *Jung and the post-Jungians.*

Sansone, R. A., Chu, J., & Wiederman, M. W. (2007). Self-inflicted bodily harm among victims of intimate-partner violence. *Clinical Psychology & Psychotherapy, 14*(5), 352–357.

Scharff, D. E. (1996). *Object relations theory and practice: An introduction.* Rowman & Littlefield.

Scotland-Coogan, D., & Davis, E. (2016). Relaxation techniques for trauma. *Journal of Evidence-informed Social Work, 13*(5), 434–441.

Seligman, M. E. (1972). Learned helplessness. *Annual Review of Medicine, 23*(1), 407–412.

Seligman, M. E., & Beagley, G. (1975). Learned helplessness in the rat. *Journal of Comparative and Physiological Psychology, 88*(2), 534.

Seligman, M. E., Rosellini, R. A., & Kozak, M. J. (1975). Learned helplessness in the rat: time course, immunization, and reversibility. *Journal of Comparative and Physiological Psychology, 88*(2), 542.

Serrat, O. (2017). Understanding and developing emotional intelligence. In *Knowledge solutions* (pp. 329–339). Springer, Singapore.

Shapiro, F. (1989). Eye movement desensitization: A new treatment for post-traumatic stress disorder. *Journal of behavior therapy and experimental psychiatry, 20*(3), 211–217.

Shapiro, F. (2012). *Getting past your past: Take control of your life with self-help techniques from EMDR therapy.* Rodale.

Shapiro, F. (2017). *Eye movement desensitization and reprocessing (EMDR) therapy: Basic principles, protocols, and procedures.* Guilford Publications.

Silberg, J. L., Dallam, S. J., & Samson, E. (2013). *Crisis in family court: Lessons from turned around cases.* Final Report submitted to the Office of Violence Against Women, Department of Justice (supported under award #2011–TA-AX-K006).

Skinner, B. F. (1963). Behaviorism at fifty. *Science, 140*(3570), 951–958.

Skinner, B. F. (1971). Operant conditioning. *The Encyclopedia of Education, 7*, 29–33.

Snoyman, P., & Aicken, B. 2011. Self-reported impulsivity in male offenders with low cognitive ability in New South Wales prison. *Psychology, Crimes and Law, 17*: 151–164

Spidel, A., Vincent, G., Huss, M. T., Winters, J., Thomas, L., & Dutton, D. (2017). The psychopathic batterer: Subtyping perpetrators of domestic violence. In *The psychopath: Theory, research, and practice* (pp. 327–340). Routledge.

Springer, K. W., Sheridan, J., Kuo, D., & Carnes, M. (2003). The long-term health outcomes of childhood abuse. *Journal of General Internal Medicine, 18*(10), 864–870.

Springs F. E., & Friedrich, W. N. (1992). Health risk behaviors and medical sequelae of childhood sexual abuse. *Mayo Clin Proc.* *67*:527–32.

Stack, P. F. (February 16, 2018). Mormon bishops are told to 'believe the sisters' when they learn of marital abuse—but they don't always do so. Salt Lake Tribune. Retrieved April 22, 2021 from https://www.sltrib.com/religion/2018/02/16/believe-the-sisters-but-mormon-bishops-dont-always-do-so-when-they-learn-of-marital-abuse/

Stark, C. R., Riordan, V., & O'Connor, R. (2011). A conceptual model of suicide in rural areas. *Rural and remote health*, *11*(2), 220.

Stenz, L., Schechter, D. S., Serpa, S. R., & Paoloni-Giacobino, A. (2018). Intergenerational transmission of DNA methylation signatures associated with early life stress. *Current Genomics*, *19*(8), 665–675.

Stiles, M. (2002). Witnessing domestic violence: The effect on children. *American Family Physician*, *66*(11), 2052.

Sturge-Apple, M. L., Skibo, M. A., & Davies, P. T. (2012). Impact of parental conflict and emotional abuse on children and families. *Partner Abuse*, *3*(3), 379–400.

Sweet, P. L. (2019). The sociology of gaslighting. *American Sociological Review*, *84*(5), 851–875.

Terzi, S. (2013). Secure attachment style, coping with stress and resilience among university students. *The Journal of Happiness & Well-Being*, *1*(2), 97–109.

The Duluth Model (2021)

Tomaka, J., Thompson, S., & Palacios, R. (2006). The relation of social isolation, loneliness, and social support to disease outcomes among the elderly. *Journal of aging and health*, *18*(3), 359–384.

Thornton, D., & Matravers, A. (2013). The Machiavellian sex offender. *Sex Offenders in the Community*, 144.

Thurschwell, P. (2009). *Sigmund Freud*. Routledge.

Treleaven, D. A. (2018). *Trauma-sensitive mindfulness: Practices for safe and transformative healing.* WW Norton & Company.

Trickett, P. K., Mennen, F. E., Kim, K., & Sang, J. (2009). Emotional abuse in a sample of multiply maltreated, urban young adolescents: Issues of definition and identification. *Child Abuse & Neglect, 33*(1), 27–35.

Trocmé, N., & Bala, N. (2005). False allegations of abuse and neglect when parents separate. *Child abuse & neglect, 29*(12), 1333–1345.

Twohig-Bennett, C., & Jones, A. (2018). The health benefits of the great outdoors: A systematic review and meta-analysis of greenspace exposure and health outcomes. *Environmental Research, 166,* 628–637.

Uchtdorf, D.F. (November, 2013). Come, join with us. *Ensign.*

U.S. Department of Health and Human Services (2010). *Child maltreatment 2010.* Retrieved from https://www.acf.hhs.gov/archive/cb/data/resource/child-maltreatment-2010 on March 16, 2021.

Valtorta, N. K., Kanaan, M., Gilbody, S., Ronzi, S., & Hanratty, B. (2016). Loneliness and social isolation as risk factors for coronary heart disease and stroke: systematic review and meta-analysis of longitudinal observational studies. *Heart, 102*(13), 1009–1016.

Van der Kolk, B. A. (1994). The body keeps the score: Memory and the evolving psychobiology of posttraumatic stress. *Harvard Review of Psychiatry, 1*(5), 253–265.

Van der Kolk, B. A., Hodgdon, H., Gapen, M., Musicaro, R., Suvak, M. K., Hamlin, E., & Spinazzola, J. (2016). A randomized controlled study of neurofeedback for chronic PTSD. *PloS One, 11*(12), e0166752.

Viatte, S., Plant, D., & Raychaudhuri, S. (2013). Genetics and epigenetics of rheumatoid arthritis. *Nature Reviews Rheumatology, 9*(3), 141.

Vonderlin, R., Kleindienst, N., Alpers, G. W., Bohus, M., Lyssenko, L., & Schmahl, C. (2018). Dissociation in victims of childhood abuse or neglect: A meta-analytic review. *Psychological Medicine, 48*(15), 2467–2476.

Warner, C. T. (2001). *Bonds that make us free: Healing our relationships, coming to ourselves* (p. 336). Salt Lake City, UT: Shadow Mountain.

Walker E. A., Keegan D., Gardner G., Sullivan M., Bernstein D., & Katon W. J. (1997). Psychosocial factors in fibromyalgia compared with rheumatoid arthritis: II. Sexual, physical, and emotional abuse and neglect. *Psychosom Med. 59*:572–7

Washington, A., & Boundy, D. (1989). *Willpower's not enough: Recovering from addictions of every kind.* Harper Perennial, New York.

Webster, V., Brough, P., & Daly, K. (2016). Fight, flight or freeze: Common responses for follower coping with toxic leadership. *Stress and Health, 32*(4), 346–354.

White, M., & Epston, D. (2004). Externalizing the problem. *Relating experience: Stories from Health and Social Care, 1*, 88.

Winters, J., Clift, R. J., & Dutton, D. G. (2004). An exploratory study of emotional intelligence and domestic abuse. *Journal of Family Violence, 19*(5), 255–267.

Yehuda, R., Daskalakis, N. P., Bierer, L. M., Bader, H. N., Klengel, T., Holsboer, F., & Binder, E. B. (2016). Holocaust exposure induced intergenerational effects on FKBP5 methylation. *Biological psychiatry, 80*(5), 372–380.

Yehuda, R., & Lehrner, A. (2018). Intergenerational transmission of trauma effects: putative role of epigenetic mechanisms. *World Psychiatry, 17*(3), 243–257

You, J. S., & Jones, P. A. (2012). Cancer genetics and epigenetics: two sides of the same coin?. *Cancer Cell, 22*(1), 9–20.

Zahn, M. A., Block, R. B., Sharps, P., Campbell, J. C., Campbell, D., Gary, F., . . . & Witte, J. (2003). Intimate partner homicide. *National Institute of Justice Journal, 250*, 2–48.

ABOUT THE AUTHOR

Ryan Anderson, PhD, LMFT, MedFT, received his master's degree from Brigham Young University in marriage and family therapy. He earned a PhD in medical family therapy at East Carolina University and completed his internship at Duke, with a focus on family therapy in psycho-oncology. He has provided therapy for individuals, groups, and families in community mental health clinics, university settings, inpatient psychiatric units, and hospitals, as well as in the wilderness and in residential treatment centers.

He is also one of the cofounders of Telos U, where he and his team help young men and young women with mental health struggles transition into adult roles.

Ryan is the author of various professional articles, textbook chapters, and books, and is also a regular speaker at regional and national conferences in his field.